The KIDS' COLLEGE Almanac

A First Look at College

FOURTH EDITION

Barbara C. Greenfeld and Robert A. Weinstein

JIST Works
America's Career Publisher

The Kids' College Almanac, Fourth Edition
A First Look at College

© 2010 by Barbara C. Greenfeld and Robert A. Weinstein

Published by JIST Works, an imprint of JIST Publishing
7321 Shadeland Station, Suite 200
Indianapolis, IN 46256-3923
Phone: 800-648-JIST   Fax: 877-454-7839   E-mail: info@jist.com

Visit our Web site at **www.jist.com** for information on JIST, tables of contents, sample pages, and ordering instructions for our many products!

Quantity discounts are available for JIST books. Please call our Sales Department at 800-648-5478 for a free catalog and more information.

Trade Product Manager: Lori Cates Hand
Development Editor: Heather Stith
Cover Designer and Page Layout: Toi Davis
Proofreaders: Linda Seifert, Jeanne Clark
Indexer: Cheryl Lenser
Printed in the United States of America
14 13 12 11 10   9 8 7 6 5 4 3 2 1

Library of Congress Cataloging-in-Publication Data

Greenfeld, Barbara C.
  The kids college almanac : a first look at college / Barbara C. Greenfeld
  and Robert A. Weinstein. -- 4th ed.
      p. cm.
  Includes index.
  ISBN 978-1-59357-736-0 (alk. paper)
  1. College student orientation--United States--Juvenile literature.
  2. Universities and colleges--United States--Juvenile literature.
  3. College choice--United States--Juvenile literature. I. Weinstein, Robert A. II. Title.
  LB2343.32.G75 2010
  378.73--dc22

                                    2010007055

We have been careful to provide accurate information in this book, but it is possible that errors and omissions have been introduced. Please consider this in making any career plans or other important decisions. Trust your own judgment above all else and in all things.

Trademarks: All brand names and product names used in this book are trade names, service marks, trademarks, or registered trademarks of their respective owners.

ISBN 978-1-59357-736-0

Contents

An Introductory Note to Parents...

I frequently attend meetings of college admissions officers from across the country. Those who attend express concern about my generation of parents pushing our kids to achieve. We push them to excel in sports. We insist on piano or dance lessons; we encourage them to be involved in religious youth groups. We urge them—rather strongly at times—to take the hardest courses in school. We suggest that they enroll in courses to earn college credit while in high school so that they can get a jump start on higher education.

My colleagues and I acknowledge that this takes place and that it is not always good. Kids should have time to be kids. They have plenty of time to worry about college and career.

So why am I writing a foreword to a book that encourages middle and junior high school kids to think about college? Because I believe strongly, as do the authors, that kids should be aware of their future. The more they learn now about what college is, the better the choices they will make when the time comes.

During my 36 years of helping high school students make their transition to college, I have seen a profound change in the way students and parents make their selections. In today's society, uninformed choices are often made about colleges based on their ranking, their reputation, their football team, or simply their name.

What happens less frequently is a careful assessment of a student's learning and social interaction style, and an effort to discover a set of colleges that will best serve a particular student's educational and social development. Colleges that are not name brands, that do not have "sweet 16" basketball teams, and that are not "ivy" or "ivy-like" are often overlooked.

In *The Kids' College Almanac*, Barbara Greenfeld and Robert Weinstein demystify college. They give kids a thoughtful introduction to the universe of choices they will have when the application process begins. The authors succeed beautifully in going beyond the "name brands" to explain the strengths of different categories of schools. They talk about what actually happens at college, how students learn, and what students do during this important period of their lives. They review the application process and discuss how students can make informed choices.

The real value of *The Kids' College Almanac*, however, is that it makes students (and I hope their parents) aware that a logical discovery process indeed takes place during the college search. The book offers valuable insight into the steps required to identify and refine choices. It lends advice about how to engage college representatives who can provide help along the way. Finally, by discussing how financial aid can make just about any college affordable, *The Kids' College Almanac* dispels the myth that college is only for the well-off. The college selection process is far more than just looking at the rankings or at "where my friends are going." The process, in fact, is a life event which requires care and thought.

I had the honor of serving as vice president of enrollment and college relations at Dickinson College in Carlisle, Pennsylvania, and dean of enrollment at The Johns Hopkins University in Baltimore. I am also privileged currently to serve as vice president for communications at Lafayette College in Easton, Pennsylvania.

These are three excellent schools, but Johns Hopkins is very different from undergraduate colleges such as Dickinson and Lafayette. Johns Hopkins is a major research university with a heavy graduate and research emphasis in which some undergraduates thrive. Dickinson and Lafayette are smaller undergraduate colleges where teaching and student development are emphasized. A student who would benefit from Hopkins might find the close mentoring relationships at Lafayette and Dickinson too intrusive. The student who would grow significantly at a smaller undergraduate college might be unhappy with the fast pace of a research university.

Although one kind of institution may be better known than the other, the choice between these schools must be based on substance, not visibility, and on what is right for the particular student. That is what *The Kids' College Almanac* sets out to explain in a comprehensive way, in terms that students in grades 5 through 9 will understand and, eventually, appreciate.

Back to our role as parents. We must guide and motivate our children. But we must also encourage them to discover their future. It is, after all, theirs to be had.

I guarantee that the final year before college will be much calmer and less stressful if parents and students approach it from an informed standpoint, and always with some sense of humor. *The Kids' College Almanac* will help your family get there.

Robert J. Massa, Ed.D.
Easton, PA
January 2010

Preface

Kids think and dream about the future—or at least other worlds different from the ones they occupy at any particular moment. They experiment with all sorts of roles. Young children run around with capes, hats, and other dress-up clothes, pretending to be superheroes and fictional characters found in books, movies, television, and cyberspace. As they grow older, experimentation moves to the more traditional: doctors, teachers, police officers, musicians, moms, dads, and other roles borrowed from the adult world. Anything and everything seems possible.

When you're in fourth or fifth grade, it seems quite reasonable to be a professional athlete who then becomes a doctor and finds the cure to a terrible disease, or a movie star who is also an astronaut. Through middle school, kids continue to talk about challenging, meaningful, and even daring careers.

Kids are the ultimate optimists, often even in the face of extreme adversity. Some literally embrace the motto "The sky's the limit!" They achieve goals that bear a striking resemblance to their earlier role-playing. Many achieve goals similar to the spirit, if not the specifics, of their youthful dreams; many will occupy careers not even yet in existence. But for others, the dreams and the possibilities of making those dreams come true are lost or, at least, misplaced somewhere along the way.

The Kids' College Almanac has been written to help youngsters ages 10 to 15 keep their dreams in sight. Let us be clear: We firmly believe that childhood is a time to be treasured and enjoyed. This book is not intended to pressure youngsters to follow one particular path or another. Instead, our primary goals are to demystify college and to answer the kinds of questions about their future that young people think about at this age. Most important, we want to motivate youngsters with varying backgrounds and experiences to take advantage of the many opportunities available to them.

Throughout the book, we introduce vocabulary and concepts that elementary, middle, and high school students may have heard but not necessarily understood. We have provided a number of interesting facts, charts, and profiles that we hope will prove to be surprising and fun. We have also taken care to address the needs and interests of young people who face special challenges, as well as those with special talents.

In the fourth edition, we have reworked information about paying for college and financial aid in chapters 10 and 11, keeping it current with ongoing changes. Charts and tables have been thoroughly updated. Our coverage of the role of technology has been expanded and continues to be fully integrated throughout the book. The fourth edition also reflects recent changes to college entrance exams.

In most other ways, the book retains the features of the previous editions that our readers valued. Youngsters can read this book from cover to cover. We hope many will. They can also read individual chapters that interest them—no special sequence is required. We think the book's most important design feature is that it can be picked up, opened to any page, read, and understood, regardless of which other pages the reader has seen. This feature enables young readers to pick and choose what interests them at any point in time.

We address topics in a direct, conversational style. We have also tried to provide a level of detail that will appeal to more sophisticated readers. At the same time, the book lays a foundation that prepares students to use other college resources in their junior and senior years of high school. By focusing on the 50 states and a wide variety of colleges, we believe our readers will see the full range of possibilities and opportunities—and learn some geography in the process!

Parents, teachers, guidance counselors, librarians, and others will find *The Kids' College Almanac* to be a valuable reference tool for answering questions kids ask. Many parents and educators have spoken to us about their own concerns that, having gone to college many years ago, they do not feel they have the right information to advise kids about today's opportunities. Similar concerns have been expressed by those who never attended college, who attended in another country, or who speak English as a second language. We are confident that this book enhances their ability to motivate, encourage, and prepare young people, while learning something new and interesting themselves.

Acknowledgments

One's major goals and accomplishments are rarely achieved alone. We are no exception to this rule. Our gratitude begins with our wonderful parents, who proved to us that we could do whatever we wanted to if we believed in ourselves and were willing to work hard. Larry Greenfeld has always provided faithful and ongoing support. Sofia Rose Greenfeld has brought joy to our family life and reinforces the very foundation for this book—helping children achieve their dreams. The many students of all ages, stages, and places we have met throughout our careers continue to inspire us, demonstrating over and over that young people of all backgrounds think, plan, hope, dream, and even worry about the future—far more than is often recognized.

Our reviewers for all four editions contributed valuable suggestions and insight. In addition to providing valuable advice for all our editions, Dawn Mosisa, from The Johns Hopkins University Carey School of Business, guided our revision of chapters 10 and 11. Robert Massa, Lafayette College, has been a special champion of our efforts. His dedication to creating opportunities for young people striving for access and success to postsecondary education is inspiring. Others contributed in important ways to this book, including Julie Kerr, who provided enthusi-astic support from the first word. For photographs, we are grateful to Colby Communications, Eddie George, Michelle Kwan, Gregory Jbara, Kip Evans, Paul Bither, Judy Blume, and many others. Throughout this project, we received guid-ance from hundreds of college employees throughout the country. Special thanks to our editors Heather Stith and Lori Cates Hand, along with Bob Grilliot, and their many supportive colleagues at JIST Publishing.

Barbara adds: Our book's success is possible because of the love and support of family and friends. My sweetest Sofia Rose has lovingly and patiently allowed me to test and validate my abiding belief that children are joyful about learning. Being her Bubbe is my greatest pleasure. Moishe Greenfeld provided wonderful companionship during long hours at the keyboard. I am indebted to my loyal brother and co-author Robert. I have been privileged to work with wonderful col-leagues throughout my career, particularly those at Howard Community College. I extend thanks to those who have shared and supported my interest in helping youngsters see the way forward to successful and fulfilling futures. Bob Massa is an extraordinary man of his word and a can-do person. He has supported this book through every edition and helped in so many other ways to transform aspirations and ideas into opportunities for so many students. Dawn Mosisa too has been a constant source of support and expertise, a truly faithful friend and colleague. I continue to be inspired by young people of all ages and stages whose enthusiasm and love of learning and discovery have been the foundation of my career and for this book.

Robert adds: I start by acknowledging my wonderful teachers, including Joan C. Keenan, Mary Lee Ruddle, and Fred Geib. Gerson Publishing Company has provid-ed years of continual support. I've been blessed with loyal family whom I treasure, and I can't imagine this journey without my sister and co-author Barbara. My heartfelt thanks to Wendy B., Debs, Sandi, Julie, Adele, and Paula. Cyberspace has brought me full-circle with my Oak Hill Park and Northwood families who inspired me to reach higher—a special nod, in particular, to Donald and Leslie, Lenni, and Colette and Cathy. My colleagues at Oasis Players provide creativity, laughter, and music when they are most needed. I can't say enough about John Carleo, who for over two decades has been a most trusted mentor and friend. Continued thanks to Team Dounelis for the moon. And far from least, a special nod to my beloved Red Sox for the frosting to go with the cake.

Finally, we thank our parents again. Those who were fortunate to know our dad, Gerson, realize that, at its simplest, this book is an extension of the value he always placed on a good education. As for our mom, Fran, we simply couldn't ask for a more devoted and loving parent and friend.

B.C.G. and R.A.W.

And, in the very room in which
he sat, there were books that could
take you anywhere, and things
to invent, and make, and build,
and break, and all the puzzle and
excitement of everything he didn't
know—music to play, songs to sing,
and worlds to imagine and then
someday make real. His thoughts
darted eagerly about as everything
looked new and worth trying.

Norton Juster
The Phantom Tollbooth

1

What Is College?

College provides a bridge to your future. When you go to college, you will have the opportunity to learn new things and to build skills. You will have the opportunity to learn more about yourself and to explore careers that may be part of your future. You will also have the opportunity to make new friends and to share new experiences with them.

Colleges are schools of higher education. At college you can continue your education at an advanced level, beyond what you learn in middle school or high school. Most colleges work in much the same way. Yet they can take many forms, as you will see. Because of these differences, you will have the opportunity to find a college that's right for you!

Types of Colleges

Many colleges can be described as **liberal arts colleges.** The *liberal* in *liberal arts* does not refer to politics. It means that students study a wide variety of subjects and gain experience in many areas.

Some colleges are **research colleges.** They not only teach students, but also serve as centers for original research. When you hear or read about medical break-throughs, you will find that many are made at research colleges and universities.

Other colleges are thought of as **teaching colleges.** People who teach at these colleges may do research, but they are especially interested in teaching.

Your learning goals may influence which type of college you choose.

TYPES OF COLLEGES AND UNIVERSITIES

College. Schooling after high school, often in four-year programs that offer bachelor's degrees. A college can be part of a larger university.

University. Usually a larger institution that combines one or more colleges with other schools, such as a law school; usually has graduate degree programs.

Community college. May be called junior college; provides programs that lead to associate's degrees and professional certificates. Students can complete requirements for degrees in two years, and many continue their education at four-year colleges or universities.

Technology or technical college. May be either two-year or four-year schools; these schools may give special emphasis to agricultural programs such as farming and ranching, or programs such as machine tooling, electronics, computer-aided drafting (CAD), computer engineering, Web site design, or many other areas of study.

The History of Colleges

Did you know that the origins of colleges date back thousands of years? Plato's Academy and Aristotle's Lyceum, established in ancient Greece in the fourth century B.C.E., are thought of as the first colleges. Ancient Palestine, Rome, Egypt, Babylonia, and India were centers for the study of religion, philosophy, war, and diplomacy. Two major institutions for Islamic studies, located in Egypt and Morocco, are both more than one thousand years old!

With the birth of schools such as the University of Paris, the University of Bologna, the University of Salamanca, and Oxford University in the thirteenth and fourteenth centuries, medieval Europe became the next center for colleges. Law joined religion and philosophy as an important area of study.

Medicine, science, and literature were important during the Renaissance period that followed. New colleges were established throughout Europe as well as the Americas.

Asian and African nations have seen the steady growth of colleges over the past 200 years.

Many of the major universities in Paris are located in a section frequently called the Latin Quarter. This name comes from the days when the students living there regularly studied Latin or Greek and spoke it as they went around to the cafes and shops.

The word *college* comes from the Latin *collegium,* which means society. Students would form their own societies or clubs, as they still do at many colleges. *University* comes from *union* and refers to the partnership of teachers and students. Today we often interchange the words *college* and *university.* In general, however, universities are larger and include one or more colleges.

College in the United States

The Pilgrims arrived at Plymouth Rock in 1620. Just 16 years later, the school we know as Harvard was founded. By the American Revolution (1776–1783), several more colleges had been established, including the College of William and Mary, Yale University, Princeton University, Columbia University, Brown University, Rutgers (The State University of New Jersey), and Dartmouth College.

By the Civil War (1861–1865), the number of colleges had grown. Most colleges founded in this period were privately funded rather than supported by state governments. Although many began with ties to religious organizations, most eventually loosened or cut these ties altogether. For example, in 1693 the College of William and Mary was set up to train clergy for the Anglican Church. It later took on broader goals and became sponsored by the Commonwealth of Virginia in 1906.

The number of colleges has continued to grow with the addition of public, private, land-grant, and community colleges. Today you can choose from more than 3,500 colleges and universities in the United States!

VIRGINIA

A decade after serving as the third president of the United States (1801–1809), Thomas Jefferson founded the University of Virginia. The university was set up in 1819 and opened its doors in 1825. Jefferson also played an important role in deciding what subjects would be taught at the university. Many of the original buildings, which Jefferson designed, are still being used today.

The University of Nebraska is one of the nation's oldest land-grant colleges. University Hall (left) was the university's first building. It was built on the north edge of the city of Lincoln in 1869, the same year the University of Nebraska held its first classes.

Land-Grant Colleges

In 1862 and 1890, the Morrill Acts (Land-Grant Acts) led to major changes in American education. The laws gave land and money to each state. The land and money were used to fund, support, and maintain colleges that specialized in the study of agriculture and mechanic arts (engineering). These **land-grant colleges** were established to provide educational opportunities and training to the working classes.

Today, more than 3.6 million students attend the various state universities and land-grant colleges.

The 1890 law divided grants between colleges for white students and colleges for black students in states practicing segregation. Many historically black colleges were founded in the late 1800s with these grants.

Well before the Morrill Acts were passed, the University of North Carolina was established by the General Assembly of North Carolina in 1789 as the country's first state university. Located in Chapel Hill, the university now has more than a dozen colleges and schools. With its faculty of 3,200 teachers, the University of North Carolina serves more than 28,000 students.

NORTH CAROLINA

What Is My State's Oldest College?

State	College or University	Year Founded
Alabama	Athens State University	1822
Alaska	University of Alaska–Fairbanks	1917
Arizona	Arizona State University	1885
	University of Arizona	1885
Arkansas	University of the Ozarks	1834
California	Santa Clara University	1851
	University of the Pacific	1851
Colorado	University of Denver	1864
Connecticut	Yale University	1701
Delaware	University of Delaware	1743
Florida	Florida State University	1857
Georgia	University of Georgia	1785
Hawaii	University of Hawaii	1907
Idaho	Brigham Young University–Idaho	1888
Illinois	McKendree University	1828
Indiana	Vincennes University	1801
Iowa	Loras College	1839
Kansas	Highland Community College	1858
Kentucky	Transylvania University	1780
Louisiana	Centenary College of Louisiana	1825
Maine	Bowdoin College	1794
Maryland	Washington College	1782
Massachusetts	Harvard University	1636
Michigan	University of Michigan	1817
Minnesota	University of Minnesota	1851
Mississippi	Mississippi College	1826
Missouri	Saint Louis University	1818
Montana	Rocky Mountain College	1878

NORTH CAROLINA

Salem College, an all-women's college in North Carolina, opened in 1772 as a school for girls. The Moravians, a Protestant denomination, founded it with the belief that women deserved an education comparable to the one given to men.

What Is My State's Oldest College?

State	College or University	Year Founded
Nebraska	Peru State College	1867
Nevada	University of Nevada–Reno	1874
New Hampshire	Dartmouth College	1769
New Jersey	Princeton University	1746
New Mexico	New Mexico State University	1888
New York	Columbia University	1754
North Carolina	Salem College	1772
North Dakota	Jamestown College	1883
	University of North Dakota	1883
Ohio	Ohio University	1804
Oklahoma	Northeastern State University	1846
Oregon	Willamette University	1842
Pennsylvania	University of Pennsylvania	1740
Rhode Island	Brown University	1764
South Carolina	College of Charleston	1770
South Dakota	Augustana College	1860
Tennessee	Tusculum College	1794
Texas	Southwestern University	1840
Utah	University of Utah	1850
Vermont	Castleton State College	1787
Virginia	College of William and Mary	1693
Washington	Whitman College	1859
West Virginia	Marshall University	1837
	West Liberty University	1837
Wisconsin	Beloit College	1846
	Carroll University	1846
Wyoming	University of Wyoming	1886
District of Columbia	Georgetown University	1789

In 1779, the University of Pennsylvania received its fourth name! Benjamin Franklin founded it as the Charity School in 1740. In 1749, it became the Academy of Philadelphia. Then it changed again, to the College of Philadelphia in 1755.

PENNSYLVANIA

More Colleges That Are Over 200 Years Old...

State	College or University	Year Founded
Pennsylvania	Moravian College	1742
Virginia	Washington and Lee University	1749
New Jersey	Rutgers University	1766
Pennsylvania	Dickinson College	1773
Virginia	Hampden-Sydney College	1775
Pennsylvania	Washington and Jefferson College	1781
Maryland	Saint John's College	1784
North Carolina	Louisburg College	1787
Pennsylvania	Franklin and Marshall College	1787
Pennsylvania	University of Pittsburgh	1787
Pennsylvania	York College	1787
North Carolina	University of North Carolina	1789
Vermont	University of Vermont	1791
Massachusetts	Williams College	1793
Tennessee	University of Tennessee	1794
New York	Union College	1795
New York	Hartwick College	1797
Kentucky	University of Louisville	1798

Community and Junior Colleges

Louisburg College in North Carolina is the oldest two-year college in the United States. It was founded in 1787.

Some two-year colleges have been around since the eighteenth and nineteenth centuries. However, the real rise of two-year colleges came more recently. After World War II, there was a great demand for local colleges that could meet the changing educational and training needs of the community. These colleges could also meet the needs of people who could not go to school full-time for four years. Soldiers returning from war, the entrance of more women into the workforce, and the growth of the suburbs were all factors that led to the founding of community colleges across the United States. Ever since then, increasing numbers of students have chosen community colleges.

Community colleges serve people with a wide range of educational goals. They offer lower costs, closeness to home, and more personal instruction and services.

Many students start their college education at a community college immediately after high school. They may prepare for transfer to a four-year college or for immediate employment. Community colleges make it possible for students to continue their education while managing work or family responsibilities. These colleges also provide opportunities to learn specific career skills, prepare for a job, or take a course for pleasure.

In many cases, the two years you spend in full-time study at a community college are equivalent to the first two years you would spend at a four-year college.

Vincennes University in Indiana was founded in 1801 by William Henry Harrison, who was later elected president of the United States. Although the word *university* is in its name, Vincennes is primarily a two-year college. The college was formally chartered as Vincennes University by the Indiana Territory Legislature in 1806 (before Indiana became a state). As a tribute to its heritage, Vincennes has kept University in its name.

INDIANA

Like many community colleges, Flathead Valley Community College in northwestern Montana got its start in the 1960s. Flathead Valley (left) is an example of a college that brings educational opportunities to students who live in less-populated rural areas.

Technology Colleges and Institutes

Chapter 5 describes many fields of study in more detail.

Passage of the Land-Grant Acts in the nineteenth century led to the founding of many new colleges that provide education in technology, architecture, engineering, agriculture, and the sciences. Students who attend **technology colleges** learn how to develop new technologies as well as how to find new uses for existing technology.

In addition, many other fine schools specializing in technology have been established through the years. One of the first of these schools was Rensselaer Polytechnic Institute (RPI), founded in 1824 in Troy, New York. Other leading technology colleges include Case Western Reserve University (1826), Cooper Union (1859), Massachusetts Institute of Technology (1861), California Institute of Technology (1891), Carnegie Mellon University (1900), and Harvey Mudd College (1955).

Many two-year colleges offer a wide variety of courses in technology and agriculture. In some cases, students go directly into the workplace after completing their program. But many others will continue on to four-year colleges and universities.

Industrialist Andrew Carnegie founded Carnegie Mellon University in 1900. In its early years, it prepared Pittsburgh students for work in local industries. Over the years, it has become a leading research university. But you can study more than technology there. For example, it is the only school in the nation that offers a full program in bagpipe music!

Technical Institutes and Career Schools

Technology programs often emphasize the theories behind the way things work. Technical and career programs focus instead on the hands-on part of how things work. For instance, in a technology course you might study how to design a faster, more capable computer. But in a technical or vocational course, you are likely to learn how to build, repair, operate, and maintain computers. Many community colleges offer a combination of technology and technical courses.

When you attend technical and career schools, you learn specific job skills that will prepare you for work. For example, an English class may focus on writing memos, letters, and reports rather than studying poetry and literature. An accounting class may focus on bookkeeping skills rather than interpreting a company's financial reports.

Some schools may offer a wide variety of career programs related to computers, business, auto repair, culinary arts, allied health, and other areas. Others may focus on one particular area such as electronics or cosmetology. Some two-year schools, such as community colleges, offer programs that prepare students to continue their education at four-year colleges and universities.

*Private career schools that are run for profit are often called **proprietary schools**.*

Carefully compare technical and career schools with local colleges, especially community colleges. Ask your guidance counselor about their reputations and talk to students who have attended them. See chapter 14 for more information.

The Culinary Institute of America is a technical college with branches in New York, California, and Texas that is devoted entirely to cooking, baking, and other courses for food-service professionals. The Medix School (located in Maryland and Georgia) is a private technical school that prepares its students to work in health-care facilities in jobs such as medical assistants, dental assistants, and patient care technicians.

Statewide Systems

Many states link a variety of colleges and universities together in a statewide system. For example, the State University of New York (SUNY) includes 4 universities, 13 state colleges, 8 technology colleges, and 30 community colleges. It also includes health-science centers and other specialized colleges. More than 420,000 students are enrolled at the various SUNY colleges. Of these, about half attend one of the community colleges located throughout the state.

Other states have extensive statewide systems as well. California has two sets of universities—the University of California system (including Berkeley and UCLA) and the California State University system (including Cal State Fullerton).

Some systems, in addition to various colleges located throughout the state, have one major school that is their leading or flagship university. The University of Maryland at College Park and the University of Wisconsin at Madison, both large research universities, are examples of flagship universities within statewide systems.

The University at Buffalo is a major research institution that is one of four university centers in the SUNY system. The South Campus (shown here) is near a residential section of Buffalo. It houses most of the university's health science programs. It can be reached easily by public transportation.

The Campuses of the State University of New York (SUNY)

University Centers

Albany

Binghamton

Buffalo

Stony Brook

State University Colleges

Brockport

Buffalo

Cortland

Empire State College

Fredonia

Geneseo

New Paltz

Old Westbury

Oneonta

Oswego

Plattsburgh

Potsdam

Purchase

Colleges of Technology

Alfred

Canton

Cobleskill

Delhi

Farmingdale

Institute of Technology

Maritime

Morrisville

Additional Colleges

Ceramics

Environmental Science and Forestry

College of Optometry

Community Colleges

Adirondack

Broome

Cayuga

Clinton

Columbia-Greene

Corning

Dutchess

Erie

Fashion Institute of Technology

Finger Lakes

Fulton-Montgomery

Genesee

Herkimer County

Hudson Valley

Jamestown

Jefferson

Mohawk Valley

Monroe

Nassau

Niagara County

North Country

Onondaga

Orange County

Rockland

Schenectady County

Suffolk County

Sullivan County

Tompkins-Cortland

Ulster County

Westchester

Health Science Centers

Downstate Medical Center (Brooklyn)

Upstate Medical University (Syracuse)

What Is Affiliation?

Affiliation is a type of connection, association, or relationship. For instance, a college might have close ties with its founders, maybe a religious organization, such as the Roman Catholic Church. A college's affiliation may indicate the students it serves (for example, women's colleges). An affiliation may also indicate the careers, such as technology or the military, for which a college prepares students.

In some cases, a women's college and a men's college have joined together. For instance, Jackson College (for women) and Tufts College (for men) were once separate colleges, but are now joined as a university using the Tufts name.

Affiliations may change over time. For example, military colleges such as The Citadel or the U.S. Naval Academy once educated only men. Now they educate both men and women. Many other colleges that once accepted only men or women now accept both. In some cases, financial challenges led the colleges to enroll both in order to increase enrollment. Changing times have led many other colleges to change their affiliations.

Many colleges that have a specific affiliation do not require all students to belong to that specific group. Boston College in Massachusetts and Marquette University in Wisconsin are two of many colleges affiliated with the Jesuit Order of the Roman Catholic Church. Although many of their students are Roman Catholic, not all of them are. These colleges' programs are, however, influenced by Jesuit philosophies of education, which emphasize the liberal arts, service to others, and leadership.

A college's affiliation can be very formal, as is the case with military colleges. It can also be so informal that few people are aware of it. A college's affiliation is an important factor to consider when you are applying to colleges.

COLLEGE AFFILIATIONS

Public vs. private. Public colleges are supported by taxpayers; are under the supervision of federal, state, or local governments; and are usually less expensive for local students than for out-of-state students. Private colleges are independent, supported by private funds, under much less government supervision, and usually have higher costs than public colleges.

Religion. Many colleges are affiliated with religious groups. In some cases, the group has much say about how the college is run; other times, the affiliation is much looser and students from other religious groups attend.

Gender. Some colleges accept only or mostly male students or female students. Coeducational (co-ed) colleges accept both female and male students. Many colleges have become coeducational to attract more students.

Race and ethnicity. Some colleges have strong ties to particular racial or ethnic groups; for example, historically and predominantly black colleges accept mostly African-American students, though others may attend. Many of these colleges were established at a time when black students were denied the opportunity to study at other colleges. Tribal colleges include several dozen land-grant colleges established to respond to the higher-education needs of American Indians. Within the larger institution, many colleges have individual programs that address the specific needs of the community.

Military. These schools train students for careers in the military. They can be under federal or state supervision. Many other colleges offer ROTC (Reserve Officer Training Corps) programs as part of overall studies.

Mount Holyoke College and Smith College, both in Massachusetts, are two of the oldest women's colleges in the country. However, many classes are coeducational, with students attending from other nearby colleges.

MASSACHUSETTS

Examples of Colleges with Religious Affiliations

State	College or University	Affiliation
Alabama	Samford University	Southern Baptist
Arkansas	Philander Smith College	United Methodist
California	Pepperdine University	Churches of Christ
Florida	Bethune-Cookman University	United Methodist
Georgia	Agnes Scott College	Presbyterian
Hawaii	Chaminade University	Roman Catholic
Illinois	Eureka College	Disciples of Christ
Indiana	Earlham College	Religious Society of Friends (Quakers)
Iowa	Coe College	Presbyterian
Kansas	McPherson College	College of the Brethren
Maryland	Mount St. Mary's University	Roman Catholic
Massachusetts	Boston College	Roman Catholic
Michigan	Hope College	Reformed Church in America
Missouri	College of the Ozarks	Presbyterian
Minnesota	Macalester College	Presbyterian
Montana	University of Great Falls	Roman Catholic
Nebraska	Creighton University	Roman Catholic
New Jersey	Drew University	United Methodist
New Mexico	College of Santa Fe	Roman Catholic
New York	Jewish Theological Seminary	Jewish
North Carolina	Salem College	Moravian
Ohio	The College of Wooster	Presbyterian
Oregon	Willamette University	United Methodist
Pennsylvania	Ursinus College	United Church of Christ
South Dakota	Augustana College	Lutheran
Tennessee	University of the South	Episcopal
Texas	Texas Christian University	Disciples of Christ
Utah	Brigham Young University	Latter-Day Saints (Mormon)
Virginia	Mary Baldwin College	Presbyterian
Washington	Pacific Lutheran University	Lutheran
West Virginia	West Virginia Wesleyan College	United Methodist
Wisconsin	Marquette University	Roman Catholic
District of Columbia	American University	United Methodist

Some Historically/Predominantly Black Colleges

State	College or University	Year Founded
Alabama	Alabama State University	1874
Alabama	Tuskegee University	1881
Arkansas	Philander Smith College	1877
Delaware	Delaware State University	1891
Florida	Florida A&M University	1887
Georgia	Morehouse College	1867
Georgia	Spelman College	1881
Louisiana	Grambling State University	1901
Maryland	Morgan State University	1867
Mississippi	Alcorn State University	1871
Mississippi	Jackson State University	1877
North Carolina	Fayetteville State University	1867
Ohio	Central State University	1887
Ohio	Wilberforce University	1856
South Carolina	South Carolina State University	1896
Tennessee	Fisk University	1866
Tennessee	The LeMoyne-Owen College	1862
Texas	Prairie View A & M University	1876
Texas	Texas Southern University	1947
Virginia	Hampton University	1868
District of Columbia	Howard University	1867

Many colleges with Wesleyan in their name, such as Kansas Wesleyan University, are (or once were) affiliated with the United Methodist Church. The name comes from John Wesley, the founder of Methodism. Several historically black colleges, including Rust College (Mississippi) and Claflin University (South Carolina) also have their roots in the United Methodist Church, which was strongly antislavery in the years leading up to the Civil War.

How Does a College Work?

In many ways, you can think of a college as a business. A college offers a product and services to its customers. In this case, the product is a good education. The customers are the students.

Behind the scenes are the people and facilities that help the college make its product available to students. The administration is the management team of the college. The faculty bring the product—the good education—directly to the students. You can think of classrooms, labs, and libraries as the factories where the education is produced. College services make sure that everything runs smoothly and that students are able to take full advantage of their education (see page 21 for examples). The alumni and community, including government and local businesses, provide support that helps make the college successful.

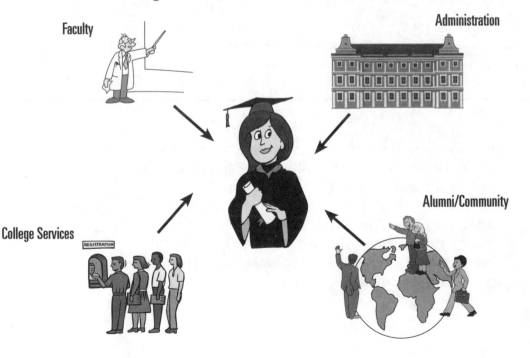

Faculty

Administration

College Services

Alumni/Community

What Is the Student Body?

The name given to all the students as a whole is the **student body.** At a four-year college, students are divided into four groups, just as in high school. The first-year students are freshmen, and second-year students are sophomores. Students in their third year are juniors. Those in their fourth or final year are seniors. Juniors and seniors are also referred to as **upperclassmen.**

*Students who have not yet graduated from college are **undergraduates.** Students who have graduated from college and study at an even more advanced level are **graduate students.***

Who Runs the College?

You may have heard about the president's administration—the people who run the United States government. In a similar way, a college's **administration** handles both the daily running of the college and its long-term planning. The exact way colleges are set up differs from one college to another.

*The head of a very large university or of a university that has several locations is sometimes called a **chancellor** or a **provost.***

WHO'S IN CHARGE?

Board of trustees. Sometimes called the board of directors or board of regents, the board of trustees is a group of people who hire and supervise a college's president and, sometimes, other key employees. The board of trustees determines the college's budget; approves new buildings, new academic programs, and major spending; and establishes broad goals for the college.

President. The president hires and manages the people who run major portions of the college. The president works closely with the board of trustees on important issues affecting the college's future and raises money for the college from businesses, alumni, the community, and other sources.

Deans. Also called vice presidents, deans are responsible for major portions of the college. The dean of faculty (or dean of instruction) hires and supervises the teachers and the subjects that are taught. The dean of students oversees student services such as counseling, athletics, and housing; and also oversees important policies and procedures that affect students, such as the honor code (policies about honesty and conduct).

Who Are the Faculty?

The people who teach at colleges are the **faculty.** **Professors** are full-time teachers who have a long-term relationship with the college. Professors may be given tenure if they meet teaching, research, or publishing requirements set by the college. **Tenure** is a guarantee of job security at the college.

Depending on how long they have been teaching at the college, or how much they have accomplished in their field, professors might be full professors, associate professors, or assistant professors. When outstanding professors retire, they are often awarded the title *professor emeritus.* Sometimes they still teach an occasional class at the college.

Instructors are usually entry-level teachers. Sometimes they fill in for professors who are on leave. Other times, the instructors are still finishing their advanced studies at another university. Lecturers and adjunct (part-time) instructors often teach one or two classes for the college.

Graduate assistants and **teaching assistants** are graduate students at the college who help teach introductory courses. Sometimes they help professors in other ways, such as grading papers and tests. They spend most of their time, however, on their own studies.

Teaching assistants, also called TAs, help professors who teach large classes. TAs often meet with students in smaller study groups. Sometimes TAs teach their own classes.

What Are College Services?

Every college has a group of people who help you get the most out of your time at college. Some, like advisors and counselors, work directly with students. Others work behind the scenes to help keep things running smoothly. Some of the major services they offer are described on the following page.

EXAMPLES OF COLLEGE SERVICES

Admissions. Informs students about the college, assists students who are applying to the college, and determines who may attend.

Financial aid. Helps qualified students get federal and state financial aid. Distributes scholarships, grants, and loans to qualified students and also helps coordinate job programs that enable students to work at the college.

Registration. Registers students for their classes. Maintains student records, including grades. Provides official information to students about their transcripts (their college records), which students often need when applying for graduate schools or jobs.

Testing and placement. Evaluates students' abilities, usually in math and English, and determines which classes students are ready to take.

Counseling and advising. Helps students select their classes, plan their schedules, and arrange for tutoring and review classes. Assists students who are transferring to or from another college. Also helps with personal concerns, as well as study and organizational skills. May also include other services such as career services and off-campus study.

Special services. Works with students who have physical challenges or learning disabilities such as dyslexia; also works with students who have other individual needs.

Student center and student activities. Works with the Student Government Association. Provides recreational activities on and off campus. Organizes special student activities such as guest lectures and concerts. May oversee the student newspaper and other publications. Works with clubs to arrange meeting space or funding.

Health center. Also called the infirmary; provides medical care.

Other offices. Buildings and Grounds maintains college facilities and landscaping. Security provides a safe environment. Food Service oversees dining halls, meals, and special events. There are also many other services.

Who Are the Alumni?

People who have already graduated from a particular college are the **alumni** of that college. Alumni are an important resource. They contribute money that helps keep your costs down. They help recruit and interview students who are still deciding where to go to college. You often have chances to meet alumni at college fairs and other special events. Alumni advise the administration about long-term policies for the college. They are also an important part of a college's school spirit.

How Important Is the Community?

Many colleges open their events and facilities to local residents. Museum tours, concerts, and use of the college's athletic facilities, such as the swimming pool or ice-skating arena, help to build a bond between the college and the community.

In many ways, the most important relationship that any college has is with the people and businesses in its community. Faculty and students live in the community. Many alumni also live in the community. Local businesses often hire students from a nearby college, both while they are still students and after they graduate. Local businesses may also help fund special programs at the college. Colleges help attract people to a community and the community helps attract students to the college.

Comparing Your School with College

Your School	College or University
School board	Board of trustees
Superintendent	Provost/chancellor
Principal	President
Vice principal	Deans/vice presidents
Teacher	Professor
Guidance counselor	Career counselor
Guidance counselor	Advisor/counselor
Nurse's office	Infirmary/health center
Library/media center	Learning resource center

2

Why Should I Think About College?

Some kids have always known that college is in their future. Is this true for you?

Or are you someone who has never thought much about college? Maybe you think that you're not smart enough, that you could never afford college, or that going to college wouldn't be very useful. Perhaps none of your friends are thinking about college—so why should you?

Your decisions about college are among the most important ones you will ever make. And to make these decisions, you will need information.

Learning Opportunities

So far, your education has focused on learning many skills, including reading, writing, math, and technology. You have studied many subjects, such as science and social studies. However, you haven't yet had much choice about what subjects you study or when you take them. For the most part, you and your classmates have studied the same things. You may have studied them at different levels, but the subjects have still been the same.

This pattern begins to change in high school. At that time, you have more choices about what classes to take. You begin to learn about the subjects and careers that really interest you.

College provides even more choices. You can learn technical skills, such as how to listen to a patient's heart or how to repair a computer. You can also study at a broader level, learning how the human heart works or how computers are designed to run different programs or to network with other computers.

In college, you can also choose certain courses just because they're fun, different, or interesting—whether or not they're related to your major area of study or the work you plan to do.

College can prepare you for your chosen career. And it definitely prepares you for a lifetime of learning at work, in school, or in the community. Going to college will help you become an expert learner.

In many ways, the most important skill you can learn in college is how to learn. If you master this skill, you can succeed throughout life. After all, you may find some point in your life when you want to—or have to—make changes. In the scientific and high-tech world in which we live, knowledge and careers change. Skills often need to be updated.

Becoming a lifelong learner will make you confident. You'll know you can learn whatever you want or need to know throughout your life!

Career Opportunities

College isn't just about studying specific subjects. In college you also learn more about yourself and what interests you. And you learn what doors of opportunity are waiting to be opened by someone just like you.

What If I Don't Know What I Want to Do?

If you're not sure about what you want to do or what opportunities are available to you, you're not alone. Most kids aren't sure. That includes college kids, too. Learning about your career opportunities is one important way that college can be helpful to you.

You don't have to know exactly what you want to be right now. It's more important for you to understand some basic things about careers. Some careers require a college education, but others do not. If you want to be an architect, you *must* complete college. Running your own business may not require you to have a college education, but the college courses you take can improve your chances of success.

For many careers, college is just the beginning. For example, to be a lawyer, you must first go to college and then to law school. To be a doctor, you have to go to medical school after college.

You can enter other careers with different levels of education. And various jobs within career fields may require different amounts of education. For example, to be a school teacher, you must be a college graduate. Most school teachers continue their studies after college. To be a principal or a college professor, however, you must have advanced studies beyond college. The following chart gives more examples of careers and the education you need to prepare for them.

Careers and College Education

Careers Requiring at Least Two Years of College or Technical School

Air traffic controller	Funeral director
Broadcast technician	Interior designer
Chef	Legal secretary
Computer support specialist	Medical records technician
Dental hygienist	Police officer
Fashion designer	Radiologic technologist
Fish and game warden	Registered nurse

Careers Requiring at Least Four Years of College

Accountant	Mechanical engineer
Computer engineer	Meeting and convention planner
Construction manager	Network systems analyst
Forensic science technician	Public relations manager
Human resources manager	Surveyor
Landscape architect	Teacher
Loan counselor	Technical writer

Careers Requiring More Than Four Years of College

Astronomer	Librarian
Chiropractor	Minister, priest, or rabbi
Clinical social worker	Optometrist
Dentist	Pharmacist
Doctor	Physical therapist
Guidance counselor	Professor
Judge	Urban planner
Lawyer	Veterinarian

Many occupations require you to be licensed by the state— to go through a formal process in which the state grants you permission to work in the field. Licenses or certification may be required in such diverse fields as teaching, nursing, social work, law, plumbing, insurance, medicine, real estate, and counseling.

The amount of education you need is not the only thing that differs from one career to another. Some careers, such as those in business and engineering, require specific skills. You will also need to take specific courses to develop these skills.

Other careers have less specific requirements. You can enter them with a broader range of courses and skills. For example, if you go into sales, you might have a background in business, economics, liberal arts, or communications. If you want a career in a helping profession such as social work, you could have a background in education, medicine, or social sciences.

Learning what people in a career really do, and what education and skills they need, is important for planning your future.

The images we have of careers are not always accurate. We often get our sense from the movies, television, or the news. For instance, most people's image of the Federal Bureau of Investigation (FBI) is shaped by action films and television programs featuring undercover agents in dangerous, high-speed chase situations. Would it surprise you, therefore, to know that the FBI is especially interested in hiring people who have studied accounting, science, computers, foreign languages, and art? People with these backgrounds are often able to do the behind-the-scenes work that not only helps catch criminals, but also helps make sure they are convicted. For example, an accounting background helps you research tax and business records to discover wrongdoing. Scientists perform laboratory work such as DNA analysis to study evidence, and artists help re-create crime scenes. Popular television series such as *CSI* (Crime Scene Investigation) have brought attention to the scientists who work with police forces to solve crimes.

Where Can I Find Career Information?

Every other year, the United States Department of Labor publishes the *Occupational Outlook Handbook (OOH)*. This useful guide describes types of careers, specific jobs, and information about the training needed for these jobs. It also lists jobs that are expected to be the most in demand in coming years.

The reference librarian at your school or in your community can help you find this resource. You can also find much of this information by computer. The Internet address for the *Occupational Outlook Handbook* is

> *www.bls.gov/oco/home.htm*

JIST, the publisher of *The Kids' College Almanac*, also publishes the *OOH*, as well as a useful resource called *Young Person's Occupational Outlook Handbook*, which is easy to read and describes about 270 jobs.

Some job titles even change their meaning over time. Today, a network administrator can mean someone who manages a group of broadcast stations; but it can also mean someone who manages a company's computer systems.

The Department of Labor's home page on the Internet provides links to a lot of useful information about careers. Its Web address is www.dol.gov. The department also has a Web page with links for kids. Its address is www. bls.gov/k12/.

Every year, new jobs are created. In the 1980s and early 1990s you would not have studied Web design (the creation of pages for the World Wide Web) because the Web itself did not exist. Similarly, e-commerce, the use of the Internet for buying and selling products and services, is continuing to create new jobs that never existed before.

Fast-Growing Occupations

Occupation	Projected Increase in Number of Jobs, 2006–2016
Registered nurses	+587,000
Postsecondary teachers	+382,000
Accountants and auditors	+226,000
Computer software engineers, applications	+226,000
Elementary school teachers	+209,000
Management analysts	+149,000
Computer systems analysts	+146,000
Network systems and data communications analysts	+140,000
Preschool teachers	+115,000
Computer software engineers, systems software	+99,000
Network and computer systems administrators	+83,000
Financial analysts	+75,000
Secondary school teachers	+59,000
Dental hygienists	+50,000
Physical therapists	+47,000
Computer and information systems managers	+43,000
Database administrators	+34,000
Medical records and health information technicians	+30,000
Veterinary technologists and technicians	+29,000
General and operations managers	+26,000
Respiratory therapists	+23,000
Occupational therapists	+22,000
Physical therapist assistants	+20,000
Physician assistants	+18,000
Environmental science and protection technicians	+10,000

Source: Occupational Outlook Handbook.

How Will Education Affect My Earnings?

Your education is likely to affect your future income. The more education you have, the higher your earnings are likely to be, not only in any one year, but over your entire lifetime.

Income is an important consideration when you make career and academic decisions. However, it should not be the only consideration. Quality of life, job satisfaction, work hours, job stability, where you will be able to live, and many other factors are also important to consider.

Whatever occupation you choose, if you become a life-long learner, you will increase your earning potential and have more choices and flexibility about how you will make a living. The following chart shows how your education level can affect your income. (See chapter 5 for more information about academic degrees.)

Education and Income

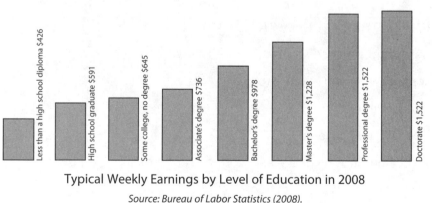

Typical Weekly Earnings by Level of Education in 2008

Source: Bureau of Labor Statistics (2008).

Who Can Tell Me About Careers?

Information about jobs that people do is all around us. Yet we usually miss it. For example, have you ever thought of asking your doctor questions like the following: Why did you become a doctor? What do you have to do to become a doctor? Where did you go to school? How did you choose which kind of doctor to be? What do you like best about your job? What do you like least?

Many of us never ask these kinds of questions. But why not? Most people enjoy talking about themselves and will gladly give you answers.

People all around you—family, friends, parents of classmates, teachers, and neighbors—can help you learn more about careers. Don't be afraid to ask hard questions. Yet understand that the people you ask won't be able to give you magic answers that make your decisions for you. However, the answers you get will help you find your own direction.

BE A CAREER DETECTIVE: ASK QUESTIONS

Why did you choose this career?

Did you always know what you wanted to be?

What would you do differently?

What kinds of jobs did you have before this one?

How have your previous jobs helped you in your current job?

Do you need any special skills or education?

How did you prepare for your career?

If you had it to do over again, would you make the same choice?

What advice do you have for kids who are interested in your career?

What Are Career Days?

Your school probably offers many opportunities for you to learn more about careers. It may even have a **career day** every year. Career days are special days when people from your community share information about their jobs, either at your school or when you visit their workplaces.

Many people have careers that you would quickly think of if you were asked to make a list of jobs—lawyer, doctor, police officer, teacher, and so on. Others have careers you may not think of quite so quickly—editor, college registrar, Web master, criminologist, microbiologist, fashion designer, factory supervisor, or surveyor.

If you go to a career day, talk to as many people as you can. Listen closely and ask questions. Some people have always known what they wanted to do. Others have made choices based on experiences and opportunities that came along. People often go in different directions than they expected.

Some people want to be their own boss. Some prefer working for others, letting them worry about running the company. Some people want to travel. Others want to stay closer to home. Some people want to do a job that has little to do with their personal hobbies. Others want to combine their interests with their job.

Job shadowing provides another way to learn about specific careers. You learn more about careers by following (or shadowing) and observing people as they go about their day-to-day business.
To learn more, go to www.jobshadow.org.

When Paul Bither went to college, he planned to study French. During his freshman year, his mother suffered a serious eye injury. This experience led Paul toward the sciences—and exploring eye care. After college, he went to optometry school. He is now an optometrist and specializes in helping patients who have low vision.

What Kinds of Career Programs Are Available?

Many business, civic, and professional groups and other organizations have programs that can help you learn about careers. Several government agencies have programs that can help, too. Some of these programs are offered at your school while others are offered at different locations. Such programs may help you explore a specific career (such as *reporter*) or an entire field (such as *publishing*).

Mentoring is discussed again in chapter 15.

These programs include summer camps, *mentoring* (working one-on-one with an adult), school and after-school programs, jobs, tours, and activities that teach you leadership skills. Many of these programs, especially those run directly through your school, are free or low cost. Others can be expensive. Even these, however, often can provide financial help to students who need it.

Southwest Airlines began its Adopt-A-Pilot program in 1997. In the program, which reaches more than 30,000 students in more than 1,250 fifth-grade classrooms across the country, classes "adopt" pilots. The students have special lessons in geography, math, science, aviation, and other classes. They learn what it's like to be a pilot and also about planes, airports, and the different places the pilots fly.

Space Camp at the U.S. Space and Rocket Center in Huntsville, Alabama, runs weeklong programs for different age groups. Activities include simulating a space shuttle mission and working in the International Space Station, using astronaut training equipment, and touring NASA's space centers. The camp also offers programs for blind and visually impaired students, as well as deaf and hard of hearing students. For more information, call 1-800-63-SPACE or visit *www.spacecamp.com*.

Preparing for Careers at Different Colleges

Career	Example of a College Where You Can Prepare for This Career
Archaeologist	Cornell University (NY)
Art therapist	Southwestern College (NM)
Astronomer	University of Arizona
Court reporter	University of Mississippi
Dance therapist	Drexel University (PA)
Earthquake engineer	University of California–Berkeley
Entomologist	Iowa State University
Fire protection engineer	University of Maryland
Flight trainer	Embry-Riddle Aeronautical University (FL)
Forest ranger	Oregon State University
Homeland security specialist	Johns Hopkins University (MD)
Interior designer	O'More College of Design (TN)
Journalist	Northwestern University (IL)
Librarian	University of Chicago (IL)
Marine biologist	University of California–Santa Barbara
Medical illustrator	Cleveland Institute of Art (OH)
Mining engineer	Colorado School of Mines
Opera singer	Indiana University
Pharmacist	Philadelphia College of Pharmacy (PA)
Social worker	Columbia University (NY)
Theater designer	Carnegie Mellon University (PA)
Veterinarian	Louisiana State University

Two-year colleges offer a wide range of career programs. At Tarrant County College in Texas, your choices include automotive collision repair, construction management, dental hygiene, fashion merchandising, management, nursing, postal service administration, radio and television broadcasting, sign-language interpretation, and welding.

TEXAS

What Are Career Centers?

Every college has an office that provides students with information and advice about careers. At these career development or career counseling centers, you can find information about careers through many sources, including books and audio, video, and computer resources.

These centers help you explore different career paths. You can learn about the different jobs that are available in various fields. You can also learn about the kind of preparation you need for these jobs.

Your school's career center, which may be in the guidance office or the library, may have access to software and Internet programs that can help you learn more about careers.

Career testing and counseling can help you find out things about yourself that might be important when you choose a career. These services help you identify your interests and strengths. Through a combination of conversations, surveys, and tests, a career counselor can help you learn more about your personal likes, dislikes, and skills and how these compare with the likes, dislikes, and skills of people who work in different jobs.

For example, you might find you have an interest in art, but you don't know how you could turn it into a career. Art is a broad field with different opportunities in areas such as advertising, sales, entertainment, computer-aided design, fashion, architecture, and many others— including sculpting and painting.

A **career counselor** can help you find a good fit. Suppose you are an outgoing person who enjoys meeting new people. You may want to go into sales. If you are a creative or artistic person who is clever with words and new ideas, advertising may be a better choice for you. If you like the idea of combining art with math and engineering, then architecture might be an area to consider.

Many job placement offices offer students workshops on writing resumes, interviewing, and job search skills, including using the Internet. At many colleges, students have the opportunity to interview for jobs with hundreds of businesses, government agencies, and other organizations that come to recruit students.

What Is Job Placement?

Most career centers have a **job placement** office. This office invites employers to the college to interview students. Most companies that talk to students prefer to hire those who are ready to graduate. But in some cases, companies hire students for the summer. In this way, the companies can see whether the student is someone they would want to hire for full-time work after college. Part-time or summer work, as well as special summer programs offered by many colleges, also gives students opportunities to explore whether certain jobs, careers, and companies are a good match for them.

Job placement services are among the most important services offered by proprietary schools, technical institutes, and other specialized programs. Before deciding where to attend, learn about these services and the school's success in helping students get jobs.

Is College the Only Way to Prepare for a Career?

In some cases, college is the only way. But for some careers, your options include vocational and proprietary schools, technical institutes, and other specialized programs. These schools often focus on specialized areas such as electronics, culinary arts, plumbing, cosmetology, and so on.

Remember: No one can take education and skills away from you. The more you have, the better off you will be!

Artistic Opportunities

Colleges give students opportunities to develop acting, directing, musical, and artistic skills. In most cases, students simply enjoy these experiences and continue them after graduation through church and local choirs, community theater, or for personal relaxation. Some students, however, choose professional careers in the arts. If you are interested in the arts as a career, you should look for colleges that offer special programs in your area of interest.

Some colleges focus primarily on the performing arts. Among them are Berklee College of Music, American Musical and Dramatic Academy, the Conservatory of Music at Oberlin College, and Westminster Choir College of Rider University.

Other colleges emphasize the visual arts. These include the School of the Art Institute of Chicago, Rhode Island School of Design, San Francisco Art Institute, and Ringling College of Art and Design.

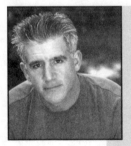

Gregory Jbara first majored in communications and minored in physics at the University of Michigan, even though his passion was acting. He ultimately transferred in his fourth year to the Juilliard School, Drama Division, in New York City. Since gaining his BFA, Gregory has worked steadily in commercials and voiceovers, in film and television, and on Broadway (2009 Tony Award for his role as Jackie Elliot in *Billy Elliot the Musical*). Gregory recommends a college education, noting, "Few people are prepared to make choices about careers right out of high school. Remember, you can always change schools or career options or even your hair color! You always have the option to change your course in life." Gregory's Web page can be found at *www.gregoryjbara.com*.

Athletic Opportunities

Students headed for athletic careers—especially in sports such as basketball, football, hockey, baseball, and tennis—use their college years to develop their skills. Top athletes in other sports, such as swimming, soccer, gymnastics, and track and field, often compete at the college level. College also provides opportunities for people who are interested in coaching, sports therapy, sports psychology, and sports marketing and management.

For most students, athletics simply enrich their college years. Even if you don't play on an official team, you can participate in a wide range of sports activities.

Most colleges have **intramural sports.** Students form teams and play other teams from within the college. Intramural teams, often called club teams, are usually open to anyone who wants to play. Also, many colleges have excellent facilities where all students can play racquetball, lift weights, exercise, swim, run track, and play basketball in their free time.

Only a small number of college athletes move to the professional ranks. Goals and dreams are important. But it's also important to have a backup plan and prepare for another career.

Eddie George won the 1995 Heisman Trophy and other awards as a record-setting running back for The Ohio State University. A first-round draft choice of the Tennessee Titans (then the Houston Oilers), he was the National Football League's Offensive Rookie of the Year in 1996, was a Pro Bowl selection for the next four years, and played in 2000's Super Bowl XXXIV. Eddie prepared for life after football by studying landscape architecture in college. He is a founding partner of EDGE, a company that develops public parks, town centers, retirement communities, school athletic facilities, and more. Eddie is also involved in numerous charities, camps that provide fitness training, and other businesses. He has gone back to graduate school to study at Northwestern University's Kellogg School of Management.

Life Opportunities

When you think about college, you may think first about studying and preparing for a career. But college also enriches your personal life. It helps you make important transitions.

Living Independently

Like many students, you may find that your first real opportunity to live away from your parents and family comes when you go to college. You will have to take greater personal responsibility on a day-to-day basis.

For example, you may be used to someone asking you every day whether you've finished your homework. Maybe you're not allowed to do certain things—watch TV, play computer games, talk on the phone—until your homework is done.

When you go to college, you probably won't be asked about homework all the time. You won't be told when to do it. Although you might like this freedom, you might find that being asked about homework helped you stay on track. Now you will have to motivate yourself to succeed. You will have to set your own schedule.

For every freedom that you gain, you also gain a responsibility. Learning to balance these two—freedom and responsibility—is just one part of college. But it is a very important life skill.

You'll find lots of support at college for making this transition. Professors will tell you when assignments are due and exams are scheduled. And lots of college services will be nearby, ready to help you organize your time.

Establishing Goals

You don't have to be sure about what you want to do after college in order to start college. But college gives you the chance to think about what is important to you and what you want your life to be like.

Starting college is like starting a new year and making resolutions. You may have goals that include preparing for a career, getting good grades, trying new activities, learning new skills, making new friends, or even learning for its own sake. Setting goals will help you get more out of the college experience.

Meeting a Wide Range of People

When you go to college, you have the chance to meet people with backgrounds different from your own. Your classmates may be from other parts of the state or country. They may be from other parts of the world. Their cultural or religious backgrounds may be very different from yours.

You will meet people of all ages with various points of view. Your classmates and teachers will have experiences different from yours. Therefore, you will be exposed to new ideas, viewpoints, and lifestyles.

You will want to think carefully about how other people's perspectives fit with your own opinions, goals, and values. You will be able to use this experience to learn more about yourself and others.

And you will make new friends. Some of the friends you make in college may become important to you in other ways, for example, in helping you find a job later in life. Others will become lifelong friends, enriching your life for years to come.

Exploring New Opportunities

Perhaps the most exciting part of college is the chance to try new experiences. You can take some courses simply for enjoyment or to satisfy your curiosity. You can try a new sport—perhaps rowing or lacrosse—or a recreational activity that may not have been available to you before.

You may be able to perform in a play, work on a newspaper, or join student government. You might get involved in the college community, perhaps coordinating a food drive, helping build housing for the homeless, organizing a political rally, or raising money for charity.

You will have the opportunity to listen to and meet artists, journalists, political leaders, researchers, and others who visit the college. Some of the people you meet may be able to offer you advice about careers and maybe even a job! You may have the chance to travel, studying in other parts of the country or the world. Every day of college will provide new opportunities that will help you grow in new and exciting ways!

3

Who Goes to College?

Two hundred years ago, the typical college student in the United States was a young, white man. Women and students of color were rarely found at college. Not until the 1830s did changes begin to happen. For instance, when Oberlin College in Ohio was founded in 1835, the trustees expressed a clear interest in educating students of color. And in 1841, the first three women in the United States to receive A.B. degrees (see chapter 5) graduated from Oberlin.

How times have changed! Today anyone who wants to go to college has the opportunity to go. Perhaps before long, you'll be going, too!

The Basics

If you decide to attend college someday, you will not be alone. Every year about 18 million students attend college.

Four-Year and Two-Year Students

Enrollment in two-year colleges has skyrocketed in the past 50 years. Today about 37 percent of college students attend community colleges.

COLLEGE STUDENT ENROLLMENT

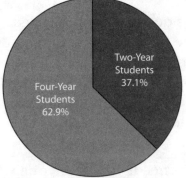

Two-Year Students 37.1%

Four-Year Students 62.9%

Source: U.S. National Center for Educational Statistics, most recent data available (2005).

Some colleges require all freshmen to live in college-run housing. Many believe that these students have enough of an adjustment to make without adding the responsibility of managing a home. After their first year, students have more choice about where they live.

Residential Students and Commuters

At some colleges, the majority of students live in housing owned and operated by the college. This is true especially at private colleges that require you to attend full time. Living at the college with other students is often considered an important part of the college experience.

Other colleges do not offer college-run housing. At these colleges, students live at home or on their own. They must *commute* (travel) to and from college each day. This is most often the case at two-year colleges.

Full-Time and Part-Time Students

Students who go to a four-year college on a full-time basis can usually graduate in four years. Similarly, students who go to a two-year college on a full-time basis can usually graduate in two years. Students may need more time to graduate if they take extra classes or decide to change their major field of study. Others may need less time if they take extra courses and study year-round.

Many people cannot attend college full-time. They may have other commitments such as holding down a job or taking care of their family. For some, money is an issue. Many students simply prefer to take one or two courses at a time rather than a full load of classes. Most colleges, though not all, allow you to attend part-time. If you want this option, double-check that the colleges of interest to you will let you attend part-time.

An increasing number of programs—in fields such as engineering and architecture, for instance—are five-year programs.

Day and Evening Students

Many colleges give you a lot of choices about when to take your classes. Community colleges in particular have developed their schedules to meet the needs of the working student. Students can attend evening classes or even weekend classes. Some classes meet only once a week. Many colleges also offer early morning classes that you can take before work.

Distance education, which is discussed in chapter 4, allows you to take your classes at any hour of the day.

Scottsdale Community College (SCC) in Arizona, like many other colleges, offers courses at a variety of times throughout the day. For example, you can take an English composition class as early as 7:30 a.m. For students who can attend classes only at night, SCC offers the same course starting as late as 7:15 p.m.

ARIZONA

Today's Students

Unlike the students of 200 years ago, today's students come from many different backgrounds.

Age

Today's college students come from all age groups. Most full-time students are younger than 24 years old. But most part-time students are older than 24.

Older students, many of whom have already been to college, take college courses for a variety of reasons. Rapid changes in technology require some workers to update their knowledge. People planning to change careers need new information and skills. Others enjoy taking courses for enjoyment or personal accomplishment.

Gender

Community colleges have traditionally served more women than men.

In recent years, a big change has been the number of women who attend college. In the 1950s, twice as many men attended college as women. By the 1970s, women were catching up. Now, women outpace the men, with about 2.5 million more women attending college than men.

Male and Female College Enrollment

Year	Male Students	Female Students
1955	1,733,000	920,000
1965	3,630,000	2,291,000
1970	5,044,000	3,537,000
1980	5,874,000	6,223,000
1985	5,818,000	6,429,000
1990	6,284,000	7,535,000
1995	6,343,000	7,919,000
2000	6,722,000	8,591,000
2005	7,456,000	10,032,000

Number of Women and Men at U.S. Colleges

College or University	Women*	Men*
Alabama State University	2,773	1,871
Pima Community College (AZ)	18,775	15,361
University of San Francisco (CA)	3,392	2,007
Colorado School of Mines (CO)	720	2,590
U.S. Coast Guard Academy (CT)	263	712
Florida State University	17,546	14,049
Spelman College (GA)	2,310	20
DePaul University (IL)	8,340	6,684
Indiana University–Bloomington	15,519	14,875
Kirkwood Community College (IA)	8,078	7,163
Kansas State University	8,973	9,572
Bates College (ME)	857	803
United States Naval Academy	914	3,529
Massachusetts Institute of Technology	1,857	2,315
University of Michigan	13,067	13,016
University of Mississippi	5,000	4,800
Dana College (NE)	315	375
Colby-Sawyer College (NH)	618	330
The College of New Jersey	3,622	2,583
Westchester Community College (NY)	7,063	5,550
Duke University (NC)	2,990	3,280
The Ohio State University	17,700	19,700
Reed College (OR)	801	663
Lehigh University (PA)	1,968	2,788
Roger Williams University (RI)	2,117	2,236
Furman University (SC)	1,534	1,216
University of South Dakota	4,287	2,557
Vanderbilt University (TN)	3,436	3,096
Austin Community College (TX)	20,405	15,393
Radford University (VA)	4,625	3,398
Marquette University (WI)	4,350	3,650
Western Wyoming Community College	1,745	2,133

Estimated number of full-time and part-time undergraduate students, fall 2007.

Who Went Where to College?

Graduate	College
Scott Adams (cartoonist, *Dilbert*)	Hartwick College (NY)
Daniel Akaka (senator)	University of Hawaii
Christiane Amanpour (broadcast journalist)	University of Rhode Island
Sean Astin (actor, director)	University of California–Los Angeles
Evan Bayh (senator)	Indiana University
Jeff Bezos (founder, Amazon.com)	Princeton University (NJ)
Sabeer Bhatia (founder, Hotmail)	California Institute of Technology
Joe Biden (U.S. vice president)	University of Delaware
Gloria Borger (broadcast journalist)	Colgate University (NY)
Benjamin Bratt (actor)	University of California–Santa Barbara
Sergey Brin (cofounder, Google)	University of Maryland
Ken Burns (filmmaker, historian)	Hampshire College (MA)
Eric Cantor (congressman)	George Washington University (DC)
Benjamin Carson (neurosurgeon)	Yale University (CT)
Kenneth Chenault (chairman, American Express)	Bowdoin College (ME)
Kristin Chenoweth (actress, singer)	Oklahoma City University
Kenny Chesney (singer)	East Tennessee State University
Steven Chu (Nobel Prize–winning scientist)	University of Rochester (NY)
Bryan Clay (athlete, decathlon)	Azusa Pacific University (CA)
Hillary Rodham Clinton (secretary of state)	Wellesley College (MA)
Tom Cole (congressman)	Grinnell College (IA)
David Cook (singer)	University of Central Missouri
Anderson Cooper (broadcast journalist)	Yale University (CT)
Jeff Corwin (host, Animal Planet)	Bridgewater State College (MA)
Bill Cosby (entertainer, author)	Temple University (PA)
Candy Crowley (broadcast journalist)	Randolph College (VA)

Growing up in San Diego, explorer Robert Ballard developed an early interest in scuba diving and marine life. He studied marine geology at the University of California–Santa Barbara. His studies and early jobs led him to deep-ocean exploration. Among his many achievements, he located and explored *Titanic,* the great ocean liner that sank in 1912.

Who Went Where to College?

Graduate	College
Taye Diggs (actor)	Syracuse University (NY)
Jamie Dimon (chairman, JPMorgan Chase)	Tufts University (MA)
Rita Dove (poet)	Miami University (OH)
Tim Duncan (athlete, basketball)	Wake Forest University (NC)
Louise Erdrich (poet, writer)	Dartmouth College (NH)
Gloria Estefan (singer)	University of Miami (FL)
Russ Feingold (senator)	University of Wisconsin–Madison
Tina Fey (comedian)	University of Virginia
Renee Fleming (opera singer)	SUNY–Potsdam (NY)
Brendan Fraser (actor)	Cornish College of the Arts (WA)
Phyllis Frelich (actress)	Gallaudet University (DC)
Nomar Garciaparra (athlete, baseball)	Georgia Institute of Technology
Jennifer Garner (actress)	Denison University (OH)
Robert Gates (secretary of defense)	College of William and Mary (VA)
Doris Kearns Goodwin (historian, writer)	Colby College (ME)
John Grisham (writer)	Mississippi State University
Sanjay Gupta (doctor, medical reporter)	University of Michigan
Mia Hamm (athlete, soccer)	University of North Carolina
Anne Hathaway (actress)	New York University
S.E. Hinton (writer)	University of Tulsa (OK)
Gwen Ifill (broadcast journalist)	Simmons College (MA)
Hugh Jackman (actor)	University of Technology, Sydney (Australia)
Jesse Jackson, Jr. (congressman)	North Carolina Agricultural and Technical State University
Phil Jackson (basketball coach)	University of North Dakota
Quincy Jones (musician, producer)	Berklee College of Music (MA)
Andrea Jung (chairman, Avon)	Princeton University (NJ)

In 2009, Dr. Andrew Feustel flew on the final Space Shuttle mission to service the Hubble Space Telescope. He began college at Oakland Community College in Michigan while working as an auto mechanic. He continued his education at Purdue University in Indiana and Queen's University in Canada.

Who Went Where to College?

Graduate	College
Muhtar Kent (chairman, Coca-Cola)	University of Hull (United Kingdom)
Charles Krauthammer (journalist)	McGill University (Canada)
Brian Lamb (founder, C-SPAN)	Purdue University (IN)
Spike Lee (film director)	Morehouse College (GA)
John Lewis (congressman)	Fisk University (TN)
Maya Lin (architect)	Yale University (CT)
Gary Locke (secretary of commerce)	Yale University (CT)
Keith Lockhart (conductor, Boston Pops)	Furman University (SC)
Yo-Yo Ma (cellist)	Harvard University (MA)
David Mamet (playwright)	Goddard College (VT)
Peyton Manning (athlete, football)	University of Tennessee
John McCain (senator)	U.S. Naval Academy (MD)
Audra McDonald (actress, singer)	Julliard School of Music (NY)
Idina Menzel (actress, singer)	New York University
Leslie Moonves (president, CBS)	Bucknell University (PA)
Toni Morrison (writer)	Howard University (DC)
Ralph Nader (consumer activist)	Princeton University (NJ)
Michelle Obama (first lady)	Princeton University (NJ)
Ellen Ochoa (astronaut)	San Diego State University (CA)
Brad Paisley (singer)	Belmont University (TN)
Sarah Palin (former governor)	University of Idaho
Candace Parker (athlete, basketball)	University of Tennessee
Itzhak Perlman (violinist)	Juilliard School (NY)
Natalie Portman (actress)	Harvard College (MA)
Colin Powell (general, former secretary of state)	City University of New York
Condoleezza Rice (former secretary of state)	University of Denver

Where did authors of popular books for kids attend college? Theodor Geisel—Dr. Seuss—attended Dartmouth College in New Hampshire. Judy Blume, author of *Tales of a Fourth Grade Nothing* and many others, went to New York University. In 2004, she became the first children's author to receive an honorary National Book Award.

Who Went Where to College?

Graduate	College
Mitt Romney (businessman, former governor)	Brigham Young University (UT)
Ileana Ros-Lehtinen (congresswoman)	Florida International University
J.K. Rowling (author)	University of Exeter (United Kingdom)
Ken Salazar (secretary of interior)	Colorado College
Adam Sandler (actor)	New York University
Howard Schultz (chairman, Starbucks)	Northern Michigan University
Donna Shalala (president, University of Miami)	Western College for Women (OH)
Eric Shinseki (secretary of veterans affairs)	U.S. Military Academy (NY)
Ruth Simmons (president, Brown University)	Dillard University (LA)
Olympia Snowe (senator)	University of Maine
Stephen Sondheim (composer)	Williams College (MA)
Sonia Sotomayor (Supreme Court justice)	Princeton University (NJ)
Steven Spielberg (director, producer)	California State University–Long Beach
Debbie Stabenow (senator)	Michigan State University
Meryl Streep (actress)	Vassar College (NY)
Susan Stroman (Broadway choreographer)	University of Delaware
Amy Tan (writer)	San José State University (CA)
Isaac Tigrett (cofounder, Hard Rock Cafe)	Centre College (KY)
Neil deGrasse Tyson (astrophysicist)	Harvard College (MA)
Carrie Underwood (singer)	Northeastern State University (OK)
Nydia Velázquez (congresswoman)	University of Puerto Rico
Denzel Washington (actor)	Fordham University (NY)
Meg Whitman (former president, eBay)	Princeton University (NJ)
Oprah Winfrey (talk show host, producer)	Tennessee State University
Kevin Youkilis (athlete, baseball)	University of Cincinnati (OH)

Ed Pastor represents Arizona's fourth district in Congress and is a past chairman of the Congressional Hispanic Caucus. The first member of his family to attend college and law school, he graduated from Arizona State University. Before entering politics, he was a high school chemistry teacher.

Race and Ethnicity

Hispanic students now make up at least one-fourth of the student body at more than 260 colleges.

The racial and ethnic mix of college students has changed considerably over the past several decades. In 2007, 32 percent of college students were minorities, compared with 15 percent in 1976.

The civil rights movement of the 1950s and 1960s helped to open up educational opportunities to people of all races and ethnicities. Since then, colleges have worked hard to better represent the diversity in their communities and in the general population. Many colleges have designed programs that focus on attracting students from many different backgrounds and experiences and ensuring the success of those who attend.

MONTANA

About three dozen colleges that focus on the needs and concerns of American Indians have been established throughout a dozen states in the West and Midwest. Several of these colleges, including Blackfeet Community College, Fort Peck Community College, and Little Big Horn College, are located in Montana.

ALABAMA

In 1881, Tuskegee University was founded in Alabama to provide industrial training for black students. Famous American educator Booker T. Washington headed the school until 1915 and transformed it into an important industrial and agricultural center. The university has continued to expand its offerings into a variety of professional and liberal arts areas as well. In 1896, George Washington Carver moved to Tuskegee. While there, he conducted his famous experiments with peanuts and other crops. Important agricultural research continues at Tuskegee to this day.

Geography

The number of people who live in each state varies quite a bit across the country. In a similar way, the number of students who attend college in each state also varies.

By a wide margin, California has more college students than any other state. Almost 300,000 freshmen begin college in California each year. Other states with more than 100,000 college freshmen include Texas, New York, Florida, Pennsylvania, Illinois, and Ohio. States with the fewest number of college students include Alaska, Wyoming, Vermont, Delaware, North Dakota, and Hawaii. Of course, these are also states that have relatively small populations.

When you're ready to go to college, you will be able to apply to schools in your own state as well as schools in other states. Most students—about 80 percent—stay in their own state. This is true in part because most states have large state university systems that cost less if you are a resident. Therefore, you can go away to college without going too far from home or spending too much. For many, this is the best of both worlds!

Massachusetts, Pennsylvania, and New York bring in a lot of students from out of state. All three states have many nationally known private colleges. For example, each fall, more than 26,000 freshmen *come* to Massachusetts from out of state, while about 19,000 freshmen *leave* for colleges in other states.

College provides an opportunity to explore living in another state or another part of the country.

New Jersey's pattern is different. More students leave New Jersey to go to college than come to New Jersey from other states. This is not surprising, though. Together, nearby Pennsylvania and New York have almost 300 four-year colleges. Thus, New Jersey students have many choices close to home.

How Many Students Are in My State?

State	College Students in 1970*	College Students in 2005*
Alabama	104,000	256,000
Alaska	9,000	30,000
Arizona	110,000	546,000
Arkansas	52,000	143,000
California	1,257,000	2,400,000
Colorado	123,000	303,000
Connecticut	125,000	175,000
Delaware	25,000	52,000
Florida	236,000	873,000
Georgia	127,000	427,000
Hawaii	39,000	67,000
Idaho	35,000	78,000
Illinois	452,000	833,000
Indiana	193,000	361,000
Iowa	109,000	228,000
Kansas	102,000	192,000
Kentucky	99,000	245,000
Louisiana	121,000	198,000
Maine	34,000	66,000
Maryland	150,000	314,000
Massachusetts	304,000	443,000
Michigan	393,000	627,000
Minnesota	161,000	362,000
Mississippi	74,000	151,000
Missouri	184,000	374,000
Montana	30,000	48,000

*Rounded to the nearest thousand.

In 1970, about 67,000 students were enrolled at colleges in Puerto Rico and the American territories of American Samoa, Micronesia, Guam, the Marshall Islands, the Northern Marianas, Palau, and the U.S. Virgin Islands. By 2005, the number of students had grown to more than 223,000.

How Many Students Are in My State?

State	College Students in 1970*	College Students in 2005*
Nebraska	67,000	121,000
Nevada	14,000	110,000
New Hampshire	29,000	70,000
New Jersey	216,000	380,000
New Mexico	44,000	131,000
New York	806,000	1,152,000
North Carolina	172,000	484,000
North Dakota	31,000	49,000
Ohio	376,000	616,000
Oklahoma	110,000	208,000
Oregon	122,000	200,000
Pennsylvania	411,000	692,000
Rhode Island	46,000	81,000
South Carolina	70,000	210,000
South Dakota	31,000	49,000
Tennessee	135,000	283,000
Texas	442,000	1,241,000
Utah	82,000	201,000
Vermont	22,000	40,000
Virginia	152,000	439,000
Washington	184,000	348,000
West Virginia	63,000	100,000
Wisconsin	202,000	335,000
Wyoming	15,000	35,000
District of Columbia	77,000	105,000

*Rounded to the nearest thousand.

The biggest increase in college enrollment over the past 30 years has come from states such as Florida, Texas, and California. These states have rapidly growing populations. Their statewide systems have also added many new colleges.

Economic Background

College was once a place only for students from wealthy backgrounds. The land-grant colleges built in the latter half of the nineteenth century were intended to make college more available to students from all economic groups. Community colleges have also increased accessibility. They provide low-cost education and flexible scheduling. The increase of federal assistance through loan programs and grants has also made college more accessible.

Socioeconomic background refers to the education, occupations, and incomes of groups or individuals.

As recently as 1982, more than 29 percent of students from the lowest socioeconomic backgrounds did not plan to attend college. By the 1990s, this number fell to 8.1 percent. Even more dramatic: In 1982, about 38 percent of this same group planned to go to college directly after high school. But by the 1990s, more than 80 percent planned to go to college directly after high school.

International Students in the United States

Every year a large number of students come from other countries to study in the United States. For the most part, the number has grown through the years. Now more than 600,000 students from other countries study at U.S. colleges and universities. (In addition, many American students study in other countries each year—see chapter 4.)

The single largest group of international students is from South and East Asia. In 2007, more than 94,000 students came from India and at least 81,000 more came from China. These students, along with those from South Korea, Japan, Taiwan, Thailand, Indonesia, and Malaysia, represent more than half of all international students who come here to study.

International Students in the United States

Country or Region of Origin	Number of Students in the United States in Fall 2007	Percentage of International Students in 2007
Brazil	7,578	1.2
Canada	29,051	4.7
China	81,127	13.0
Colombia	6,662	1.1
France	7,050	1.1
Germany	8,907	1.4
Hong Kong	8,286	1.3
India	94,563	15.2
Indonesia	7,692	1.2
Japan	33,974	5.4
Kenya	5,838	0.9
Malaysia	5,428	0.9
Mexico	14,837	2.4
Nepal	8,936	1.4
Nigeria	6,222	1.0
Pakistan	5,345	0.9
Russia	4,906	0.8
Saudi Arabia	9,873	1.6
South Korea	69,124	11.1
Taiwan	29,001	4.6
Thailand	9,004	1.4
Turkey	12,030	1.9
United Kingdom	8,367	1.3
Venezuela	4,446	0.7
Vietnam	8,769	1.4

Where Did U.S. Presidents Go to College?

President	College
George Washington	Did not attend
John Adams	Harvard College (MA)
Thomas Jefferson	College of William and Mary (VA)
James Madison	College of New Jersey (now Princeton)
James Monroe	College of William and Mary (VA)*
John Quincy Adams	Harvard College (MA)
Andrew Jackson	Did not attend
Martin Van Buren	Did not attend
William Henry Harrison	Hampden-Sydney College (VA)
John Tyler	College of William and Mary (VA)*
James K. Polk	University of North Carolina
Zachary Taylor	Did not attend
Millard Fillmore	Did not attend
Franklin Pierce	Bowdoin College (ME)
James Buchanan	Dickinson College (PA)
Abraham Lincoln	Did not attend
Andrew Johnson	Did not attend
Ulysses S. Grant	U.S. Military Academy (NY)
Rutherford B. Hayes	Kenyon College (OH) Harvard Law School (MA)
James A. Garfield	Hiram College (OH)* Williams College (MA)
Chester Alan Arthur	Union College (NY)
Grover Cleveland	Did not attend
Benjamin Harrison	Miami University (OH)
William McKinley	Allegheny College (PA)*
Theodore Roosevelt	Harvard University (MA)

Attended but did not graduate.

Before being elected president of the United States, Woodrow Wilson served as president of Princeton University (NJ) and Dwight Eisenhower served as president of Columbia University (NY).

Where Did U.S. Presidents Go to College?

President	College
William Howard Taft	Yale University (CT) Cincinnati Law School (OH)
Woodrow Wilson	Davidson College (NC)* College of New Jersey (now Princeton) University of Virginia Law School
Warren G. Harding	Ohio Central College
Calvin Coolidge	Amherst College (MA)
Herbert Hoover	Stanford University (CA)
Franklin D. Roosevelt	Harvard University (MA) Columbia University Law School (NY)
Harry S. Truman	Did not attend
Dwight D. Eisenhower	U.S. Military Academy (NY)
John F. Kennedy	Harvard University (MA)
Lyndon B. Johnson	Southwest Texas State Teachers College (now Texas State University)
Richard M. Nixon	Whittier College (CA) Duke University Law School (NC)
Gerald Ford	University of Michigan Yale University Law School (CT)
Jimmy Carter	Georgia Southwestern College* Georgia Institute of Technology United States Naval Academy (MD)
Ronald Reagan	Eureka College (IL)
George H. W. Bush	Yale University (CT)
Bill Clinton	Georgetown University (DC) Oxford University (Britain) Yale University Law School (CT)
George W. Bush	Yale University (CT) Harvard Business School (MA)
Barack H. Obama	Occidental College (CA) Columbia University (NY) Harvard Law School (MA)

Attended but did not graduate.

President Herbert Hoover was in the first freshman class at Stanford University, where he studied geology and mining and met his wife, Lou Henry—the only woman geology student.

Students with Disabilities

The number of students with physical and learning disabilities has increased in recent years. Colleges are now more accessible than ever to students with special needs. Ramps, elevators, and other conveniences have been added. Academic and other special services for students have been added as well.

Medical advances, legal protections, and cultural changes have opened doors for many students with disabilities. Technology, especially computers, is a big part of the story, too. Not too long ago, people with disabilities were often looked at in terms of what they *could not* do. The focus today is more often on what people *can* accomplish regardless of their disabilities.

First-Generation Students

Students whose parents did not attend college are often referred to as **first-generation students.** This term may also apply to those students who are immigrants to the United States.

Many colleges recognize that, in some cases, first-generation students have special needs when they apply to college and begin their studies. Some of these colleges have set up special programs that help make college more accessible to people who thought they would never be able to attend college.

The Bottom Line

If you *want to go* to college, you *can go* to college. If you want college in your future, it is there for you. And even though you may not go to the first choice on your list, you will still go to college—one that offers you a good education and real opportunities.

4

Where Are Colleges Located?

Colleges are located everywhere! As the number of colleges in the United States has increased, so has the variety of colleges.

Today, colleges and universities come in all sizes and settings. For example, you can find extremely large colleges in small towns and very small colleges in big cities.

You may not even need to leave home to get a college education. Instead, college can come to you, especially through your computer, your television, and occasionally the mail!

What Is a Campus?

If you hear that a college has a beautiful **campus,** you are hearing about the college's physical setting as well as its buildings. Sometimes these are referred to as buildings and grounds.

College campuses are located in a wide range of settings. Some colleges, like DePaul University in Chicago and Wayne State University in Detroit, are located in the heart of a big city. These are examples of urban colleges.

Other colleges have rural campuses and might be located in ranch or farm country. Eastern Wyoming College in Torrington, Wyoming, and Castleton State College in Castleton, Vermont, are examples of rural colleges.

Many colleges, especially community colleges, have campuses located in the suburbs. Cuyahoga Community College in Ohio and Northern Virginia Community College are examples of suburban colleges.

The Wolfson Campus, one of Miami-Dade College's eight campuses, is located in the heart of downtown Miami and serves students in a highly populated urban area.

Still other colleges, such as Clarkson University in New York and Williams College in Massachusetts, are located in the heart of small towns. The relationships between the towns and the colleges are extremely close.

College campuses vary in other ways. Some are hilly; others are flat. The buildings are close together on some campuses. On others, the buildings are spread apart, with lots of space for walkways, fields, trees, gardens, or ponds. The layout of the campus makes some colleges more accessible than others to students with physical disabilities or to students who commute.

The architecture also varies. For example, at many older colleges, you will see a lot of traditional redbrick or stone buildings. Many colleges feature modern architecture. Some even have dramatic sculptures located around campus.

How you feel about a college's campus may be an important factor when you decide where to attend.

The Business Administration Building, like other buildings at the University of Texas at El Paso (UTEP), is designed in the style of buildings from the Himalayan kingdom of Bhutan. UTEP's campus provides one of the only examples of this ancient architecture in the Western Hemisphere.

63

What Are Branch Campuses?

Sometimes a college has more than one location. The college may have a main or central campus. However, to meet the needs of other students, the college sets up additional campuses in other locations. These campuses are often called **branch campuses** or **extension centers.** Branch campuses often start with temporary buildings or rented space. Permanent buildings are added later when student demand grows.

Two or more colleges may work together to provide opportunities to a broader range of students in underserved locations. In some cases, one college may use space on another's campus to benefit the students from both colleges.

Education centers are generally smaller than campuses. They may even be as simple as one or two rooms in a storefront or office building. Their location provides students with added convenience.

For example, Shoreline Community College's main campus is about 10 miles north of Seattle, Washington. In recent years, the population east of Seattle has grown dramatically. In response, Shoreline opened the Northshore Center in Bothell. That center then relocated to Lake Forest Park, so that Shoreline can better meet the high-tech training needs of the region.

Sometimes branch campuses become equal in size or importance to the original campus. The college may become a multicampus college. The campuses may or may not share a common administration. However, they often operate independently from each other.

MARYLAND

The University System of Maryland created The Universities of Shady Grove campus to better serve one of Maryland's fastest-growing regions. Students can take classes at one or more of the nine Maryland public colleges that share buildings and certain services.

Can I Learn Away from Campus?

You no longer need to go to a traditional campus to study at the college level. Many alternative choices are available, making it possible for more people than ever to go to college.

What Is Distance Learning?

Students can learn at a distance, and more and more are doing so. They can take courses from home, from the workplace, and from many other locations—even from the South Pole or an aircraft carrier in the middle of the ocean!

Distance learning is instruction that takes place when the student and the teacher are not in the same location all or most of the time. The Internet, television, DVDs, CDs, audiotapes, videotapes, video streaming, and print-ed materials all are used in distance learning.

Sometimes students are able to interact with the teacher in *real time*—when a class is actually being taught. In fact, a class might be made up of dozens of students in different locations, even from all over the world. Yet the students are learning at the same time. In other cases, e-mail and the Internet make it possible for students to set their own schedules. They interact with their teachers and other students on an individual basis.

To find out more about Seminole State College's distance learning pro-gram, visit its Web site at www.seminolestate.edu/dl/.

Seminole State College, in central Florida, offers many different kinds of distance learning programs in a wide range of subjects. Students can choose different forms of learning, though not every course is offered in more than one way. Students can complete all or most of their aca-demic requirements through distance learning classes.

When Is Distance Learning a Good Choice?

Distance learning is an excellent choice for mature, self-disciplined students. This learning option allows some students—for instance, those who have to work, travel, or help care for family members—to take more classes than they could if they had to attend traditional classes. Distance learning also provides great opportunities to take classes that are not available nearby or at a convenient time. Students can also develop career skills or simply enjoy the fun of learning.

Online Studies

Before the Internet, correspondence courses were the major form of distance learning. Course materials, homework, and tests were sent back and forth through the mail.

Many colleges now offer online courses. Some require students to attend class on campus for some portion of the time while studying online the rest of the time. In some cases, the classes are entirely online, although students may need to take exams on campus or at an approved test center. Many colleges offer entire degrees online. The University of Phoenix, Excelsior College, Rio Salada College, and Governor's State University are examples of colleges that offer many or all of their degree programs online.

SAMPLE ONLINE COURSES AT THE UNIVERSITY OF PHOENIX

Business Law	Organizational Leadership
Human Nutrition	eBusiness
Criminology	Creative Writing
Statistics	Pop Culture and the Arts
Public and Community Health	Introduction to Psychology
Web Design	Astronomy

Military Choices

Distance learning has opened up many opportunities for members of the armed forces and their families. People who work for the military may move a lot or are often stationed in distant or remote locations. As a result, they do not always stay long enough at one specific college to complete its graduation requirements. In addition, they may need specific courses, especially in engineering and electronics.

Military bases often have education centers in which one or more colleges offer classes. Some colleges have branches on or near military bases or other government facilities.

For example, the University of Maryland University College (UMUC) has numerous international locations that serve students from all 50 states and on all 7 continents. You can take courses through UMUC, even if you are stationed as far away as Antarctica.

To learn more about these opportunities, visit the SOC Web site at www.soc.aascu.org.

The military also has special partnerships with more than 1,800 colleges. Partner colleges are called *Servicemembers Opportunity Colleges* (SOCs). These partnerships help military personnel and their family members complete college programs.

The Community College of the Air Force serves more than 300,000 members of the Air Force, the Air National Guard, and the Air Force Reserve. You must be in one of these to attend. The courses that students take include those that are part of their regular Air Force training, as well as other courses offered by approximately 100 civilian technical schools and colleges in many different locations.

How Many Colleges Are in My State?

State	Four-Year Colleges*	Two-Year Colleges*
Alabama	31	26
Alaska	5	2
Arizona	19	22
Arkansas	22	25
California	174	129
Colorado	27	16
Connecticut	28	17
Delaware	6	5
Florida	72	53
Georgia	54	56
Hawaii	9	8
Idaho	8	3
Illinois	94	55
Indiana	57	18
Iowa	38	19
Kansas	29	29
Kentucky	35	16
Louisiana	27	47
Maine	20	10
Maryland	36	16
Massachusetts	95	22
Michigan	67	34
Minnesota	45	33
Mississippi	20	17
Missouri	68	30
Montana	10	14

These numbers are based on a survey conducted by the National Center for Education Statistics during the 2006–2007 academic year. They include only public and private not-for-profit schools.

In addition to the colleges in the 50 states, there are many colleges in Puerto Rico. Colleges are located in the U.S. territories of American Samoa, Guam, the Northern Marianas, and the U.S. Virgin Islands as well.

How Many Colleges Are in My State?

State	Four-Year Colleges*	Two-Year Colleges*
Nebraska	24	12
Nevada	6	3
New Hampshire	19	8
New Jersey	37	28
New Mexico	14	20
New York	212	75
North Carolina	60	62
North Dakota	12	8
Ohio	100	46
Oklahoma	30	33
Oregon	35	18
Pennsylvania	146	58
Rhode Island	12	3
South Carolina	37	22
South Dakota	14	9
Tennessee	54	42
Texas	97	69
Utah	10	8
Vermont	21	2
Virginia	50	28
Washington	28	37
West Virginia	22	15
Wisconsin	42	23
Wyoming	1	7
District of Columbia	13	1

These numbers are based on a survey conducted by the National Center for Education Statistics during the 2006–2007 academic year. They include only public and private not-for-profit schools.

Almost every state offers a full mix of colleges, including four-year and two-year, public and private, large and small. Metropolitan areas such as Philadelphia, Boston, New York, Chicago, and Los Angeles offer dozens of choices.

The Largest Four-Year Colleges

State	Largest College or University	Number of Students*
Alabama	Troy University	21,299
Alaska	University of Alaska–Anchorage	10,471
Arizona	Arizona State University	41,626
Arkansas	University of Arkansas–Fayetteville	14,948
California	California State University–Fullerton	31,750
Colorado	University of Colorado–Boulder	25,521
Connecticut	University of Connecticut	16,112
Delaware	University of Delaware	15,378
Florida	University of Central Florida	41,320
Georgia	University of Georgia	25,204
Hawaii	University of Hawaii–Manoa	13,827
Idaho	Boise State University	16,925
Illinois	University of Illinois–Urbana	30,895
Indiana	Purdue University–West Lafayette	31,186
Iowa	Iowa State University	21,354
Kansas	University of Kansas	20,828
Kentucky	University of Kentucky	17,000
Louisiana	Louisiana State University–Baton Rouge	23,393
Maine	University of Maine–Orono	9,596
Maryland	University of Maryland–College Park	25,857
Massachusetts	University of Massachusetts–Amherst	18,812
Michigan	Michigan State University	35,678
Minnesota	University of Minnesota–Twin Cities	29,110
Mississippi	Mississippi State University	12,555
Missouri	University of Missouri–Columbia	21,652
Montana	University of Montana	11,504
Nebraska	University of Nebraska–Lincoln	18,053

*Based on total undergraduate students in fall 2007.

In the fall of 2007, 10 different four-year colleges in California each had more than 20,000 undergraduate students. In 22 other states and the District of Columbia, no college campus has as many as 20,000 undergraduate students.

The Largest Four-Year Colleges

State	Largest College or University	Number of Students*
Nevada	University of Nevada–Las Vegas	21,692
New Hampshire	University of New Hampshire	12,067
New Jersey	Rutgers University	26,829
New Mexico	University of New Mexico	19,986
New York	New York University	21,327
North Carolina	North Carolina State University	24,145
North Dakota	North Dakota State University	10,160
Ohio	The Ohio State University–Columbus	37,411
Oklahoma	University of Oklahoma	19,707
Oregon	University of Oregon	16,674
Pennsylvania	Pennsylvania State University–University Park	36,815
Rhode Island	University of Rhode Island	12,173
South Carolina	University of South Carolina	18,827
South Dakota	South Dakota State University	10,257
Tennessee	University of Tennessee–Knoxville	21,369
Texas	University of Texas–Austin	37,459
Utah	Brigham Young University	30,798
Vermont	University of Vermont	10,504
Virginia	Virginia Polytechnic University	23,044
Washington	University of Washington	28,570
West Virginia	West Virginia University	20,145
Wisconsin	University of Wisconsin–Madison	30,618
Wyoming	University of Wyoming	9,468
District of Columbia	Strayer University	11,785

Based on total undergraduate students in fall 2007.

The two largest campuses in the United States in the fall of 2008 were The Ohio State University in Columbus and Arizona State University in Tempe. Each enrolled more than 50,000 undergraduate, graduate, and professional students. Other campuses with more than 50,000 students included University of Florida, University of Minnesota, University of Central Florida, and University of Texas in Austin.

TEXAS

OHIO

Exchange Programs and Consortiums

Many colleges give you the opportunity to study at another college for up to a year. Your studies at the second college count toward your graduation requirements at the first. Two colleges may have an arrangement with each other for an **exchange program:** They exchange groups of students for one or more terms. The students get to broaden their experience at another type of campus, take courses that might not otherwise be available to them, and make new friends.

For more information about this consortium, visit its Web site at www.fivecolleges.edu.

Sometimes when several colleges are located near each other, they form a group called a **consortium.** Students at one college can take classes at the other colleges participating in the consortium. For example, Amherst College, Hampshire College, Mount Holyoke College, University of Massachusetts, and Smith College are located within a few miles of each other. If you attend one of these colleges, you will be able to take certain courses at the other four colleges. You get some of the educational advantages of an exchange program without going away from your main college for a long period of time.

Pomona College in Claremont, California, and Colby College in Waterville, Maine, have an exchange program. A group of Pomona students spends half a school year studying at Colby while a group of Colby students studies at Pomona. In addition, Pomona College is one of the Claremont Colleges, a consortium that includes Claremont McKenna College, Harvey Mudd College, Pitzer College, Scripps College, Claremont Graduate University, and Keck Graduate Institute of Applied Life Sciences. You can learn more about this consortium by visiting its Web site at *www.claremont.edu/*.

In some cases, colleges work together to provide opportunities for students that they might not be able to offer individually. For example, the Great Lakes Colleges Association (GLCA) has 13 member colleges from Michigan, Indiana, Ohio, and Pennsylvania.

Among the programs that GLCA supports is the Philadelphia Center. This program, founded in 1967, provides opportunities for students from GLCA member colleges, as well as other colleges from across the country, to spend half a school year in Philadelphia.

Students spend four days a week in various work environments throughout Philadelphia. They attend a couple of seminars every week that are led by the center's faculty. In addition, the students take an evening course that focuses on the cultural concerns of a large city.

For more information about the GLCA, visit its Web site at www.glca.org.

The Philadelphia Center is now managed by Hope College, a GLCA member. You can learn more about the center at its Web site, www.tpc.edu.

Members of the Great Lakes Colleges Association

School	Location
Albion College	Albion, Michigan
Allegheney College	Meadville, Pennsylvania
Antioch College	Yellow Springs, Ohio
The College of Wooster	Wooster, Ohio
Denison University	Granville, Ohio
DePauw University	Greencastle, Indiana
Earlham College	Richmond, Indiana
Hope College	Holland, Michigan
Kalamazoo College	Kalamazoo, Michigan
Kenyon College	Gambier, Ohio
Oberlin College	Oberlin, Ohio
Ohio Wesleyan University	Delaware, Ohio
Wabash College	Crawfordsville, Indiana

Colleges Outside the United States

Increasingly, colleges are encouraging students to spend time studying outside of the United States. No matter what your field of study, you can benefit from traveling and studying abroad. If you study a foreign language, you will probably want to study in a country where that language is spoken. If you are studying business, medicine, history, or government, then an international perspective would be of value to you. Even students who focus on American studies can benefit from learning how other countries view the United States.

Students at Howard Community College in Maryland have opportunities to study throughout the world. They can also study through partnerships with other colleges and even design their own study abroad experience.

Many colleges coordinate their own study or travel abroad programs for their students. Some colleges open their programs to students from other colleges. And some have partnerships and exchanges with international colleges and other organizations. Most often, study abroad programs are led by faculty. Students travel in groups. In other cases, students make arrangements to study independently.

If you attend Middlebury College in Vermont, you will have the opportunity to study throughout the world in diverse locations such as Montevideo, Uruguay; Irkutsk, Russia; Segovia, Spain; and Hangzhou, China. Students at Hollins College in Virginia are able to study in countries such as Argentina, Ghana, Ireland, Japan, and South Africa, among others.

The American University of Paris and The American University in Cairo are two examples of American colleges located in other countries.

Students who want to spend all their college years outside the United States can apply directly to colleges based in other countries. They can also apply to American colleges based in other countries. Choose wisely if you plan to study outside the United States. Be sure your degree will be valid in the United States.

When Should I Study Abroad?

Many international study programs are designed especially for college juniors. These programs are often referred to as **junior year abroad.** Students may spend an entire year studying in another country, though many go away for only part of a year.

Shorter term study abroad programs are also popular and a good first experience. They are often two to four weeks long and scheduled in the winter or summer. They work very well for students studying at four-year colleges and for students who cannot be away for longer periods. Your advisor may be able to help with your plans and to make sure that your program is approved. You may also be able to participate in another U.S. college's overseas program.

Dickinson College in Carlisle, Pennsylvania, places a high emphasis on international study. Almost 60 percent of its students study abroad, usually during their junior year. Dickinson has numerous centers in Australia, China, Italy, Germany, Spain, Mexico, Russia, Japan, England, France, Cameroon, South Korea, and New York City. Faculty members from either Dickinson or the host college supervise the program. Dickinson also offers many other international opportunities for study in Argentina, Brazil, Costa Rica, Egypt, India, and Israel. Students have still more opportunities to go abroad during the January break and the summer, where they can study in many of the same countries, as well as numerous other countries. In some cases, students from other two- and four-year colleges can participate in many of Dickinson's study abroad programs.

PENNSYLVANIA

Colleges Around the World

Country/Province	College or University	Year Founded
Argentina	University of Buenos Aires	1821
Australia	University of Sydney	1850
Brazil	Federal University (Rio de Janeiro)	1920
Canada, Ontario	University of Toronto	1827
Canada, Quebec	McGill University	1821
China	Beijing University	1898
Costa Rica	University of Costa Rica	1843
Czech Republic	Charles University	1348
Egypt	Al-Azhar University	970
England	Merton College (Oxford)	1264
France	The Sorbonne	1257
Germany	University of Heidelberg	1386
India	University of Mumbai	1857
Ireland	Trinity College	1592
Israel	Hebrew University–Jerusalem	1918
Italy	University of Bologna	1088
Japan	University of Tokyo	1877
Kenya	University of Nairobi	1956
Mexico	National Autonomous University of Mexico	1551
Morocco	Al-Qarawiyin	859
The Netherlands	Leiden University	1575
Nigeria	University of Ibadan	1948
Philippines	University of the Philippines	1908
Poland	University of Krakow	1364
Portugal	University of Lisbon	1288
Russia	St. Petersburg State University	1819
Scotland	University of St. Andrews	1413
South Africa	University of Cape Town	1829
Spain	The University of Salamanca	1218
Switzerland	University of Basel	1460
Taiwan	Soochow University	1900
Ukraine	L'viv University	1661
Venezuela	Central University of Venezuela	1721

5

What Can I Learn at College?

You can learn anything and everything at college! Even the smallest colleges offer many areas of study and hundreds of different classes. Some classes provide a broad overview of a subject. Others focus on a very specific part of a subject.

Colleges have basic requirements that you must meet in order to graduate. At college you also choose a subject of special interest to study. You then take classes that focus on that subject. In this chapter, we'll take a look at both basic requirements and major areas of study.

College Degrees

After you meet high school requirements, you graduate and receive a high school diploma. Similarly, when you meet the requirements for the college you attend, you will receive a college diploma. You will also earn a degree, a title that the college awards you. The title indicates you have completed a specific level and program of study that the college offers.

What Is a Bachelor's Degree?

People earn a bachelor's degree when they complete graduation requirements for a four-year college. The two degrees that are awarded most often in the United States are the B.A. (Bachelor of Arts) and the B.S. (Bachelor of Science).

Some students are able to earn their bachelor's degrees in less than four years. Many others need longer, especially if they have changed colleges or changed their field of study.

Many smaller colleges offer only one degree, most often the B.A. In fact, graduating students may receive that title even if they have taken mostly science courses. Larger schools often offer both degrees. The student's area of study determines which degree is awarded at graduation.

Some schools offer other types of bachelor's degrees for students who have specialized in such areas as engineering, music, literature, fine arts, nursing, or theology.

What Other Kinds of Degrees Can I Earn?

Two-year colleges also award certificates. These indicate that a student has completed about a year of work in a specific career field.

Most two-year colleges provide the freshman and sophomore years of college. They grant associate's degrees, in most cases either Associate of Arts (A.A.) or Associate of Science (A.S.). A few two-year colleges offer the junior and senior years of college and award bachelor's degrees.

Students with bachelor's degrees can continue their studies at an advanced level. You can earn a master's degree by completing an additional year or two of specialized studies. For example, if you study business administration at an advanced level, you may earn the title M.B.A., or Master in Business Administration. With an additional two to five years of very specialized and advanced study, you can earn a doctorate degree. The Ph.D., which stands for Doctor of Philosophy, is one of the more commonly earned doctorates.

What Is an Undergraduate?

Students who have not yet earned their college degrees are called **undergraduates.** Once they have earned their bachelor's degrees and are enrolled in advanced studies, they are **graduate students.** Universities are usually made up of one or more undergraduate colleges, as well as graduate schools that offer advanced degrees (see chapter 1).

What Is an Honors Graduate?

Colleges honor their top students at graduation by awarding them a mark of distinction. You can graduate *cum laude* (Latin for "with praise"); *magna cum laude* ("with great praise"); or *summa cum laude* ("with highest praise"). These honors follow you throughout your life. They can help you continue your studies and get hired in your chosen field.

When you hear that someone is a doctor, you might think automatically of a medical doctor. However, not all doctors are medical doctors. The chart on the next page lists some other types of doctors. Note that the Ph.D. is awarded for advanced studies in a wide variety of subjects, not just philosophy.

Grades are the most important factor in determining who graduates with honors.

In the 2006–2007 school year, almost 1.5 million students earned bachelor's degrees at U.S. colleges. During that same year, colleges awarded more than 728,000 associate's degrees, about 605,000 master's degrees, and about 61,000 doctorate degrees.

Different Kinds of College Degrees

Degree	Full Name of Degree
A.A.	Associate of Arts
A.A.S.	Associate of Applied Science
A.A.T.	Associate of Arts in Teaching
A.S.	Associate of Science
A.B. or B.A.	Bachelor of Arts
B.B.S.	Bachelor of Business Science
B.C.L.	Bachelor of Civil Law
B.F.A.	Bachelor of Fine Arts
B.Lit. or B.Litt	Bachelor of Literature
B.S. or B.Sc.	Bachelor of Science
B.S.N.	Bachelor of Science in Nursing
Lit.B.	Bachelor of Literature
L.L.B.	Bachelor of Laws
Mus.B.	Bachelor of Music
M.A.	Master of Arts
M.A.T.	Master of Arts in Teaching
M.B.A.	Master of Business Administration
M.C.E.	Master of Civil Engineering
M.F.A.	Master of Fine Arts
M.P.A.	Master of Public Administration
M.S.	Master of Science
M.S.W.	Master of Social Work
D.D.	Doctor of Divinity
D.D.S.	Doctor of Dental Surgery
D.S. or D.Sc.	Doctor of Science
D.V.M.	Doctor of Veterinary Medicine
Ed.D.	Doctor of Education
J.D.	Doctor of Jurisprudence (Doctor of Law)
L.L.D.	Doctor of Laws
M.D.	Doctor of Medicine
Ph.D.	Doctor of Philosophy

Courses and Credits

Right now you probably study anywhere from five to seven subjects during the school year. Think of each subject as a course. As you enter high school, you have more flexibility about which courses you take than you do in junior high or middle school. For example, you probably will have to study science in high school. However, you may be able to choose which science courses you take.

College courses are similar to courses you already take. They're just taught at a higher level; but you should be ready for that level when you get to college. Full-time college students take three to six courses at a time. Courses generally meet three times each week for 50 minutes, or twice each week for 75 minutes at a time. Some classes meet only once a week, but for a three-hour session. Many science classes have an additional session each week in which students gain practical experience in a **laboratory.**

For each course that you take, you earn **credits.** Think of college credits as time. Most colleges assign one credit for each hour that the course meets during the week. You earn three credits for most courses and four credits for many science courses, because of the laboratory session. However, some colleges assign one credit or unit for each course you take, regardless of how many hours per week it meets.

Although most courses have three or four credits, some have fewer or more. Some courses— for example a review of basic concepts or a physical education course—might run for just a few weeks and award only one or two credits. Other classes, especially in math and foreign languages, meet four or five times a week, and may count for more credits.

At colleges that assign three credits for a class that meets three hours each week, you will need about 120 credits altogether to graduate. This equals 40 classes that are three credits each—and fewer classes if you take courses with more credits. The actual number of credits, classes, and time spent in class depends on the college you attend, your program of study, and the class teaching method.

What Are Distribution Requirements?

These required courses are sometimes called core curriculum, foundation courses, or general education requirements.

As part of graduation requirements, colleges often require you to take courses in a variety of different fields. Although you might be allowed to choose the specific courses you take to meet these requirements, you must choose them from the categories the college selects. Because these courses are distributed over several subject areas, they are often called **distribution requirements.**

Colleges may also have other general required subjects for their graduates, such as English, math, diversity, foreign language, and technology.

Colleges divide subjects into different groups such as natural sciences, social sciences, and humanities. These divisions are described later in this chapter. To fulfill distribution requirements, you must often take a certain number of courses in each of these areas.

SAMPLE DISTRIBUTION REQUIREMENTS

To earn a bachelor's degree at Ohio Wesleyan University, students must meet requirements in English, writing, cultural diversity, quantitative reasoning, and foreign language. They must also complete courses in the following areas:

Social sciences. Three courses selected from subject areas such as black world studies, economics, geography, history, journalism, politics and government, psychology, sociology/anthropology, and women's and gender studies.

Natural sciences. Three courses selected from subject areas such as botany/microbiology, chemistry, computer sciences, geology, mathematics, physics/astronomy, and zoology.

Humanities. Three courses selected from subject areas such as black world studies, English, modern foreign languages, humanities and classics, philosophy, religion, theatre and dance, and women's and gender studies.

Arts. One course selected from subject areas such as English, fine arts, music, theatre, and dance.

Majors, Minors, and Electives

While you are in college, you choose an area of study in which you will concentrate most of your time. This area is called your **major.**

Choosing a major is often called declaring a major.

How Do I Choose a Major?

During your freshman or sophomore year, you will meet with your **advisor**—a teacher or staff member assigned to help you choose a major. Your advisor helps you complete paperwork and other requirements to make your choice official.

At some larger universities, you must apply during your freshman year to be accepted into a specific program of study.

How Do I Complete a Major?

Departments are groups of professors who teach the same subject area. Each department sets up requirements for a major field of study. For instance, to major in English, you might need to take a minimum of 10 English courses. The department may require you to take at least one world literature course and one Shakespeare course. You may also be required to take related courses. For instance, you might take three or more courses about American literature or poetry.

*Students can graduate with a **double major** by completing requirements for two majors. Students who want to teach high school often major both in education and in the subject they want to teach.*

Requirements for English majors vary from college to college. Requirements for other majors also vary. Sometimes you have a lot of choice about the courses you take. But in other cases, the department tells you what to take.

What If I Change My Mind?

After taking several courses, many students find they would like to switch to another major. You are allowed to change your mind. If you do, however, you must complete the requirements for the new major. This switch might require you to stay in school longer.

Your advisor or the registration office can help you complete any procedures required for changing your major.

At the University of North Carolina at Chapel Hill, students are first admitted to the General College. As freshmen and sophomores, they concentrate on completing their general education requirements. During the last half of their sophomore year, they are accepted into an upper-level college in which they complete their major requirements. These colleges include a college of arts and sciences, a school of education, a school of pharmacy, and the Kenan-Flagler Business School.

What Is a Minor?

Some majors and minors prepare you for graduate studies. For instance, a pre-medical (pre-med) major prepares you for medical school and a pre-law major prepares you for law school.

In addition to your major, you may want to concentrate in a second area because it interests you or because it helps you in your major field of study. However, you may not want to complete all the major requirements needed to major in this other field.

Many colleges provide opportunities to **minor** in subjects. You still need to complete certain requirements, but they are fewer, for instance, 6 courses instead of 10. Suppose you decide to major in Spanish. You may also be interested in Hispanic music or drama. In that case, you might choose to major in Spanish and minor in theater.

What Are Electives?

Some elective requirements are specific. You might be required to take a history course, for instance, but you can pick which one. Other electives are general—you can choose any course you want.

In addition to required courses, you will be able to take other courses that you get to choose. Courses you elect to take—which you are not required to take—are called **electives.** They provide opportunities for you to take additional courses in your major, courses taught by a particularly noted professor, or courses just for fun. Students can also use electives to meet requirements for their minor or for a second major.

Divisions, Disciplines, and Departments

Colleges combine subject areas into groups called divisions. At larger universities, these divisions might be entire colleges or schools, such as a college of arts and sciences or a school of journalism.

Each subject area is a discipline. The people who teach in that discipline make up a department. Sometimes a department covers more than one discipline. For example, the disciplines of French, Spanish, and other languages may make up the modern languages department.

The way departments are combined varies. One college may have a *modern* languages department, which includes only currently spoken languages. The professors who teach Latin and Greek might be in a separate department, such as Classics. At another college, the Latin and Greek professors may be combined with the French and Spanish professors in a *foreign* languages department.

Some subjects are **interdisciplinary** because they combine two or more disciplines into one. For example, human development often combines biology and psychology to look at the nature of humans.

The way divisions are organized also varies. The business administration program at some colleges is so large that it is its own division made up of management, marketing, accounting, finance, human resources, and production disciplines. Elsewhere, the program may be so small that it is a single discipline within social sciences. Mathematics may be grouped with natural sciences, engineering, computer science, or humanities.

When you look at colleges, look at how departments are organized. Be sure the college you choose offers the specific area in which you are interested.

Natural and Physical Sciences

Many disciplines focus on the way the natural or physical world works. They are grouped together in natural science or physical science divisions. Many science courses require you to spend time in a lab conducting hands-on experiments. You will have to memorize new vocabulary, much of it unfamiliar. Math skills are very important when you study the sciences.

Biology

Biology is the study of human, animal, and plant life. For example, *botany* focuses on plant life while *zoology* focuses on animal life. The smallest units of life—molecules and cells—are not considered to be either animal or plant. *Molecular biology* and *cellular biology* focus on these building blocks of life.

Other important branches of biology study entire organisms, looking at their structure *(anatomy),* growth and development *(developmental biology),* and function *(physiology). Microbiology* looks at the smallest organisms and viruses. The field of *population biology* combines two fields: *ecology* (the study of populations in their environment) and *genetics* (the study of heredity). *Marine biology* studies the plants and animals of the ocean.

Chemistry

Chemistry is the study of substances that make up the natural world and how adding or removing energy from these substances changes them. *Analytical chemistry* looks at what makes up substances. *Inorganic chemistry* focuses on the properties and reactions of all chemical substances except for those that contain carbon and hydrogen. Carbon compounds (substances that contain carbon)—the building blocks of life—are the focus of *organic chemistry.*

Physics

Physics looks at how all the parts of the universe inter-
act. *Classical physics* focuses on physical forces such as
gravity, electricity, and magnetism. *Modern physics* moves
beyond the traditional theories and looks at the atomic
world, semiconductors, and modern communications.
Major fields within physics include *mechanics,* the study
of objects in motion; *thermodynamics,* the study of heat
and energy transformation; and *optics,* the study of light.

Earth and Atmospheric Sciences

Several important fields make up these sciences. The
most prominent field is probably *geology,* the study of the
planet Earth. *Physical geology* looks at the composition
of the planet, while *historical geology* looks at the earth's
evolution (how the earth has changed over millions of
years). Other fields include *paleontology,* the study of
prehistoric life; *petrology,* the study of rocks; *mineralogy,*
the study of minerals; and *oceanography,* the study of
the oceans. *Meteorology* is the study of the earth's atmosphere and weather over the short term, whereas *clima-
tology* takes the long-term view of these topics.

Astronomy

Astronomy studies the bodies of the universe, such as
planets, meteors, comets, and stars. Some fields within
astronomy track the positions of these bodies and study
their chemical composition and physical forces. An
important branch of astronomy is *cosmology,* which looks
at the universe as a whole.

Combined Sciences

Many fields combine two branches of science. For example, *geophysics* studies the effect of physical forces on the
earth (for example, earthquakes). *Biochemistry* studies the
chemical composition of living organisms.

Social and Behavioral Sciences

The way the physical world works is central to the natural sciences. By contrast, the social sciences center on the way the human world works. The social sciences look at individuals and society—human behavior and the interactions people have with each other and with the institutions we've set up to organize our lives.

Psychology

The behavior of individuals is the main focus of psychology. Animal behavior is also important. *Child* and *developmental psychology* look at how age and experiences affect behavior. *Abnormal psychology* emphasizes behavior that is not what is commonly expected and accepted. *Experimental psychology* uses lab and field studies to learn more about patterns of behavior. *Industrial psychology* explores behavior in the workplace. *Educational psychology* looks at how people learn and ways to help people make educational and career decisions. Counseling and therapy—helping people with problems—are at the heart of *clinical psychology*.

Sociology

Sociology emphasizes groups and society. It looks at group behavior and the role of institutions such as marriage, the family, religion, schools, the legal system, and organizations. Roles that people are expected to play—based on factors such as profession, religion, class, gender, and age—are also studied. *Demography* is the study of populations. Other areas include *criminology,* the study of legal systems and crime; *deviance,* which looks at behaviors that go against society's expectations; *urban sociology,* which focuses on behavior in cities; and *gerontology,* which focuses on the roles and behaviors of elderly people.

Social Psychology

This interdisciplinary field draws on both sociology and psychology. It looks at the relationship between individuals and groups. Psychologists examine how behavior is affected by groups and institutions. Sociologists focus on small-group behavior and the ways that groups and institutions affect individuals.

Anthropology

Anthropology looks at the physical and cultural development of humans. It also involves natural sciences and history. *Physical anthropology,* which draws on biology, studies the evolution of humans and how they adapt to their environment over time. *Cultural anthropology* studies the development of societies, language, and culture.

Political Science

Political science is the study of government. *Comparative government* looks at governments around the world. *Political theory* examines the ways in which governments—such as democracies, dictatorships, and monarchies—are organized. *Politics* looks at how things get done: how elections are conducted and how laws are made. *Public administration* is the study of how people govern, create budgets, and put policy into action. *Institutions* such as the presidency, Congress, the judicial system, lobbyists, and the media are also studied.

Economics

Economics studies systems of money and how goods and services are produced, distributed, and consumed. *Microeconomics* looks at the supply and demand of goods and services. *Macroeconomics* focuses on broad issues such as employment and national income. *Money and banking* focuses on how money is created and how the banking system is structured.

Arts and Humanities

The ways in which humans use their imagination to express themselves creatively make up the arts. The ways in which humans think about themselves and their place in the world make up the humanities.

History

Most colleges place history with either the social sciences or the humanities. History is the study of all that has taken place in the past. Special emphasis is given to activities of individuals and societies. You can specialize by studying certain regions; for instance, Asian or African history. You can also specialize by studying time periods, for example, nineteenth-century history throughout the world. You can specialize in other ways too, studying the history of war, women, science, industrialization, and so on.

Philosophy

Philosophy is the study of the basic principles of our lives and the world around us. Major branches include *metaphysics,* which tries to define reality; *epistemology,* the study of knowledge; *aesthetics,* the study of how we define what is beautiful; and *ethics,* the study of how we make moral judgments. *Logic* is an important branch that looks at how we can build arguments that reach valid conclusions.

Religion

Religion looks at people's views about God and the universe and how their beliefs shape their way of life. Many colleges offer courses that compare different religions such as Christianity, Judaism, Islam, Hinduism, Buddhism, and many others. Many programs offer courses that prepare students to be members of the clergy.

Classics

Most programs in the classics focus on the study of ancient Greece and Rome, as well as other ancient cultures. You are often expected to learn either Latin or Greek. You might study the history and culture of great civilizations as well as the outstanding works of literature they produced.

English

Students who major in English usually focus on either *writing* or *literature*. Those who specialize in writing may take many courses on the art of constructing novels, short stories, plays, and poems. Those who specialize in literature learn to analyze plots, themes, characters, and style. Most literature courses focus on works that were written in English. *World literature* courses introduce students to the works of great authors regardless of the language or culture in which they wrote.

Performing and Applied Arts

Many courses in drama (or theater) and film are similar to literature courses: You read or view the great works of others. Other courses focus on performance. These courses train actors, directors, sound and lighting technicians, stagehands, and other behind-the-scenes workers.

Courses in *music, art,* and *dance* can be history or studio courses. In history classes, you might take survey courses that give you broad overviews of the works of others. You might also take courses that narrow the focus. For example, you might study Italian opera, French Impressionist painting, or Russian ballet.

Studio courses give you direct experience. You might spend time in a studio singing, practicing an instrument, composing music, sculpting, painting, or choreographing a new dance.

Engineering

How scientific and mathematical theories are applied to meet the challenges of our everyday world is central to engineering. There are more than 25 major specialties within engineering. Many of these have their own subdivisions. Common specialties are described below.

Chemical Engineering

Chemical engineering students learn to develop the processes and equipment that are used to make new materials and products. The transformation of petroleum (oil) into plastics and other materials, the development of alternative fuels, the creation of synthetic rubber, and the process of removing salt from ocean water (desalination) all fall within the field of chemical engineering.

Civil Engineering

Civil engineering focuses on structure—buildings, foundations, construction, road paving, and so forth. Civil engineering also deals with infrastructure—the design of networks of roads, bridges, and tunnels; and planning how reservoirs, dams, water lines, and sewer lines work together to serve a community. Major fields within civil engineering include *construction, surveying, soils, urban planning,* and *transportation.*

Electrical Engineering

The field of electrical engineering focuses on the use of electric power and signals. It includes telecommunications, medical technology, computers, and broadcast media. Branches include areas such as *electric power and machinery,* generating and distributing electric power; *electronics,* transmitting and processing information by circuits and devices; *communications and control,* using information to perform tasks; and computer engineering.

Mechanical Engineering

Machines are at the heart of mechanical engineering. Some mechanical engineers specialize in *machines* themselves, their design and operation, and the materials used to build them. Others might specialize in either *fluid* or *thermal* (heat) *sciences. Robotics,* the use of machinery to perform human tasks, is a fast-growing field within mechanical and electrical engineering.

Industrial Engineering

Closely tied to fields within business administration (production and operations), industrial engineering looks at the management of industrial production. Cost, safety, budgeting, quality control, and planning for the efficient use of machines and human resources are all concerns of industrial engineering.

Other Engineering Fields

Aeronautical engineering focuses on the development of aircraft for both civilian and military use. *Aerospace engineering,* which is concerned with vehicles flown outside the earth's atmosphere, is closely related. Often part of civil engineering, *environmental engineering* is concerned with matters such as water supply, air pollution, disposal of solid and hazardous wastes, and the use and protection of natural resources. *Materials science* engineers specialize in the use of resources such as metals, ceramics, and plastics to create products. Their expertise is very important to engineers in other fields. *Military engineering* applies the tools of engineering to military purposes. *Mining engineers* study ways of finding and extracting mineral deposits. *Nuclear engineers* work on developing and using nuclear energy as a power source and for other purposes. *Safety engineers* work in all the engineering fields developing ways to prevent accidents and improve job and public safety.

Mathematics and Statistics

Mathematics departments may be found within science, humanities, or engineering divisions, depending on the college. They are also often linked with computer science departments. In most cases, statistics courses are taught as part of the math department's offerings. A higher percentage of students take math courses than any other type of course, with the possible exception of English.

Mathematics

Most students are required to take math courses in college. For many, the tools learned in algebra, geometry, trigonometry, and calculus form an important foundation for work in other fields. Logic skills developed in math courses are important to all disciplines, including the humanities.

Many *applied math* courses cover mathematical techniques and models used to solve problems in engineering and the natural and social sciences. Other applied math courses emphasize tools needed for business administration studies.

Pure math courses focus on the theories of math. Research focuses on discovering and solving new mathematical formulas and developing new computational techniques and mathematical models.

Statistics

Like mathematics, statistics supports studies in other disciplines, such as sociology and economics. Courses focus on understanding and solving real-world problems by designing surveys and experiments, summarizing the data gathered, and interpreting the resulting information. Many individual departments also offer their own statistics courses.

Computers and Information Systems

Computer science and computer technology departments may be separate at many colleges. They may also be linked with math, engineering, technology, or business departments. Students who major in the computer field generally choose between programs that focus on the science (theory) of computers and those that focus on the technology (techniques and tools).

Students often choose to study either the *hardware* or the *software* side of computers. The hardware side, which can be taught through computer engineering, looks at the technology itself, the design of computers and systems, and the manufacture, repair, and maintenance of computer components. The software side emphasizes computer languages and applications. You can learn existing languages or learn how to develop new ones. As the Internet has grown, so have Web design and the use of languages and applications such as HTML, Java, Flash, Visual Basic, and countless others.

The rapidly growing field of *information systems* often combines hardware and software tools. In *networking* courses, students learn to manage a group of computers within or even across organizations. In *systems analysis* courses, students look at how computers function to meet the needs of an organization. *Computer security* and *forensics* are other important areas—developing programs that help protect information stored on computers and ensure that it is private and safe. Because computers are so important to so many fields, computer studies often combine with fields such as business, education, graphic design, architecture, criminal justice, medicine, the arts, transportation, law, and mass media.

Computer science students *are more likely to study how to create new computer languages or more efficient ways to manipulate existing languages.* Computer technology students *are more likely to apply programs written in certain languages so that others can perform specific tasks.*

Technology and Trades

Technology students learn to use science for practical reasons such as developing new or improved products. Students learning trades focus on specific, applied job skills that may involve building, installing, operating, and repairing equipment or providing practical services. For example, in biomedical technology, students may learn biology, physics, and engineering in order to design better medical equipment. Meanwhile, biomedical technicians learn how to use and repair different kinds of medical equipment. Two-year colleges and vocational, technical, and other career schools offer a wide variety of choices.

Chapter 14 covers trades and other education choices in more detail.

Applied Trade	Description
Automotive technology	Repairing and maintaining automobiles and other vehicles
Construction technology	Planning, supervising, and building homes, offices, and other buildings
Cosmetology	Caring for hair, nails, and skin
Culinary arts	Preparing meals and desserts, purchasing food supplies, managing kitchen workers, planning menus
Graphic arts	Designing Web pages, brochures, books, advertising, and other materials
Office technology	Preparing letters and documents, filing, scanning, scheduling, and handling e-mail, voice mail, and office calls
Plumbing	Installing and repairing pipes and equipment that carry water, gas, air, and chemicals
Public safety	Policing, planning for major emergencies
Real estate	Buying and selling land and buildings
Surveying	Measuring construction sites and collecting information for maps and charts
Travel and tourism	Arranging travel for individuals, groups, and businesses or promoting travel destinations

Languages

At many colleges, students must study a foreign language in order to graduate. Each college sets up its own requirements. If you study a foreign language in high school, you may be able to meet this requirement before entering college.

Knowing another language can be helpful to you in many careers. Business students can improve their job opportunities with international firms if they speak a second language. Knowing a second language will be helpful to you if you have an interest in research, whether in history, music, archaeology, psychology, or any other field. For instance, if your field is music, then German and Italian are especially important.

Although Spanish and French have traditionally been the most commonly taught languages, today you can learn almost any language you want. *Critical languages* are ones such as Arabic, Chinese, and Korean that our nation needs to have more people learn.

Many colleges group French, Spanish, Italian, and Portuguese together in a Romance languages department. These languages are called Romance languages because they developed from the Latin spoken in late Roman times.

Heritage languages are the native languages that immigrants continue to speak and want their families to learn.

LANGUAGES TAUGHT AT BYU

Brigham Young University (BYU) in Provo, Utah, offers a particularly wide range of languages, including

Afrikaans	Danish	Icelandic	Swahili
American Sign	Dutch	Italian	Swedish
	Farsi	Japanese	Thai
Arabic	Finnish	Korean	Ukrainian
Bulgarian	French	Norwegian	Urdu
Cantonese	German	Polish	Vietnamese
Chinese (Mandarin)	Hebrew	Portuguese	Welsh
	Hindi	Russian	
Czech	Hungarian	Spanish	

Medicine and Allied Health

Some programs in medicine and allied health prepare you to work immediately after college. In other cases, your courses lay the foundation for advanced studies. In *clinical courses,* you work with patients and equipment to develop your skills.

Medicine

If your goal is to be a doctor, dentist, ophthalmologist, or veterinarian, you will take courses that prepare you for professional school. Students in these fields often major in biology in college. Once they are in professional school, they develop further academic, technical, and clinical skills. They may then select a specialty for further study.

Nursing

Nurses provide direct patient care, working closely with patients and their families. Nurses work in hospitals, doctors' offices, nursing homes, public health clinics, schools, businesses, and even in patients' homes.

Some courses help prepare you for special exams you must pass to earn a license or certificate to practice in that field in your state.

Many colleges prepare students for different levels of nursing. Some community colleges and technical schools have one-year nursing programs that prepare students to be *licensed practical nurses (LPNs)*—these nurses can provide basic care to patients under the supervision of a registered nurse or physician. Other colleges (and some hospitals) have two-year or four-year programs that prepare students to be *registered nurses (RNs)*—they provide a higher level of care than LPNs and are more independent.

Advanced practice nurses—clinical nursing specialists, nurse practitioners, and nurse anesthetists—provide the most specialized care, are the most independent, and require the highest level of education.

Allied Health and Medical Technology

Technology students learn to perform tests and to operate medical equipment needed to diagnose and treat illnesses and injuries. Therapy students learn to help patients prevent medical problems and to recover from illnesses and injuries. Studies include *physician assistant*, *dental hygiene, radiology technology, physical therapy, respiratory therapy, laboratory science*, and *emergency medical technology* (including paramedics). *Occupational therapists* help people with disabilities learn daily living skills. Along with *gerontologists*, they also work with elderly people, helping them maintain and improve their quality of life.

Health and Wellness

Pharmacists prepare and dispense medication. *Speech and language pathologists* and *audiologists* work with people who have speech, language, hearing, and swallowing problems. The field of *public health* looks at how to prevent disease and promote health at the community and society level.

Careers are growing rapidly in wellness, an area dedicated to preventing illness and improving overall health and quality of life. *Nutrition* is a broad-based field in which you study how food and minerals affect the body. *Dieticians* learn to prepare healthy and specialized diets. *Weight management* is a related area, where the focus is on helping people lose, maintain, or even gain weight.

Exercise science is a field that helps people improve or maintain fitness. *Personal trainers* help clients develop healthy exercise programs. *Athletic trainers* work with individual and team athletes to prevent or recover from injuries and to strengthen the body to meet the demands of individual sports.

Individual doctors will work with patients who have the flu. Public health officials look ahead at the type of flu that is coming in the next season. They make sure enough vaccines are produced for the community, coordinate with doctors and hospitals to make sure vaccines are ordered, and educate the public about getting vaccinated and other steps citizens can take to avoid the flu.

Chiropractors, acupuncturists, and massage therapists help patients ease pain and reduce stress. Personal coaches help people manage and balance their work and personal life.

Business

Some business programs offer a general overview of managing a company. Other programs allow you to specialize in an area such as finance or marketing.

Management

People who start up their own companies (or enterprises) are often called entrepreneurs. Courses and programs that address their needs are increasing in popularity.

Students learn how to coordinate the resources, policies, and operations of a company. *Human resource management* studies hiring, training, and managing benefits. *Organizational behavior* looks at how a company is structured so that people can work effectively. *Production and operations management* centers on how goods and services are produced, parts and supplies are ordered, machinery is maintained, and work is scheduled.

Accounting and Finance

Accounting students learn to organize, record, report, and interpret an organization's financial records. Finance looks at how a company manages its overall financial resources and gets the money it needs to operate.

Marketing and Sales

Marketing students learn to research what customers want, develop products and customers, present products to customers, set prices, and distribute products. They also study advertising, public relations, and promotion. *Sales* courses teach selling techniques and managing customer information. *E-commerce* courses look at ways in which business is conducted on the Internet.

Other Business Fields

Management information systems (MIS) classes teach how to organize and maintain a company's information. *Business law* teaches students about the laws and regulations affecting businesses. *International business* focuses on business in the global economy.

Education and Library Sciences

Teachers must be certified by the state in which they teach. Elementary and preschool teachers usually have several required courses that prepare them to teach different subjects such as reading, arithmetic, and science. Middle and high school teachers take courses both in education and in the field in which they plan to teach, such as history, English, science, or math.

In most cases, education students take courses in the history or philosophy of education, child psychology (how children learn), and methods classes—techniques for the classroom. During their senior year, students are assigned as student teachers to a nearby school and are supervised by the main classroom teacher. Most teachers take additional courses after they've been hired in order to keep their certification up to date.

Early childhood education studies prepare you to teach preschool through third grade; *elementary education* focuses on first through sixth grades; *secondary education* prepares you to teach middle, junior, and senior high school grades. *Special education* focuses on working with students who have disabilities. *English as a Second Language* prepares you to teach students who need to learn English while studying other courses. *Education administration* courses are often at the graduate level; they prepare students for careers such as principal, dean, headmaster, guidance counselor, and curriculum developer.

Library sciences are about more than books. They focus as much on *information* and *instructional technology*. Librarians might work in schools and media centers, public libraries, universities, hospitals, and corporations. Their challenging studies include *reference*, information used for research; *circulation*, the way the library's resources are made available to users; and *collections*, techniques for building the library's resources.

Not all colleges have programs that meet state standards for elementary and preschool teachers. More have programs for middle and high school teachers.

Many states require students to take a national exam before they take their education courses or before they graduate to make sure they have the required academic knowledge and skills.

101

Other Programs

In addition to the areas of study already described, you can choose from many others, depending on the college you attend.

Agriculture and Forestry

Students can specialize in several areas. *Agricultural business* focuses on how to manage a farm or a ranch. *Agronomy* emphasizes crop production. *Animal science* emphasizes breeding and raising farm animals and live-stock. *Horticulture* focuses on ornamental plants, fruits, and vegetables; landscaping design is a related program. Students might also study *water management.*

Students in *forestry* learn to manage forests for environ-mental and recreational purposes. They can also study how to harvest timber, maple syrup, and other forest products; land surveying; animal and human protection; and urban forestry—the use of trees and other plants in cities.

Hospitality and Tourism

Students in this field learn how to make people com-fortable when they are not at home, whether they are traveling on long business trips or simply going out to a local restaurant. They may also learn to coordinate large gatherings such as conventions, meetings, and wed-dings. *Hotel and restaurant management* covers areas such as supervising employees, making reservations, billing, ordering supplies, maintaining the facility, and han-dling security. *Culinary arts* teaches students to prepare meals and desserts. *Food service management* focuses on health, safety, and nutrition for hospitals, schools, nurs-ing homes, fast-food chains, and other locations involved with large-scale food preparation and catering.

Communications and Mass Media

If you are interested in how information is exchanged and used to influence individuals and groups, you may want to study communications. *Speech communications* focuses on what is said, how it is said, and how speech is understood. *Public relations* and *marketing* look at the way in which the public or other audiences think about a product, service, individual, or point of view. *Mass communications* looks at how spoken, written, visual, and electronic information is shared by large numbers of people, often over long distances, and how the Internet affects these forms of communication. Determining an organization's current audience, the desired audience, and how to develop product loyalty are very important.

Many communications majors study speech, writing, radio and television broadcasting, the Web, or journalism. The communications field intersects with many other fields, including graphic arts, photography, film, music, Web design and technology, politics, and business.

Military Programs

You can combine college with a military career by attending colleges run by branches of the military such as the United States Air Force. Or you may enroll in a Reserve Officers Training Corps (ROTC) program. Many colleges throughout the country offer ROTC. Most of these programs cover some or all of your college costs and let you choose your field of study while preparing to enter the service as an officer.

All branches of the military need people in many different fields. For example, the military needs doctors, nurses, lawyers, pilots, scientists, language experts, automotive mechanics, technology specialists, engineers, and police. As a result, students in the military academies and those in ROTC can select from many majors.

Interdisciplinary Studies

Many areas of study build on courses and disciplines already described in this chapter. They are known as **interdisciplinary** studies. For example, *environmental studies* builds on a combination of biology, geology, and chemistry courses, as well as anthropology and history. A focus on *environmental policy* includes a similar mix of natural sciences, but also builds on economics and government courses.

Another interdisciplinary field is *human development*, which combines biology studies with social sciences such as psychology, sociology, education, and anthropology. The field looks at the entire human lifespan from birth to death, bringing together the physical changes of the body with social and emotional abilities, learning, and cultural influences. Other interdisciplinary studies include *urban studies*, *sustainability* (using the earth's resources effectively), and *homeland security*.

Cultural Studies

Many colleges have studies in different areas of culture, ethnicity, race, and gender. At its core, *American studies* combines literature and history courses that have American themes. You then build on this core with studies from other disciplines, again with an American theme—music, art, government, geography, philosophy, and so forth.

Similar programs can be found at many colleges for *East-Asian studies*, *Latin American studies*, *European studies*, *African studies*, *Middle Eastern studies*, and others. These programs may be even more finely tuned, for example, Appalachian studies or Japanese studies.

You also have opportunities at various colleges to major in *women's studies*, *Black* or *African-American studies*, *Latino studies*, or studies based on specific religions.

What Else Can I Study?

Program	Description
Archaeology	The study of the past—especially the physical materials, such as art, tools, structures, and ritual and religious artifacts, that people and cultures left behind.
Architecture	The study of designing and constructing buildings, including homes, offices, and even entire communities. Involves strong computer, math, and drawing skills, and may include courses in civil engineering, art, urban planning, and landscape design.
Aviation	The study of airport, airlines, and flight management. Includes air traffic and ground control, air safety, radar systems, and cargo operations.
Entomology	The study of insects and closely related creatures. Overlaps with environmental, biological, and physical sciences; public health; medicine; agriculture and forestry; and economics.
Equestrian studies	The study of horses and how to care for them. Includes knowledge of horse anatomy, nutrition, breeding, training, riding instruction, equestrian events, and stable and horse farm operation.
Geography	The study of how the world's physical characteristics influence people and how people influence their environment. Important to military and security operations; cartography (mapmaking); global positioning and geographic information systems; trade, politics, and diplomacy; economics; agriculture; and public health.
Mortuary science	Combines three different areas—the science of preparing the dead for burial or cremation, the psychology of grief counseling and helping surviving family and friends, and the business of managing a funeral home.
Podiatry	A field of medicine specializing in the foot and ankle. Important specialty areas include sports medicine, diabetes care, and pediatric and geriatric care.
Sports management	A field that includes the different aspects of professional, amateur, and recreational sports and facilities. Involves accounting; finance; advertising, marketing, and promotion; facilities and transportation management; scheduling; and events planning.

Other Requirements

As you have read, you must meet various requirements to earn your college degree. You must take a number of courses and earn a specific number of credits. You may also have to show a certain level of ability in English, math, foreign language, and other subjects. You also declare a major and meet the specific requirements for that major. Some colleges have additional requirements, such as keeping your grades at or above a set level. As we have noted before, check the requirements for each individual college.

Anything and Everything!

Information about requirements can be found in college catalogs and on Web sites (chapters 7 and 8) or by talking with your advisor (chapter 12).

We started this chapter by noting that you can learn anything and everything at college. You've now read about a wide range of disciplines that you can study. In the next chapter, you'll learn about internships and independent studies. These give you an opportunity to build your own course around something of special interest to you.

Some colleges let you design an independent major. You work closely with your advisor to put together an entire program of study—not just one course—of special interest to you. If you have a clear idea of what you want to study, find a college that offers that program or find one that will let you create your own.

MASSACHUSETTS Many colleges will let individual students design an independent major. At Hampshire College in Massachusetts, all students design their own programs of study. In addition, the college requires all students to perform community service.

6

How Will I Learn at College?

You will learn in all sorts of ways! Chapter 5 describes the many different subjects you can choose from when you attend college. But it's not only the subjects you study that vary. In this chapter, we look at the different ways you can learn—in and out of the classroom.

We'll start by looking at how colleges set up their school year. We'll take a look at the different ways you can attend class. We will then look at the tools you can use to study—the library, books, computers, and multimedia tools among them. You'll find that college is much more than just sitting in a classroom and listening to a professor talk!

The College Calendar

Colleges do not all use the same school year. They have different starting and ending dates. They also have different ways to divide the school year.

Many colleges offer optional summer terms. Some students attend a different college during the summer in order to take classes that might not be available to them otherwise.

What Is a Semester?

Many college school years are divided into two terms called **semesters.** Most semesters last 16 to 18 weeks. Fall semesters start in August or September and usually end in December. Spring semesters start in January or February and end in late April or May. Most students take four or five classes each semester.

*Some colleges have a **4-1-4** or a **4-4-1** calendar. Students attend two terms, each of which lasts four months. Students also have one month of special studies, either between terms (4-1-4) or at the end of the year (4-4-1). Mount Mercy College in Cedar Rapids, Iowa, has a 4-1-4 calendar. Transylvania University in Lexington, Kentucky, has a 4-4-1 calendar.*

Are There Other Types of College Calendars?

Some colleges have three **trimesters.** Each lasts about 15 weeks. Most full-time students take classes two trimesters per year. (Attending all three can shorten the time needed to graduate.) Since trimesters are shorter than semesters, the pace of each course is a bit quicker. You cover the same amount of material, but in a shorter time span.

Colleges that use the quarter term system divide the year into four terms. Each lasts about 11 weeks. Most full-time students attend three terms per year, usually in the fall, winter, and spring. In a **quarter** term, you take fewer courses at a time. Courses are taught at a faster pace and meet more hours each week than semester courses do.

At Colorado College in Colorado, Cornell College in Iowa, and Tusculum College in Tennessee, students take one course at a time. Each course lasts about three and a half weeks, with a few days off between courses. Students take eight or nine courses each year. This type of calendar is often called a **block calendar.**

Two Sample College Calendars

The actual dates for these calendars vary from year to year.

**Semester Calendar:
The University of Missouri–Columbia**

Fall Semester

August 23	Classwork begins
August 31	Last day to register, add, or change sections
September 27	Last day to drop a course without a grade
October 29	Last day to withdraw from a course
December 10	Fall semester classwork ends
December 13–18	Final examinations
December 18	Semester ends

Winter Semester

January 10	Classwork begins
January 18	Last day to register, add, or change sections
February 14	Last day to drop course without a grade
April 4	Last day to withdraw from a course
April 28	Winter semester classwork ends
May 1–6	Final examinations
May 6	Semester ends

Summer session also available

Quarter Calendar: Northwestern University

Fall Quarter

September 21	Classes begin
September 27	Last day to add or change classes
October 29	Last day to drop a class
October 29	Last day to withdraw without academic review
December 4	Classes end
December 6–10	Final examinations

Winter Quarter

January 5	Classes begin
January 12	Last day to add or change classes
February 11	Last day to drop a class
February 11	Last day to withdraw without academic review
March 11	Classes end
March 13–17	Final examinations

Spring Quarter

March 27	Classes begin
April 3	Last day to add or change classes
May 5	Last day to drop a class
May 5	Last day to withdraw without academic review
June 3	Classes end
June 5–9	Final examinations

Summer quarter also available

Are All Classrooms the Same?

College courses can be taught in different ways based on the setting, number of students, the professor's teaching style, the subject, and other factors.

Lectures

In many courses, professors stand in front of students and talk—or **lecture**—about the topic being covered. They might use slides, films, recordings, printed materials, and other resources along with the lecture. Some may provide time during their lecture for students to ask questions. Others may even ask questions for students to answer.

Some professors give very clear personal opinions. Others offer many points of view. Expect to be challenged about your ideas and opinions—that's part of the excitement of college!

Lectures can be given in regular classrooms, much like the ones in middle and high school. The classes often have between 15 and 40 students. However, lectures may also be held in a large hall or auditorium that holds hundreds of students. In these larger lecture classes, students are often divided into smaller discussion groups that meet with teaching assistants once a week.

During lectures, students usually take lots of notes to review later. Some bring recorders or laptops, if permitted. Large lecture classes might be filmed or recorded. All these methods allow students to review the lectures at a later date.

A history professor may lecture about the American Civil War from a Union perspective, and then ask you to read from the Confederate perspective. You would then learn both points of view about the war.

Expect to have reading assignments that you must complete before class. Lectures may cover the same ground in more detail or summarize what you have read. Sometimes you may read material that differs from the point of view your professor presents in class. This contrast provides you with a wider range of views.

Discussion Classes

Not all classes are lectures. Some classes combine lectures with classroom discussions or even emphasize discussion. These classes are usually smaller so that all students can participate fully.

Discussion classes have several formats. Sometimes professors begin with a brief lecture and then invite the students' reaction and discussion. Others often begin with discussion, asking questions that help guide the students toward making discoveries on their own.

For example, in a political science class, you may look at how television influences who gets elected to public office. The professor might ask you to summarize the assigned reading about the topic. Other students add their own views about the pros and cons of television and how much of a role it has. The professor steers the discussion, making sure that all sides are covered and that certain key points are raised.

What Are Seminars?

In many ways, **seminars** are similar to discussion classes. Many colleges have freshmen seminars. Juniors and seniors majoring in the same field often attend seminars as well. Class size is small, often fewer than 15 students, so that everyone can participate fully. In fact, you are expected to participate!

Seminars usually focus on narrower topics. For example, instead of a course on "The American Novel," a seminar may focus on the novels of Mark Twain. Seminars often meet once a week for three hours. Discussions can then be detailed. Students learn from each other, challenging or supporting each other's views and defending their own.

In a seminar, you often sit in a circle or around large tables. You might even meet in a lounge or at a professor's home. The informal setting helps encourage everyone to participate.

Lab Classes

Laboratories give you hands-on experience. You go to your regular lectures and then spend time in a lab. You often earn more credits for a course with a lab than you earn in other courses.

Natural science courses frequently include labs. You might study cells under a microscope in a biology lab, find the amount of acid in a solution in a chemistry lab, or study the effects of gravity on a falling object in a physics lab.

Courses in the social sciences, engineering, and many other fields may also use labs. For example, in a psychology lab you might learn how to train an animal to behave in a particular way.

How Do Field Studies Differ from Labs?

Labs are controlled settings. Although you might not know what the results of your research will be, you are in control of all the factors: temperature, lighting, time, and so forth. **Field studies** take you away from a controlled setting and into the real world. Instead of studying a leaf under a microscope, you might observe the growth of plants in the woods. You might look at different layers of soil near an earthquake fault line or study people's behavior when a traffic light turns yellow.

Both labs and field studies emphasize how you conduct research and experiments. You are trained to use equipment and to establish the purpose of your research. You are taught how to gather your observations and then how to record them in a way that will let you reach logical conclusions. Learning how to do research properly is as important as doing the research itself.

Some labs may be scheduled. You attend on a specific day at a specific time. Other labs are open. You spend a certain amount of time each week at your convenience, or you spend as much time as you need to complete your work.

Math, computer, and foreign-language courses may also have labs. Their main purpose is to give students an opportunity to practice what has been taught.

Labs and field studies give you the chance to apply the theories you learn in the classroom.

Are There Opportunities to Study on My Own?

In addition to the classes that you take with other students, many colleges offer opportunities for you to study independently. In fact, many colleges will strongly encourage you to take at least one independent study course, especially during your junior or senior year.

Independent Study

Would you like to study something in-depth that greatly interests you, even if it is not available as a regular college course? Independent study gives you that chance.

In an **independent study** course, you work one-on-one with a professor who agrees to sponsor your work. You set goals with the professor and then develop plans for achieving your goals. Your plans include how you will study and how often you will meet.

The possibilities of what you can do are endless! You can research how pollution is affecting a nearby pond, study a disease that has affected your family, write a full-length play, build a machine, or even start a company!

Not all college courses are offered on a regular basis. Some are offered only occasionally, perhaps only once every two years. (The college catalog will have this information.) Independent study gives you the chance to study the material taught in these courses at a time that fits your schedule.

113

Studios and Practice Rooms

For many courses in the arts, you work in studios and practice rooms to develop your skills and techniques. In art classes, you draw, paint, or sculpt in studios. You often work on your own, but you may meet in groups, especially when working with a model. As a performing arts major, you spend hours alone vocalizing, practicing an instrument, learning dance steps, or even stretching muscles. You spend still more hours rehearsing with others in choirs, small ensembles, bands, orchestras, plays, and dance troupes.

Self-Paced Learning

Some classes are set up to allow you to work at your own pace. In many self-paced classes, you go to a learning lab to get your reading and homework assignments. You may be able to study in the lab itself, using computers or other equipment. You can also check out special materials, including books, DVDs, and videotapes. Tests are often administered by someone who works in the lab—an instructor or an aide. As long as you successfully complete all requirements within a set amount of time, you complete the course.

Self-paced courses enable students to complete familiar material quickly and spend more time on material that is difficult for them.

Self-paced learning is especially helpful for many **remedial, developmental,** and **preparatory** courses. These courses help students strengthen basic skills and bring them up to the college level. For example, many students need to develop their math skills to the level needed for other classes. Self-paced learning is also seen in areas such as office technology.

Self-paced classes enable some students to finish a class early and move on to the next level. They also help students who need a longer period of time to complete the course.

Distance Learning

Chapter 4 discusses distance learning, which takes place outside the traditional classroom. Some forms of distance learning, such as teleclasses and real-time online courses, are similar to traditional lecture or discussion classes. Other forms provide opportunities for self-paced learning.

TYPES OF DISTANCE LEARNING

Online course. Students take the course using the Internet. Some courses take place in real time, with the students and teacher interacting at the same time. In other cases, students use the computer at their convenience, leaving messages and questions for the teacher and classmates. Exams and assignments may be completed on the computer, on campus, or at some other location.

Hybrid course. Students take part of a course on campus and part of it on the computer using the Internet. This method is often recommended for students taking an online class for the first time. Also called *campus web*.

Telecourse. Classes have been filmed in advance. Students watch them on public or cable television or on DVD, videotapes, or videostreaming. Students meet periodically with the instructor and take exams on campus or other approved locations.

TeleWeb. Courses combine telecourse materials and online instruction. Instructional materials are usually printed or available on DVD, videotape, or videostreaming (if you have a high-speed Web connection). Course activities are usually completed online.

Teleclass. Classes are live on cable television. Students may call in to comment or ask questions.

Interactive television. Students in different locations attend class in rooms equipped with television cameras and microphones. An instructor or teaching assistant is available at each location. Students can see, hear, and interact with the course's main instructor and each other as if they were together.

Multimedia course. Course uses a combination of instructional materials that enable students to learn independently. Materials may include CDs, DVDs, slides, software, workbooks, and other print and visual materials.

Can I Combine Work with My Studies?

Many colleges have special programs that allow you to combine your education with work. The chance to apply what you've learned in class to a real-world setting is very important. For some students, having the chance to earn money to pay for college is very important. In all cases, the proven work experience you gain will be helpful when you apply for jobs after graduation.

What Is Cooperative Education?

*Cooperative education is sometimes called work-study or work-based learning. As chapter 11 explains, the term **work-study** also refers to programs that help students pay for college by working on campus.*

Students who want to combine their studies with jobs that help them pay for their education can participate in **cooperative education** (or **co-op**) programs. Students have the opportunity to gain practical experience working in their chosen field.

Many co-op students alternate between college and work. They may spend one term in classes, followed by a term at a co-op job, followed by classes again. At some colleges, they can repeat this pattern. In some cases, students combine work with studies. They take fewer classes at a given time and increase their work schedule.

Some colleges allow students to apply co-op work experience toward meeting their graduation requirements. Even when co-op work does not count toward graduation requirements, you can earn money while gaining very valuable career experience.

HAWAII

Some students who participate in cooperative education at Maui Community College in Hawaii gain work experience in areas such as carpentry, hotel operations, and auto body repair. Other co-op students gain experience in areas such as journalism, agriculture, and nursing.

Northeastern University, located in the heart of Boston, Massachusetts, is a leader in cooperative education. Its program dates back to 1909. Every year about 6,000 students work at more than 2,000 sites, not only in Boston, but throughout the country and internationally. Students who participate in the program earn their degrees in either four or five years. After completing their freshman year, students alternate work and studies for their remaining years. Therefore, each year students have two semesters of courses and two semesters of work. Among the co-op employers in the United States are John Hancock, Turner Construction, Boston Police Department, the *Boston Globe,* Boston Harbor Hotel, Walt Disney World, Perkins School for the Blind, General Electric, Gillette, Children's Hospital Boston, Mass General Hospital, PricewaterhouseCoopers, CVS Pharmacy, Greater Boston Legal Services, Raytheon, and Dana Farber Cancer Institute. Northeastern also has assignments around the world including Australia, Chile, Costa Rica, England, India, Singapore, Spain, and Turkey.

MASSACHUSETTS

In co-op programs, employers often coordinate their hiring with the college. Co-op experience can help you decide whether your chosen field is the right one for you. Even if you decide it's not, your experience will help you more fully develop job skills that apply to many fields.

If you participate in a co-op program, you may need more time than other students to complete your graduation requirements. On the other hand, your co-op experience can help you find work after you graduate. In many cases, you may even have a job already waiting for you with an employer that you worked for through the co-op program.

What Are Internships?

Like co-op programs, **internships** enable you to apply to the workplace what you have learned in your courses. They allow you to combine the spirit of independent study with the practical experience you can gain from cooperative learning and other jobs. Colleges that offer internship programs usually allow you to apply your internship toward your graduation requirements.

Some internships are paid. Many, especially those with nonprofit organizations, are not. In either case, you gain direct experience, make progress toward your degree, and develop job contacts.

IDEAS FOR INTERNSHIPS

Broadcast communications. Work for a radio station: Conduct research for news stories or special features, learn how radio programs are made.

Government and politics. Work on a candidate's campaign: Help research issues, organize volunteers, prepare for events, communicate with voters.

Business. Help a company research consumer reactions to its products: Develop a survey, gather information, analyze responses, summarize findings, report to the company's management about the results.

Performing arts. Work with a community theater: Research and write grant proposals, coordinate volunteers, publicize performances, help develop a long-term plan, assist with fundraising events.

Human services. Work for a community services organization: Develop an after-school or camp program, teach children how to read or use a computer, develop a Web site.

Science. Work as a lab assistant: Help conduct experiments, record observations and results, assist with basic research.

Students often arrange their own internships. Many companies, organizations, and government agencies offer internships to college students. For instance, engineering students at the University of Pittsburgh have opportunities to work with the U.S. Army Corps of Engineers, Westinghouse, and Cisco Systems, among others.

Some colleges open their internship programs to students from around the nation and the world. American University in the District of Columbia has a Washington Semester designed for students majoring in government, politics, foreign policy, international business, communications, law, and arts and humanities. Students participate in internships two days per week, gaining valuable work experience related to their major. They also attend seminars and have the opportunity to meet public officials and decision-makers. Students also earn college credit, experience living in the nation's capital, and make new friends and important connections.

The Smithsonian Institution in Washington, D.C., has several internship programs, including one geared especially toward Native Americans.

Internships sometimes have a special focus. For example, the Hispanic Association of Colleges and Universities (HACU) coordinates a National Internship Program for Hispanic students. Since 1992, the program has helped thousands of students find paid internships throughout the country.

For more information about HACU's National Internship Program, visit the program's Web site at www.hnip.net.

Jonathan Hamburg studies economics and loves international travel. He is exploring possible careers that involve both, including careers in government and business. His internship with the United States Citizenship and Immigration Services (USCIS) is helping him to decide the direction he will take when he graduates college.

Libraries and Learning Centers

If you think that a library is just a place where they keep a lot of books and magazines, think again! College libraries have many resources that can be of great help to you. At many colleges, the library is part of an even larger learning center that offers special services to students.

College libraries can have hundreds of thousands, even millions, of books, periodicals, and other resources. Students can access many of these resources electronically from other locations.

Most colleges have a central library where books, magazines, and other resources are housed. Many colleges have other libraries that focus on a certain field of study. For example, music and art departments often have libraries where recordings and art prints are available.

SPACES AND PLACES AT THE LIBRARY

Main desk. Command central for the library. If you don't know where to go or how to use the library, start here!

Catalog. Lists all books, periodicals, and other resources available at the library; computerized catalogs include resources available in other locations as well as electronic and online resources.

Circulation desk. Where you check out books and resources that you can take out of the library (resources that circulate); librarians can help with interlibrary loans—borrowing materials from other libraries on- and off-campus.

Reference desk. Atlases, maps, encyclopedias, DVDs, audio and video recordings, yearbooks, special guides, and other research materials are here, but are for use in the library only.

Periodicals. Magazines, newspapers, and journals (dated resources that are published periodically) are found here; some can be checked out; many are stored electronically or on microfilm or microfiche.

Stacks. Shelves where books are stored; often open to students.

Dartmouth College has numerous libraries that specialize in areas such as music, art, and biomedical sciences. Together, the libraries have 2.7 million books, 450,000 photographs, 190,000 maps, and millions of pages of digital manuscript. These resources are listed in an electronic catalog that is available throughout the world!

NEW HAMPSHIRE

What Are Special Collections?

Libraries are important centers for research. Many libraries have collections of materials on specialized subjects. These special collections help the college attract outstanding scholars to teach, to research, and to study. For instance, the University of New Mexico in Albuquerque houses the Center for Southwest Research. The Center's collections emphasize Southwestern music and architecture and books on the American West. In the Chapin Library of Rare Books at Williams College in Massachusetts, you can find official copies of the Bill of Rights, the Declaration of Independence, the Constitution, and the Articles of Confederation—an impressive combination!

Some libraries also have collections of works by local authors or college alumni.

Colleges are often called "ivory towers," a name that comes from the look of many college libraries. Colby College's Miller Library, in Waterville, Maine, provides the classic image of an ivory tower. At night, the blue light that shines near the top of the tower can be seen from miles away.

121

Computer Labs

At many colleges, students can work online right from their own rooms, classes, or the library. In fact, wireless technology is making it possible for those with laptop computers to use them just about anywhere!

Student portals are a secure section of the college's Web site just for the college's enrolled students. They highlight the most important programs and services. Individual students can add features that make the portal even more convenient.

Colleges set up rooms with computers for student use. These labs are especially important if students do not have their own computers or necessary software. Here you can write papers, design charts and graphs, and complete special projects. You can also use other equipment such as scanners and laser printers that will help you with your assignments.

Computer labs may let you connect to the college's main computer, helping you with larger projects. Social science students, for example, may have thousands of complicated surveys to analyze. They need the computer power they can access through the college's computer system.

Computer labs also provide students access to the Internet. Many college library Web sites have an **intranet,** special protected areas where research and other learning materials are continually being added from a combination of library resources, faculty, and staff, as well as by the students themselves. By using passwords that the college provides, students may have access to these areas.

Audiovisual (A-V) Centers

Most libraries have audio and video equipment for student use. You may be required to watch a documentary film, study some slides, or listen to a political speech. The A-V center provides access to these materials.

For some classes, you may need to use equipment to make an audio recording, shoot and edit a film, or take photographs. You may need a microphone, monitor, or projector for a special activity or presentation you are organizing. The A-V center can help you.

Language and Listening Labs

Modern technology makes learning languages and applying listening skills easier. Students who are learning to speak foreign languages must practice out of the classroom, and language labs provide a place to develop language skills. Many labs have computer-aided programs that help to build grammar, vocabulary, and conversation skills. For example, you might practice repeating phrases and conversations or answer questions about what you have heard. Films, DVDs, CDs, and other multimedia materials are also available in language labs. Learning about the culture of different countries helps you better understand the language.

Music students spend time in listening labs. They often listen to a music selection numerous times to analyze it for class. Some music labs have rooms in which groups can meet, listen to, and discuss a piece of music. More often, students individually listen to recordings through headphones. They will often have the music score (the printed version of the music) so that they can both hear and see what the composer wrote. Today's technology makes it easy to experiment with specific portions of the music. In some cases, students can even separate one instrument or voice from the others for further study.

Students with Special Needs

Most colleges provide services for students with special needs. These services contribute to student success and enable students to participate fully in campus life.

Physical and Learning Disabilities

Laws such as the Americans with Disabilities Act have resulted in many changes. Elevators and ramps, handicapped parking spaces, automatic doors, and other improvements help people get to class and to other activities. Technology has made a huge difference in providing equal learning opportunities.

Colleges help students who are blind get audiotaped and Braille versions of books. They can provide readers, writers, and interpreters and help with test arrangements for students who need these services. They may even help students with accessible housing and transportation.

Other Challenges

Students can face a variety of other challenges. For some students, English is not their first or native language. Many colleges offer **English as a Second Language (ESL)** programs to help students overcome language barriers. Other colleges have programs that help students who are the first in their family to go to college. Many have programs that address the needs of older students or single parents. Whatever challenges you face, check to see whether a college has the services you need to succeed.

Gallaudet University in Washington, D.C., is the leading college for students with hearing impairments. Founded in 1864, the university has about 1,000 undergraduate students and about 400 graduate students. Gallaudet's library has the world's largest collection of deafness-related resources.

Additional Help for Students with Disabilities

HEATH Resource Center is the online clearinghouse on postsecondary education for individuals with disabilities. Every year, this organization provides information to thousands of people about college.

HEATH's online information and publications cover many topics. These include college admissions, financial literacy and paying for college, independent living, making the transition to college, and many others. You can find some of the resources on the Internet.

Heath's Web site has the following Internet address and e-mail address:

> www.heath.gwu.edu
> AskHEATH@gwu.edu

You can also contact

> The George Washington University
> HEATH Resource Center
> 2134 G Street, NW
> Washington, DC 20052

LEARNING TOOLS FOR STUDENTS WITH DISABILITIES

Large-print materials	Books on tape/CD/DVD
Magnifiers	Talking calculators
Reading machines	Notetakers
Large-screen computers	Interpreters for the deaf
Enlarged print capacity	Readers (people to read aloud)
Wheelchair-accessible desks	Closed-circuit audio
Wheelchair-accessible lab stations	Tape recorders
Writers (people to write down what is said)	Closed captioning for the hearing impaired

Learning Assistance

Many students just need help getting started. Colleges have programs that make you familiar with important places and services on campus. Most have special workshops to help you increase your reading speed and understanding, take effective notes, organize your time and materials, use computers and other technology, improve your study habits, prepare for exams, write research papers, and more. The college's Web site, advising and learning centers, and library can tell you more.

Writing Centers

The ability to communicate clearly is extremely important. But many students arrive at college without the writing skills they will need to succeed in college and beyond.

Many colleges have writing centers, which can help you with your writing skills—not only for English classes, but for all classes. The faculty members and staff at the writing center can work with you on basic grammar skills. They can also help you learn to develop a comfortable style, organize your thoughts, present logical arguments, and develop plans for writing projects, including research papers. Even students who write well may need help organizing and preparing a research paper.

Tutoring

Many students, regardless of their overall ability, find they need extra help with certain courses. Most colleges have programs where these students can get help from a tutor, either one-on-one or in small groups. Tutors may be faculty members, staff, graduate students, and sometimes even other students. In many cases, tutoring is provided free to students who want or need extra help.

Learning Materials

In addition to attending classes in many different settings, you will use several types of learning materials in college.

The learning tools you will probably use most often in college are books. Many textbooks are similar to the ones you use in school now. Their level is higher, but they have built-in aids to help you learn the subject: exercises, illustrations and photos, tables and charts, chapter reviews, and more. For many courses you will be assigned one book. Some books, like a calculus book, may be used for more than one term.

In many courses, you will be assigned several shorter but more focused books to read. For example, in an American government class, you may read specialized books about the presidency, the Constitution, the legislature, the courts, power, and the media.

Learning Technology

Computers have become so important to learning that more and more colleges are requiring students to have them. Many textbooks include digital supplements with extra study material. These may be on a CD or DVD, or they may be available directly online. A growing trend is for the textbooks themselves to be digital.

Colleges that require computers often arrange for students to buy specific models at discounted prices.

Students also use computers for taking notes in class, completing and turning in homework, researching and writing papers, or studying for exams. They can often use computers to get their assignments, review their instructors' notes, check their grades, work with classmates on group projects, or get help from a tutor.

Calculators also are important learning tools. Some calculators are designed with special features for business classes. Others have features that help you in math, engineering, statistics, or science classes. Many calculators even plug into your computer.

Before you buy a calculator, find out whether one kind is recommended over another for your classes.

There is one thing you can count on. As technology continues to develop, the different ways you can learn at college will continue to grow and change.

OTHER LEARNING MATERIALS

Study guides	Chapter reviews, summaries, sample quizzes and tests, and glossaries.
Solutions manuals	Detailed solutions to exercises in the book; used a lot in math and science courses.
Notes	Professor's class notes available through the library, bookstore, or Web; can help you prepare for or follow up on classroom lectures.
Exams	Exams from earlier years kept on file for your review when preparing for tests.
Lab kits	Supplies used in laboratory sessions; for example, safety glasses or a dissecting kit.
Studio kits	Art supplies, including charcoal, crayons, drawing pencils, paints, and drawing pads.
Audiotapes/CDs	May be reviews of lectures; also used in foreign-language classes for drill or practice.
Videotapes/DVDs	May supplement the textbook; sometimes interactive; may also be a recording of lectures for students who miss class or want the review.
Digital resources	Often an electronic version of a study guide, giving you extra practice and drill on selected topics.
Simulations	May be computerized; gives you the opportunity to test real situations; for example, a business simulation may let you pretend to run a company.
Instructor Web sites	Provides class schedule, assignments, reading list, and extra readings, as well as office hours and grades.
Publisher Web sites	Often combines study guides, audiotapes, video-tapes, and additional resources into one site.

7

How Do I Gather Information?

Choosing a college is like choosing clothes to wear for a special occasion. The trick is finding something that looks good *and* fits well. Just because it's the right fit for someone else doesn't mean it's right for you.

Before you can choose a college, you need to learn as much as possible about the options that are available to you. You can find out about individual colleges from many different sources.

In this chapter, we look at ways to gather information. Then you can begin to compare colleges and find one that is right for you.

Information: There's Lots of It!

You just need to know where to look and what to ask. People, libraries, books, the Internet, multimedia materials, and the colleges themselves are all important sources of information.

Chapter 2 lists sample questions to ask people about their careers. You can ask similar questions about their college choices.

You don't have to go very far to start gathering information. It may take you a little while to decide what to ask. And you may even have to go back to some sources more than once with follow-up questions. But that's okay.

Most people are happy to help someone who is curious and interested in college. Never be shy about asking for help.

WHO CAN TELL ME MORE ABOUT COLLEGE?

Family. Did your parents go to college? How about brothers or sisters? Perhaps you can talk with an uncle, aunt, or cousins who have gone.

Friends and neighbors. Have you ever talked about college with your friends? Are any of them thinking about going to college? Maybe they have older brothers or sisters who go to college or are applying. Do you mow the lawn, babysit, or run errands for neighbors? Find out if any of them have gone to college and ask their advice.

Teachers. Your teachers have all gone to college. Ask each of them where they went. Choose a couple with whom you are close or whose opinion you value and talk to them.

Counselors. Ask your guidance counselors at school for help. They might be especially helpful in suggesting ways you can find information. They can show you important college resources in your school.

Others. Don't forget members of your religious community, your doctor, a camp counselor or youth group leader, or anyone else who comes to mind!

What Information Do Colleges Provide?

Colleges provide information in many ways. The most traditional way has been through printed materials such as **viewbooks** and **catalogs.** In addition, college representatives visit students at high schools and at college fairs. Colleges also encourage students to visit their campuses whenever possible.

With today's technology, colleges offer information in more ways than ever before. The combination of DVDs, CDs, the Internet, videostreaming, and other technology enables you to visit a campus without leaving home.

Technology also expands your ability to contact colleges. Although you can use mail and the telephone, most students use the Internet and e-mail to contact colleges for information. You can request general information from the admissions office or request specific information from specific offices. In most cases, you can even receive, complete, and return your application online!

When you contact a college's admissions office, you are letting them know you are interested. The office may add you to its mailing (or e-mailing) list so that you will receive up-to-date news that might help you when you apply. You may also hear about special events where you can learn about the college. This information may help you when you apply.

The next page describes some of the various sources of information that colleges provide. On the page after that, you will find a sample letter you could send to an admissions office to get more information. Many college guidebooks and Web sites provide contact information for admissions offices across the country.

All of these sources are helpful. But you should always try to visit the colleges in which you are most interested. A campus visit is the best way to get to know a college.

***Recruiters** are college representatives who encourage eligible students to apply to their college. They also answer questions that students have about college. The information you get from recruiters is almost always on target. However, listen most closely to what recruiters have to say about the colleges they represent rather than what they tell you about other colleges.*

COLLEGES PROVIDE INFORMATION IN DIFFERENT WAYS

College Web sites. These are an important way to send and receive information. They usually have areas specially designed for prospective students and may include virtual tours that enable you to see the campus without actually visiting it. Many colleges also correspond with students by e-mail (see chapter 8).

Viewbook. This overview booklet provides general information about the college, usually with photographs. It helps you decide whether you want to learn more about the college.

Catalog. This detailed book for current students describes majors and graduation requirements, lists and describes courses, and explains the college's rules and regulations. Many colleges don't mail these, but they're often available online.

College fair. At this kind of event, many colleges set up information booths. You can visit booths, talk with college representatives, and pick up viewbooks and other materials; you also can place your name on a mailing list for information. College representatives may work for the college (for example, college recruiters) or may be volunteers (for example, alumni). College fairs are often sponsored by high schools or school districts.

High school visits. College representatives visit high schools, usually in the fall, and provide informational materials. Students sign up through the guidance office to meet with college representatives.

DVDs and other technology. Similar to viewbooks, audiovisual introductions to colleges often give you a chance to hear student points of view. Some colleges provide DVDs to keep, and others charge a small fee or loan them. These resources are often available through high school guidance offices, libraries, or college Web sites.

Campus tours and open houses. Tours give you a chance to see the college in person. They are available year-round and are often conducted by students. Open houses and other programs are available several times per year, especially in the fall. During these events, visitors ask questions; tour the campus; and meet faculty, students, and others.

Interview and individual visit. Interviews take place on campus with an admissions counselor or off campus (often with an alumnus). They provide an opportunity for you and the college to get to know each other better.

CONTACT A COLLEGE!

You could send this letter or one like it to the admissions office or the chairperson of an academic department. You can also send it electronically, if you have the e-mail address. Whenever possible, address your letter to a specific person.

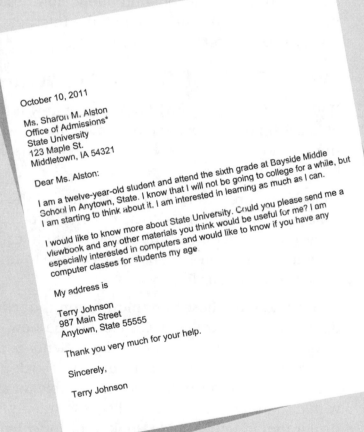

October 10, 2011

Ms. Sharon M. Alston
Office of Admissions*
State University
123 Maple St.
Middletown, IA 54321

Dear Ms. Alston:

I am a twelve-year-old student and attend the sixth grade at Bayside Middle School in Anytown, State. I know that I will not be going to college for a while, but I am starting to think about it. I am interested in learning as much as I can.

I would like to know more about State University. Could you please send me a viewbook and any other materials you think would be useful for me? I am especially interested in computers and would like to know if you have any computer classes for students my age.

My address is

Terry Johnson
987 Main Street
Anytown, State 55555

Thank you very much for your help.

Sincerely,

Terry Johnson

*Many college guides list the names of the directors or deans of admissions along with their mailing addresses. These guides frequently include e-mail addresses as well.

Where Do I Find This Information in the Library?

The librarians at both your school and public libraries are important allies as you gather information. Although anyone at the library can help you, you may want to start with the reference librarians. They can show you how to locate many useful materials. You will also find that most school and public libraries have computers that you can use to search the Internet and the library's own information databases.

What Kinds of Books Are Available?

If you go into almost any bookstore, you will find dozens of books on almost every topic having to do with college. In fact, many bookstores have entire sections devoted to books about college.

Guidebooks are available that describe all the four-year colleges in the country. Others describe two-year colleges. Some guides offer advice about getting into college or ways to pay for college. You may be able to find many of these books at your library.

Some college guides are devoted to a single topic. For example, several books explain how to write the essays you need for your college application.

Many guides are based on information that comes directly from the colleges. Others tell you how college students feel about the schools they attend. Some books rate colleges based on special categories such as the best value for your money, the most accessible for students with disabilities, or the best colleges to attend for a particular major. Other guides look at historically black colleges, summer internships, and international studies.

The list of books goes on. In fact, if you can think of a topic, someone has probably already written a book about it. And the books aren't written only for you. A lot of books are written for your parents, too, to help them know what to expect or how to plan for college expenses.

Where Else Can I Find Information?

Lots of college information is available through the Internet. Don't worry if you don't have your own computer or your own access to the Internet. You should be able to use a computer at your local or school library.

College Web sites are discussed in chapter 8.

Newspapers often have sections and articles about college. Several magazines, including *U.S. News & World Report,* have special editions just about college.

Your school's guidance office is a good place to find helpful DVDs, software, and other resources about college. The guidance office is likely to have access to college materials such as college catalogs, viewbooks, free brochures and pamphlets, and information about upcoming college-related events, including college fairs.

Social Networking

You also can find information through **social networking**, in which people share information and opinions with each other. Facebook and MySpace are sites where people can have their own home page and interact with each other. Many colleges have set up their own pages at these sites.

Be careful about which Internet sites you visit and what you write online. Talk to a parent, librarian, counselor, or college representative about reliable sites. Learn to separate fact from opinion.

Blogs and Twitter are like diaries that anyone can write onto the Internet, sharing opinions and ideas. Some colleges now have their own blogs. They invite selected students to post their thoughts and experiences in ways that will show the college in a good light.

The "information" shared through Facebook, MySpace, Twitter, and blogs is often based on the experiences and opinions of one or more people—the information may or may not be accurate and complete.

Special Programs for Learning About College

Many programs are available that can help you learn more about college. Although most of these programs are for high school students, many programs are for younger students, too.

School and College Programs

You can find specialized guides that describe summer programs across the country. You can also find information on the Internet and at college Web sites.

Schools may sponsor field trips to local colleges, meetings with guest speakers, and college fairs. Colleges have programs that bring younger students to their campuses. You may be able to participate in an academic program that gives you a feeling for a college classroom, attend a sports or arts program, or even experience living on a college campus.

TEXAS

For more information, see http://academics. utep.edu/ motherdaughter/.

Since 1986, the University of Texas at El Paso (UTEP) has run the Mother-Daughter Program. This program encourages young Hispanic girls and their mothers to see college as part of their future. The program begins in sixth grade. Teams of mothers and daughters meet one Saturday each month to participate in activities dealing with academic, personal, career, and community-life issues. During the year, the mothers and daughters tour the campus and meet with successful female Hispanic students. They participate in a career day, meeting with Hispanic women who have developed successful professional careers. The teams participate in a leadership conference and work on community-service projects. The girls also take part in an on-campus summer camp. The program does not end with sixth grade. Additional activities take place all the way through high school graduation. Similar programs are now offered at other colleges.

Government Programs

The federal government and many state governments sponsor a variety of college-preparation programs. Talent Search and Upward Bound are both designed especially for students from disadvantaged backgrounds. Talent Search helps students as early as sixth grade succeed and go on to college. Upward Bound is similar, but aimed at high school students. These programs provide students with career, academic, personal, and financial counseling. They often provide tutors and **mentors.**

Talent Search and Upward Bound are part of a group of programs called the TRIO programs. For more information, go to www.ed.gov/about/offices/list/ope/trio/.

Another important program is GEAR UP—Gaining Early Awareness and Readiness for Undergraduate Programs. GEAR UP works in partnership with cities, states, school districts, colleges, businesses, and organizations. Together they sponsor groups of mostly low-income students, usually starting in middle and junior high school. Groups of students are often supported all the way through high school with activities that help prepare them for college. In some cases, college funds are even available.

Community Programs

Many local and national organizations offer some form of early college preparation. Boys and Girls Clubs, Boy Scouts and Girl Scouts of America, the YMCA, and others sponsor special programs that include college-preparation activities.

Citizen Schools helps students in grades 6, 7, and 8 develop the skills they need to succeed in school, go to college, and become future leaders. The organization provides hands-on learning activities, including apprenticeships, exploration, homework help, and team-building; it helps thousands of students a year in dozens of locations. To learn more, visit its Web site at *www.citizenschools.org.*

What Do I Need to Know?

The United States has thousands of colleges! How can you choose among them? Start by understanding their characteristics. You will then be able to compare different colleges more easily.

Size

College guides may measure the size of the student body in slightly different ways. Be sure you check the actual number of undergraduate students.

A college's size is most often determined by the number of students it has. A college's overall size can affect class size, social life, availability of courses and resources, the range of activities, and your opportunity to participate.

Location

Location refers to where a college is. It does not refer simply to the city and state. For example, is the college close to home or far away? Is the college near an airport, train station, or bus station? How do you get to it? Is the college near anyone you know? Is the weather warm or cold, rainy or dry? What activities are near the college (museums, sports events, hiking, and so forth)?

Setting

A college's immediate surroundings make up its setting. College settings are usually described as urban, suburban, small town, or rural. Setting also refers to the campus. Does the campus have a lake or a pond? Is it flat or hilly? Is it wooded? What style is its architecture?

You can even look at setting in terms of how the campus is laid out. Is the campus big or small? Is the campus spread out or are the buildings close together? How far are the classroom buildings and the library from student housing or the parking lots? How long would it take to get from a dining hall to a classroom building? Where are the places to relax and the places to socialize?

COLLEGE SIZE AND SETTINGS

The first college listed for each category is a four-year college. The second college is a two-year college.

Size*	Setting	College or University
Small	Urban	Agnes Scott College (GA)
		Maria College (NY)
Small	Suburban	Alaska Pacific University
		New Mexico Military Institute
Small	Rural/small town	University of the Ozarks (AR)
		Lamar Community College (CO)
Medium	Urban	Oklahoma City University
		Galveston College (TX)
Medium	Suburban	Rollins College (FL)
		Berkshire Community College (MA)
Medium	Rural/small town	Middlebury College (VT)
		Mitchell Community College (NC)
Large	Urban	Brown University (RI)
		Spokane Community College (WA)
Large	Suburban	Washington University (MO)
		Clackamas Community College (OR)
Large	Rural/small town	University of South Dakota
		Atlantic Cape Community College (NJ)
Very large	Urban	Temple University (PA)
		Delgado Community College (LA)
Very large	Suburban	Arizona State University
		Washtenaw Community College (MI)
Very large	Rural/small town	Auburn University (AL)
		Cabrillo College (CA)

* Small	Less than 1,000 undergraduate students
Medium	1,000 to 5,000 undergraduate students
Large	5,000 to 10,000 undergraduate students
Very large	More than 10,000 undergraduate students

Cost

College costs vary quite a lot. Whether you attend a two-year or a four-year college affects your costs, as do other factors (such as whether you choose a public college or a private college). In chapters 10 and 11, we look more closely at college costs and ways to pay for college.

Financial Assistance

Your family may be able to provide a certain amount of help paying for college. Many types of help (also called **financial aid**) are available through **scholarships** and **grants** (money that you do not need to repay), **loans,** and jobs. Some colleges can offer more support than others. *Whether you can afford a particular college depends on more than its costs. Your true cost is also based on how much financial assistance you receive.* As you gather information, try to learn how many students receive assistance from the colleges in which you are interested and what types of assistance they receive.

Available Majors

Most colleges, especially large universities, offer many academic programs. Some specialize in areas such as performing arts, religious studies, culinary arts, or technology. Colleges have different strengths. For instance, Northwestern University's journalism program is one of its best. It is also one of the top journalism programs in the country.

Colleges often have strengths within fields of study. For example, a particular college may have a top psychology program with a special strength in experimental psychology, which is research-oriented. However, that college may not offer much in clinical psychology, which is oriented toward patients. If your interest is in the clinical areas, you may need to look elsewhere.

Academic Opportunity

In addition to knowing what programs a college offers, you'll want to know how hard it is to get into those programs. At many colleges, once you are accepted, you can major in whatever area you want. However, some areas of study, like engineering and nursing, may be limited to a certain number of students. Therefore, checking any restrictions a college may have on your favorite program is a very important part of gathering information.

Suppose Boston University is your school of choice and athletic training is your field of choice. Being accepted at Boston University does not automatically mean you can get into their athletic training program. Only a limited number of students are accepted into the athletic training program.

The Faculty

Find out how many faculty members a college has, but ask other questions, too. How many have advanced degrees? Are most classes taught by full-time professors, by their assistants, or by part-time faculty? Who has received research, writing, or teaching awards? Do any departments receive more of these awards? Are any of the departments recognized nationally?

Student-Faculty Ratio

The student-faculty ratio is the number of students at a college for each faculty member. For example, a college with a student-faculty ratio of 13 to 1 (or 13:1) has 13 students for each faculty member. This ratio is often used to indicate the opportunities that students have to interact with their professors. At a college with a 13:1 student-faculty ratio, you are likely to have more access to professors than at a college with a 25:1 ratio.

Class Size

Your learning experience will vary depending on how many students are in your classes. Teaching methods and class size often go together. A class of 300 students limits the amount of interaction with the professor. Learn the average number of students in a typical class. Also try to find out the range of class size. How many classes have more than 50 students or fewer than 20 students? Which size do you prefer?

PENNSYLVANIA

At Bryn Mawr College in Pennsylvania, few classes have more than 50 students. And almost 7 out of every 10 classes have fewer than 20 students. Bryn Mawr's student-to-faculty ratio is 8:1, or 8 students for every teacher. This means that Bryn Mawr students have a lot of access to their professors.

You should always check a college's accreditation. Most are listed in the college's catalog or in the standard college guidebooks. Your opportunities for careers, graduate schools, and professional programs could be hurt if the college you attend does not meet approved standards.

Accreditation

In order to drive a car, you must earn your license by showing the Department of Motor Vehicles that you meet a set of standards. In a similar way, a college earns its **accreditation** by showing it has met certain standards.

One type of accreditation is the kind the college earns as a whole. The college shows that it meets standards for its educational program, the services it provides, and its facilities. Many colleges are accredited by regional organizations such as the Southern Association of Colleges and Schools. Colleges can also be accredited by organizations, such as the New York State Board of Regents.

Departments also earn accreditation. For example, the National League for Nursing Accrediting Commission (NLNAC) approves nursing education programs.

College Facilities

The buildings and other facilities on the college campus are an important factor when you are comparing colleges.

Are the buildings in good shape? Are classrooms comfortable? If you are going to live on campus in a dormitory, how big are the rooms? How close to the classroom buildings are they? How are the heating and air-conditioning systems throughout the campus?

If you need or prefer a special diet, you might check whether the food service on campus can meet your needs.

Is the library up-to-date? Is it crowded? Are the chairs comfortable for studying? How are the college's technology resources? Is it easy to access the Internet from different places on campus? Do science, language, and technology labs have modern equipment? How are the college's technology services for students who don't have a computer or who live off campus?

What are the athletic facilities like? How many dining halls are there and where are they located? Where is the student union (a center of activity for students) located and what facilities does it have? All these questions and more are part of judging a college's facilities.

Health-Care Facilities

Don't overlook health facilities when you compare colleges. Learn what facilities are on campus in case you get sick or have health concerns. Is medical care available 24 hours a day? What kind of health insurance does the college offer? Where are hospitals located? Are there any hospitals on campus? Does the college charge for health-care services? If so, how much?

Campus Security

Laws now require colleges to report information each year about the safety of their campuses. For more information, see www.ope.ed.gov/security/search.asp.

Try to learn about a college's safety record. How much crime, and what kind, takes place on campus? Is the college well lit at night? Does the college have an escort service to walk students across campus at night? Does the college have its own security force? How easy is it to reach security? Are emergency phones readily available if you need to dial for help? How well protected are the parking lot and bike racks? How secure are the academic buildings and student housing?

Transportation

If you plan to live on campus, you might have questions about how easy it is to get from campus to nearby shopping, entertainment, or airports. Does the college provide buses or other transportation? Are parking spaces available to students who live on campus?

Is transportation available, especially on campus, for students with disabilities?

If you plan to live off campus and **commute** to class, you will also want to know about public transportation and parking spaces. You may want to know how close buses or trains come to campus, how often they run, what hours they run, and how much they cost. If you plan to drive to campus, you should know how much parking permits cost, how crowded the parking lots are, and how far away they are from the classrooms, the library, and any other facilities you would regularly use.

Diversity

College gives you a unique opportunity to interact closely with people whose experiences and outlook are different from your own. Many colleges try to attract students who represent the diversity of our population.

The diversity of students at many public colleges tends to be similar to the diversity of the nearby population. Some colleges draw on a small geographic area; students come from the nearby community. Other colleges are regional. Their students may include those from nearby states. Other colleges are national. They attract students from all over the United States and, in many cases, from all over the world.

Colleges vary in the racial, ethnic, and gender mix of their students. Sometimes the racial and ethnic mix reflects the local population. For example, a higher number of people of Hispanic origin live in the Southwest United States. Not surprisingly, colleges in the Southwest tend to have a higher percentage of Hispanic students than colleges in most other areas. Some colleges try to attract a broad range of students. Other colleges serve specific groups of students. For example, Spelman College in Georgia is geared toward students who are not only African-American, but also female. Similarly, Morehouse College in Georgia is geared mostly toward African-American males.

Religious diversity at colleges also varies. Some colleges aim for a broad mix of backgrounds. Other colleges are more likely to have students with similar religious backgrounds, especially if the colleges are formally affiliated with a particular religious group.

Diversity *indicates the range of people's backgrounds: age, gender, geography, race, ethnicity, religion, family income, and so forth.*

Some students can use geography to their advantage for getting into certain colleges. For example, being from North Dakota may not help you get into a college in nearby Minnesota. However, it may help you get into a New England college that's looking for a national mix of students.

Do not assume that a college affiliated with a religious group accepts only students of that religion.

Religion

You may have questions about religious observances while you are at college. If answers are not in the college materials, ask an admissions counselor. Many colleges have interfaith chapels that serve many denominations. They may also have advisors for specific religious groups. You will want to know whether services for your own faith are held on campus or in the community.

You may also have certain dietary needs. For instance, if you are Muslim or Jewish, you may want to know about the availability of kosher foods. You also may want to know about arrangements the college has to honor your needs for observances and holidays.

Students with Special Needs

Most colleges can work with you to solve or manage concerns you may have. Some colleges have extensive services to help students who have disabilities or other special needs. Many colleges provide help for students whose first language is not English. In other cases, colleges can help students who have learning disabilities with test taking or even scheduling of smaller classes.

Many students are the first person in their family to attend college. They may have special needs because they have no one in their family who has had this experience and can tell them what college is like. Their family may not always be able to give them the support and encouragement they need. As a result, they may feel that they are less prepared than other students. Colleges often have programs to address the special concerns of first-generation students.

If you are disabled or have other special circumstances, get the information you need early on about how the college can help you.

Challenge and Reputation

Some colleges are harder than other colleges. Courses are tougher, the workload is heavier, and competition is stiffer. One way to judge the difficulty of a course is to look at the skill level needed for taking the course. Some physics courses, for example, require students to have algebra skills in order to handle the math portion of the course. But other physics courses require students to have calculus skills, a higher level of math. A college where most students take calculus-based physics is generally more difficult than one where most students take algebra-based physics.

A college's level of challenge is often a matter of opinion. But there are ways to measure a college's level of difficulty and its overall reputation.

One way is to look at a college's **selectivity.** This looks, in part, at the academic record of students who enter the college. What students do after they graduate is also important. How many graduates of a four-year college continue on and get advanced degrees? How many graduates of a two-year college go on to four-year colleges?

See chapter 8 to learn more about selectivity.

Several magazines, guides, and Web sites that rate colleges are available. Some rate the overall college based on many of the factors listed in this chapter. Others are more specific. For example, you might be able to find a listing of the 10 best economics departments in the country, or colleges with the highest percentage of students going on to medical school. Talking to people is also an important way to learn about a college. Talk to graduates, students, teachers, counselors, and others.

In any rating guide, you need to understand the factors used to find the rating. For example, are the ratings based on the author's personal opinion, or are specific facts used?

Student Activities

Learn what you can about the different activities available for students. What clubs does the college have? Do many guest speakers and performers come to the college?

See chapter 13 for more information about student activities.

What opportunities does the college have for you to get involved? Will you be able to act in a play or sing in a chorus? Will you be able to be active with student government? If you like to camp or participate in debates, will you be able to pursue these activities? Can you become active with a college newspaper or other publication?

Campus activities provide a great way for students who commute to stay connected to the college.

If you like sports, will you be able to play with a college-sponsored team? Are there **intramural sports** available? If you are interested in a specific sport, such as rugby or cross-country skiing, will you be able to follow up on that interest?

You can find answers to many of these questions in college Web sites and viewbooks, alumni magazines, and various college guides, especially those that include information from students who are currently attending college.

Your Overall Feeling for the College

Some colleges may not feel right to you no matter how many strengths they have. Others have weaknesses but still feel right to you. At some point ask yourself: "What does my heart tell me about the college? Does it feel like a place where I would like to be?" You may receive lots of advice from others and, in some cases, pressure to go one place or another. Certainly the views of others are important. But at some point you must listen to your inner voice and whether it says to you, "This college will be great for me!"

8

Where Should
I Apply?

Gathering information about colleges is a great starting point. In fact, you will probably collect more information than you can imagine! Your next important step is to figure out what matters most to you. Then you can zero in on certain colleges or types of colleges where you want to apply.

Will you find one college that is perfect for you? Maybe. But you definitely will find that some colleges have advantages for you that others do not. If you know what is most important to you, choosing the right college will be much easier. This chapter will help you ask and answer the right questions about yourself and colleges. Learn how to do this and you will be well on your way!

The First Step: Know Yourself

This process of evaluating yourself is often called self-assessment.

Before you begin to decide where to apply to college, take time to think about yourself. Think about your goals, your likes and dislikes, your abilities, and your resources.

What Are Your Goals?

Think about what you would like your life to be like when you are older. Do you have special interests that may affect what you want to study or the kind of career you will want someday? If you have a particular field in mind, you should look for colleges that can help you reach that goal.

What do you do if your goals seem to conflict? For instance, you may be interested in studying business and music. Finding colleges where you can pursue them both would be a good plan. You may even be able to combine them. For example, Monmouth University in New Jersey and Middle Tennessee State University offer programs in the music business!

Maybe you have only a general idea about your future. For example, traveling, living in a certain place, making a good income, or helping your community may be very important to you, even though you're not sure how to accomplish any of these goals.

College provides wonderful opportunities for people who are not sure about their goals. You can test the waters and try out new directions. You can take courses in different areas. If you like, you can pursue those new directions or try still other opportunities.

Don't be concerned or feel pressured if you are not sure what your goals are. College is not only for people with clear goals in sight. Most people find that their goals change throughout life. Knowing yourself does not mean that you must have all the answers about your future. Being honest with yourself may mean admitting that you don't know or you're not sure about your goals. However, this understanding will help you make better decisions about where to apply to college.

Michelle Kwan is the most decorated figure skater in U.S. history and one of the most beloved of all time. Yet she never lost her commitment to earning her college degree. Her world travels and a meeting with then-Secretary of State Condoleezza Rice led to her being appointed the first American Public Diplomacy Envoy for the State Department. She attended the University of Denver (where Rice studied), earning her degree in international studies with a minor in political science. Michelle currently attends Tufts University's Fletcher School (in Massachusetts) where she is pursuing a master's degree in international affairs.

What Are Your Likes and Dislikes?

Your personal preferences about many things are important to your decisions about college. Would you rather live in a big city or a small town? Do you want to be near the ocean, rivers, lakes, or the mountains? What kind of weather do you prefer?

Do you want to go away from home—and if so, how far away? Would you rather live at or near home when you go to college? Do you want to be able to come home on weekends? Do you like being around lots of other people, or do you prefer to spend time with one or two close friends? Do you feel more comfortable with people who share your values and beliefs? Do you want to be with people whose backgrounds are different from your own?

Ask yourself the questions suggested here, as well as any other questions that are important to you. Don't worry about how someone else might respond. Being honest with yourself is what matters most!

Also consider any special needs you have. How important is having a place of worship nearby? Do you have specific dietary requirements, whether for health, religious reasons, or personal preference? Do you have specific needs because of physical or learning disabilities? You must determine how well a college and the surrounding community can meet these and other needs.

What Are Your Abilities?

Do you have special talents or hobbies related to sports, music, computers, or other areas? You will probably want to find colleges where you can pursue these activities.

Consider your strengths and weaknesses. Are you a good student? Does studying come easily to you? If the answers to these questions are "no," don't be discouraged. Just be realistic about how challenging a college you should consider. Do you have a knack for science or math? Does writing come easily to you? These kinds of questions might help lead you to areas of study and, in turn, to certain colleges.

If you know your abilities, you will be able to work with them. You will be able to build on the strengths you have identified. You will also be able to take steps to overcome or deal with any weaknesses.

What Are Your Resources?

Chapters 10 and 11 discuss college costs and ways to pay for college.

At some point, you need to consider how you and your family will pay for college. You may not have answers yet. *But don't let cost keep you from applying to a college that is right for you in every other way.*

College expenses can be met in many ways. Your family's resources and savings are one possibility. You may have your own savings that can help with college costs. Financial support is often available through the federal and state governments. Colleges themselves, as well as businesses and organizations, often provide a great deal of financial support. You may be surprised when you realize how much help is available.

Still, you need to be realistic about what you and your family can afford. As you make your list of colleges that interest you, take note of those that are more affordable than others. Note those for which you might need to get extra help.

Will you have to work while you go to college? If you have a good job, you may decide that going to college close to home or part-time makes the most sense. You may find that you can afford to be a full-time student for two years, but not for four years. Your best decision may be to attend a community college for the first two years. Earning an associate degree could then lead you to a job that will enable you to continue your education at a four-year college.

Other students reverse that order. They work while they attend a community college. They then transfer to a four-year college and attend it full-time for two years to earn their bachelor's degree. Whether you work or not, attending a community college for one or two years is one way to make your financial resources go further. It allows you to earn your bachelor's degree at a considerable savings.

Resources can affect your choices in other ways. For example, if you plan to live at home, will you have a car or access to public transportation? If you plan to go further away to college, will you be able to come home when you want, for example, for holidays and special family events?

Some government agencies have programs to help students pay for college. For example, the National Security Agency's (NSA's) Stokes Educational Scholarship pays for students to attend the college of their choice. In return, students work for the agency during summers and a certain number of years after graduating. Programs such as this may also cover housing, meals, and other living expenses. For more information, go online to *www.nsa.gov/careers/ opportunities_4_u/students/stokes.shtml.*

WHAT I THINK MATTERS!

My Goals

What subjects interest me?

What do I want to be?

Do I want to continue my education after high school?

Do I need to go to college for this career?

My Likes and Dislikes

Do I want to live away from home? If so, how far away?

How important is it that friends go to the same college I attend?

Am I comfortable around a lot of people at one time?

Do I want to be with a wide range of people or those with backgrounds like mine?

Would I prefer a city, a suburb, a small town, or a rural area?

What kind of weather do I like, or does it matter to me?

Do I have any special concerns (religious, special customs, dietary, and so forth)?

Which activities are most important to me (arts, sports, clubs, and so forth)?

Do I want to play sports when I'm at college?

Which special opportunities are important to me (study abroad, independent study, exchange programs, and so forth)?

My Abilities

What kind of a student am I?

What are my strongest and weakest subjects?

Do I have any special needs (medical, disabilities, learning, and so forth)?

How are my study skills?

How well do I handle competition and pressure?

What are my special talents?

My Resources

Are there limits to what I can pay for college?

Will my family be able to help me?

Can I go to college full-time if I want?

How will I get to classes (live on campus, drive, public transportation, and so forth)?

Build a List of Colleges

You may wonder how knowing about yourself can help you figure out where you should apply to college. That's a fair question! Let's see how it works.

Start by building a list of colleges. You can build your list in a couple of different ways. First, you can add to your list of colleges as you hear about them. Some may be colleges near where you live. Some may be colleges where family, friends, and teachers have gone. Still others will catch your interest after watching a game on television, hearing about where a famous person went to college, or even reading about an important event that took place at a college.

Learn more about these colleges. Use college guidebooks, software programs, and the Internet. Don't forget to talk to people who may be familiar with these colleges. Decide whether what you have learned is interesting to you. In short, decide whether to keep the college on your list.

Suppose you live in San Diego, California, but hear interesting things about Davidson College in North Carolina. You should first ask yourself how you feel about going to college on the East Coast, so far from home. If that idea is okay with you, start exploring Davidson more. If you don't want to go that far away, don't add Davidson or other East Coast colleges to your list.

Add Colleges That Match Your Priorities

A more focused way to build a list is to ask the questions described earlier in this chapter and in chapter 7. Decide what is important to you—then look for a college that matches your priorities. If a college has what matters to you most, add it to your list.

Few colleges will have everything that you want. But, in all likelihood, several on your list will have many of the qualities that matter most to you. These are the schools you can begin to look at more closely.

Again, suppose you live in San Diego and know that you don't want to be too far from home. Start by looking at colleges in Southern California and Arizona.

How Can I Use Technology to Build My List?

A computer with access to the Internet gives you a valuable tool that can help you build your list. You can learn a lot of valuable information about colleges through the Internet.

The Web sites of the colleges that interest you are a good place to start. The addresses for these Web sites typically include the name of the college and end in *edu*. For example, Stanford University's home page is *www.stanford.edu*.

The home page of a college Web site usually has a photo of the college and a table of contents for the major types of information you can find on the Web site, such as information about admissions, academics, and activities. Information for students thinking about going to that college is often listed under the category "prospective students."

Many Web sites use multimedia tools so that you can hear people talking and see things in motion. In many cases, these tools allow you to take a virtual tour of the campus. The tour is similar to watching a movie, but you decide where to visit! Web sites may also include blogs, diaries written by students, faculty, and others from the college. These blogs can give you insight into what individuals think about their experiences at the college.

A college's Web site tells you about that college, but it isn't as helpful for comparing colleges. College Web sites also vary in the information they provide. However, there are organizations that have both a Web site and publications that make it easy to compare information such as number of students, location and campus setting, costs, and available majors. They might even compare food on different college campuses.

As fun and interesting as using the Internet can be, remember that print materials such as college viewbooks and catalogs can be much easier and faster for finding certain types of information.

*The word **blog** comes from the phrase Web log, and is a log or journal written for the Web.*

Tools that help you search the World Wide Web, called **search engines,** include Google (*www.google.com*) and Yahoo! (*www.yahoo.com*). You can use them to help you locate more information about specific colleges. In most cases, you type the name of the college that interests you. The engine searches the Internet and comes back with a list of Web pages that contain the college's name. The college's home page will often appear near the top of the list.

A good example of this type of organization is The Princeton Review, found at *www.princetonreview.com*. You may have to register with the site, but there is no fee to use it.

If you do not have a home computer or Internet access at home, libraries, guidance offices, and career centers often have computers available for your use. In addition, software programs that provide a lot of helpful information are also available, often in your guidance office or career center.

One of the most useful Internet resources is College Navigator, a site run by the U.S. Department of Education. You can use this site to search for colleges by many different factors. A list of colleges that meet the factors you set is displayed, and you can look at each one for a brief summary. Each listing also provides a link to the college's Web site.

College Navigator also has many other features worth exploring, including the ability to compare colleges. To visit College Navigator, go to the following address on the Web:

http://nces.ed.gov/collegenavigator/

Your school's librarian or your guidance counselor should be able to help you find out more on the Internet about colleges.

A Sampling of College Home Pages on the Web

State	College or University	Web Address
Alabama	University of South Alabama	www.southalabama.edu
Alaska	University of Alaska–Anchorage	www.uaa.alaska.edu
Arizona	Scottsdale Community College	www.scottsdalecc.edu
Arkansas	Harding University	www.harding.edu
California	San Diego State University	www.sdsu.edu
Colorado	Pueblo Community College	www.pueblocc.edu
Connecticut	Trinity College	www.trincoll.edu
Delaware	Delaware State University	www.desu.edu
Florida	Brevard Community College	www.brevardcc.edu
Georgia	Georgia State University	www.gsu.edu
Hawaii	Hawaii Pacific University	www.hpu.edu
Idaho	Idaho State University	www.isu.edu
Illinois	Bradley University	www.bradley.edu
Indiana	DePauw University	www.depauw.edu
Iowa	Upper Iowa University	www.uiu.edu
Kansas	Kansas State University	www.k-state.edu
Kentucky	Centre College	www.centre.edu
Louisiana	Tulane University	www.tulane.edu
Maine	Colby College	www.colby.edu
Maryland	Howard Community College	www.howardcc.edu
Massachusetts	Clark University	www.clarku.edu
Michigan	Kalamazoo College	www.kzoo.edu
Minnesota	Normandale Community College	www.normandale.edu
Mississippi	University of Mississippi	www.olemiss.edu
Missouri	Washington University–St. Louis	www.wustl.edu
Montana	University of Montana–Missoula	www.umt.edu

The University of Delaware was one of the first universities to take full advantage of the Internet as a place to provide information to prospective students. You can visit its Web site, and take a virtual tour of the campus, by visiting *www.udel.edu*.

A Sampling of College Home Pages on the Web

State	College or University	Web Address
Nebraska	University of Nebraska–Omaha	www.unomaha.edu
Nevada	College of Southern Nevada	www.csn.edu
New Hampshire	Plymouth State University	www.plymouth.edu
New Jersey	New Jersey Institute of Technology	www.njit.edu
New Mexico	New Mexico State University	www.nmsu.edu
New York	Rensselaer Polytechnic Institute	www.rpi.edu
North Carolina	Elon University	www.elon.edu
North Dakota	Dickinson State University	www.dickinsonstate.edu
Ohio	Case Western Reserve University	www.case.edu
Oklahoma	University of Oklahoma	www.ou.edu
Oregon	Central Oregon Community College	www.cocc.edu
Pennsylvania	Lafayette College	www.lafayette.edu
Rhode Island	Brown University	www.brown.edu
South Carolina	Greenville Technical College	www.gvltec.com
South Dakota	Northern State University	www.northern.edu
Tennessee	University of Memphis	www.memphis.edu
Texas	Southern Methodist University	www.smu.edu
Utah	University of Utah	www.utah.edu
Vermont	Middlebury College	www.middlebury.edu
Virginia	James Madison University	www.jmu.edu
Washington	Gonzaga University	www.gonzaga.edu
West Virginia	Marshall University	www.marshall.edu
Wisconsin	Marquette University	www.mu.edu
Wyoming	University of Wyoming	www.uwyo.edu
District of Columbia	American University	www.american.edu

The College Board is an organization that provides a great deal of information about colleges. You can search its Web site for colleges by state, major, sports, type of school, and other characteristics. The site also has information about many other topics. The address is *www.collegeboard.com*.

Find Out More

There are lots of enjoyable reasons to visit colleges—sporting events, museums, concerts, a noted speaker, summer camps, and more.

You can find out more information about the colleges on your list in many ways. And a lot of them are fun. For starters, whenever you can, visit college campuses. The colleges you visit don't even have to be ones you want to attend. Any college you visit can give you ideas about different types of colleges.

If a college really interests you, try to visit it if at all possible. There is simply no better way to get a feel for the college. You can take a campus tour, often with student guides. You can see campus events or visit important places—the library, classrooms, the student union, and sometimes even the rooms where students live on campus.

A number of organizations help students learn more about specific colleges. In some cases, programs run by Talent Search or GEAR UP (see chapter 7) coordinate tours of local colleges. And Collegiate Choice offers videotapes of campus tours so that you can see the tour from your home. For more information, visit www. collegiatechoice.com.

You can meet with members of the admissions office. Also, many colleges have visiting days called **open houses.** When you visit, you may also be able to speak with students and professors.

Even if you can't visit, you can go to a college fair and talk to a representative. You can write a letter or e-mail the admissions office with your specific questions. You can also talk with alumni volunteers, who are happy to meet students interested in the college they attended. They can share their experiences with you, answer some questions you have, and help you get answers to others.

Family day trips or longer vacations are a great time to visit colleges. Find out whether any colleges are near where you will be traveling and visit them. For instance, if you are visiting Civil War battle sites, you may want to stop in at Gettysburg College in Pennsylvania.

Is Getting into College Hard?

As you decide where to apply, you should ask yourself "Can I get into this college?"

Colleges have different policies for deciding who can attend. They take many different factors into consideration. The way colleges select who may attend is often referred to as **selectivity.** Overall, when we look at a college's selectivity, we are looking at how easy or difficult it is to get into that college.

For the most part, college selectivity falls into three categories: **open admissions, selective admissions,** and **competitive admissions.**

Open Admissions

Open-admissions colleges provide opportunities for students who may not get into other schools. At open-admissions colleges, almost everyone who applies is accepted. Once you are admitted, your skills are evaluated. If you are ready for college-level classes, then you may take them. However, if you are not ready, you take developmental classes. These classes improve your academic and study skills so that you are prepared for college-level classes.

Most community colleges have open admissions. In addition, several state colleges as well as some private colleges have open admissions.

In addition to their college-level courses, many open-admissions colleges offer courses taught at even more challenging levels. These courses are often called **honors courses.** Sometimes entire programs are taught at the honors level.

Open admissions colleges admit a wide range of students, including honors students. However, they have the same high expectations for all of their students.

Montgomery College in Maryland is an open-admissions community college. It offers several honors programs, including different programs for incoming high school students, part-time students, and sophomores who are studying business.

161

Selective Admissions

Colleges using selective admissions have clear requirements for admitting students. As long as there is space, students who meet these requirements are usually accepted. However, students who do not meet these requirements are not admitted. Also, in cases where there are limited spaces, if you apply too late, you risk not being admitted—even if you qualify.

Grade-point average, class rank, and entrance exams are all discussed in chapter 9.

Requirements can differ quite a bit from one college to the next. Selective colleges often require you to have a certain **grade point average** or higher. For example, you may be required to have at least a B average in high school. Most colleges look at the courses you have taken in high school. Some colleges look at **class rank** (how your academic performance compares to that of your classmates). Some also look at scores on a required set of standardized tests called **entrance exams.**

Competitive Admissions

Many college guides divide competitive admissions into levels such as highly competitive and most competitive. The guides explain their levels. The levels are often based on the percentage of applicants who are accepted, as well as other requirements.

Just like colleges that use selective admissions, colleges that use competitive admissions also have clear requirements for admitting students. Their requirements are usually more strict.

Space at these colleges is limited. More students apply than can be accepted. Therefore, meeting the requirements for admission does not mean you will get in. Basically, students are competing with each other for the spaces.

Selective admissions are fairly objective. Colleges can evaluate applications in the exact same way. Competitive admissions are more subjective. Entrance exam scores and grades matter, as do more personal factors—what others say about you, essays, your activities and experiences, and special talents.

How Can I Find Out What Is Required?

Finding out what colleges look for in their students is easier than you might think. This information is available in many places. Among the easier ways is checking the books or Internet sites that describe all the colleges. Talking to your guidance counselor and representatives from college admissions offices is also helpful.

You should look for two kinds of information. First, find out what the colleges want to know about you. For instance, some colleges look closely at test scores, but others do not. Second, learn what you can about the typical students entering the college. What are their grades? How do their grades compare with those of their classmates? How well did the students score on the entrance exams?

High school counselors often keep track of which students are admitted to certain colleges each year. They can give you a good sense of what qualifications are needed at many of these schools.

Many guides provide lists that compare colleges based on how selective they are. You can find out quickly which colleges across the country are the most competitive and which have open admissions. The summary for each college also gives you more specific information about typical students.

Most colleges are willing to look at special circumstances. For example, suppose your grades suffer one year because of illness or a lot of moving. If your grades had been strong before and they bounce back later, many colleges will take your circumstances into account.

Remember that most colleges want to have a fairly diverse student body. Many people immediately think of race, religion, and geographical or economic background when they think of diversity. But most colleges also look at students' experiences when they look at diversity. Your own experiences in life may be unique and give you an advantage in the admissions process.

Do you need to be realistic about your academic achievements? Of course, but don't sell yourself short. If your qualifications are anywhere near what a college requires, do not rule out the college.

Examples of Selectivity Across the States

State	College or University	Selectivity
Alabama	University of Alabama–Birmingham	Selective
Alaska	University of Alaska–Fairbanks	Selective
Arizona	Northern Arizona University	Selective
Arkansas	Philander Smith College	Open
California	Harvey Mudd College	Competitive
Colorado	Colorado College	Competitive
Connecticut	Charter Oak State College	Open
Delaware	Wilmington University	Open
Florida	Valencia Community College	Open
Georgia	Emory University	Competitive
Hawaii	Kauai Community College	Open
Idaho	University of Idaho	Selective
Illinois	University of Chicago	Competitive
Indiana	University of Notre Dame	Competitive
Iowa	Iowa State University	Selective
Kansas	Kansas State University	Selective
Kentucky	Jefferson Community and Technical College	Open
Louisiana	University of New Orleans	Selective
Maine	Bowdoin College	Competitive
Maryland	Towson University	Selective
Massachusetts	Mount Ida College	Open
Michigan	Western Michigan University	Selective
Minnesota	Carleton College	Competitive
Mississippi	University of Mississippi	Selective
Missouri	University of Missouri	Selective
Montana	University of Great Falls	Open

TEXAS

Most states offer a wide range of selectivity. Texas's colleges cover the full range. Rice University is among the nation's most competitive colleges. Southern Methodist University is one of Texas's selective colleges. And Laredo Community College has open admissions.

Examples of Selectivity Across the States

State	College or University	Selectivity
Nebraska	Peru State College	Open
Nevada	University of Nevada–Las Vegas	Selective
New Hampshire	Keene State College	Selective
New Jersey	Union County College	Open
New Mexico	New Mexico State University	Selective
New York	Cooper Union	Competitive
North Carolina	Duke University	Competitive
North Dakota	Bismarck State College	Open
Ohio	University of Toledo	Open
Oklahoma	Rose State College	Open
Oregon	Reed College	Competitive
Pennsylvania	Millersville University	Selective
Rhode Island	Brown University	Competitive
South Carolina	Trident Technical College	Open
South Dakota	South Dakota State University	Selective
Tennessee	Vanderbilt University	Competitive
Texas	Rice University	Competitive
Utah	Utah Valley University	Open
Vermont	University of Vermont	Selective
Virginia	Washington and Lee University	Competitive
Washington	Whitman College	Competitive
West Virginia	West Liberty University	Selective
Wisconsin	Lawrence University	Competitive
Wyoming	Sheridan College	Open
District of Columbia	Georgetown University	Competitive

Brown University, Columbia University, Cornell University, Dartmouth College, Harvard University, Princeton University, the University of Pennsylvania, and Yale University are among the nation's most competitive colleges. Together these colleges are called the Ivy League, named for the ivy that grows along the walls on many of their buildings.

Narrow the Field

When you first look at colleges, the choices can seem overwhelming! But when you think about the different factors—size, setting, academics, and many others—you can narrow your list quite a bit. If your list has more than 10 colleges, you may want to narrow it more before you start applying.

How Many Colleges Should Be on My Final List?

There's no magic number. If you plan to go to a community college or a state university, you may have only one or two colleges on your list. If you are certain you will be accepted, having so few on your list is fine. But if you have not made a final decision, think about your chances of being accepted at each college. Your final list should have a range of colleges on it, including at least one college where you know you'll be accepted.

WILL I BE ACCEPTED?

No sweat. Have on your list one or more colleges where you know you will be accepted. Open admissions colleges may not have application deadlines, but you still need to apply to them early for special programs and financial support. Include selective colleges on your "no-sweat" list if you are certain you meet or exceed their admission requirements.

The right match. Include colleges that are your ideal choices and for which you are well qualified. These include colleges for which you have what is needed to be accepted and succeed, although limited space may be a factor in your acceptance.

Reach out. Include one or two colleges that you really like and where you meet or exceed many, if not all, the criteria for admission. If you do not get in, don't be too disappointed. But be willing to take at least one chance to seize a great opportunity!

Keep Track of It All

Keeping track of all the information you gather is not as hard as it seems! You can use a word processing or spreadsheet program on your computer to set up files for each college in which you are interested. You could also use file folders, a notebook, or index cards to keep track of this information. Put any information you get in these files, including favorite Web sites. Organize your files, alphabetically or by state. As you narrow your choices, you can highlight the most important files, and move the others to a back-up location.

Talk to others about how they have organized their college information. Also, think about the times you have prepared big reports and projects for school. What has worked for you?

A Chart Can Really Help!

Comparing colleges is more challenging than collecting information. Charts can help you bring together a lot of information about each college.

For example, make a list of all the criteria that matter to you most (overall size, availability of major, class size, competitiveness, and so forth). Include important points from the "Know Yourself" discussion earlier in this chapter (goals, likes and dislikes, abilities, and resources). Next, rearrange the list in order of importance to you. Now you are ready to make a chart. You can create a table with a word processing program or use a spreadsheet program to make your chart. You can also draw lines on paper to set up the rows and columns. Whichever version you use, fill in the individual boxes (or cells) with the information you gather. (See the example on the next page.) Leave room for short notes.

Your chart can be as general or specific as you would like. You can revise it as well, making it more specific or changing your priorities. When your chart is complete, your planning work is done. You're now ready to apply to college!

Comparing Colleges

Criteria	College A	College B
4-year	4-year university	4-year college
Mid-Atlantic	Pennsylvania	Washington, D.C.
Study abroad	Costa Rica, Ireland, Israel, Spain	Australia, Britain, Japan, Taiwan
Rural/suburban	Yes	No
Vegetarian meals	In one dining hall	Throughout campus
Percent receiving financial aid	50	65
Distance from home	275 miles	150 miles
Student-faculty ratio	17:1	15:1
Class size	60% of classes have fewer than 20 students	75% have 20–25 students per class
Majors available		
* Performing arts	Yes	No
* Mathematics	Yes	Yes
Grade-point average required	2.5	3.0
Public transportation available	No	Yes
Commuter/residential	Residential	Commuter
Number of undergraduates	1,900	4,300
Has ice hockey team	Yes	No
Annual tuition	$19,500	$16,900
Cool features	Nearby skiing	Bowling alleys on campus

Comments:

_____

_____

_____

_____

_____

_____

_____

_____

_____

_____

_____

9

How Do I Apply to College?

You can apply to college by following basic steps in a straightforward, organized way. With your list of colleges in hand, you are ready to begin!

If you plan to attend college right after high school, you will complete your applications during your senior year. The amount of effort this will take depends on the number of places where you are applying and their selectivity. More selective colleges have more steps and requirements than less selective colleges.

Being organized makes the process much easier. In this chapter, we explain many of the steps involved in applying to college.

The Admissions Office

At some colleges, the admissions office has other names. These include office of enrollment services and office of entry services.

The **admissions office** helps people learn about the college and works with students who are in the process of applying. It is also responsible for deciding who will be admitted.

The people who work in the admissions office—the dean, counselors, recruiters, and assistants—can answer your questions about the college, provide general materials such as viewbooks and DVDs, help you set up interviews, and arrange campus tours, open houses, and other special programs. They can also provide you with application forms if you're unable to get the forms from the college's Web site.

The Application Form

Open admissions, selective admissions, and competitive admissions are discussed in chapter 8.

Colleges require you to provide different amounts of information when you apply. Generally, colleges with open admissions require the least amount of information. Selective and competitive colleges ask for more materials.

Application forms and procedures can change from year to year. Be sure you have current forms and know the current procedures.

At its simplest, the application form is one or two pages long. This form asks basic questions about your name, address, phone number, date of birth, race, ethnic background, and citizenship. It may also ask questions about your high school background and college goals. Application forms are usually available online, and in most cases, you can submit the information online, too.

Activities outside the classroom are often called **extracurricular activities.**

More selective colleges ask for more information. They ask you about your school record, your interests and activities, and your goals in life. They may ask you to write essays and to provide standardized test scores, school records, and recommendations from teachers and others.

A Picture of Who You Are

At the heart of every application are questions the college asks to learn more about you.

What Personal Information Does a College Want to Know?

In addition to basic information, many colleges ask you about your school background. They ask where you are currently attending school and where you have gone to school in the past. Many colleges ask about your personal and academic goals.

Some colleges are interested in knowing about your family. They may ask what your parents do, whether they have attended college—and where—and whether any brothers or sisters have attended college. They may also ask about any places you have lived or traveled.

Why Do Colleges Ask These Questions?

Colleges have many reasons for asking these questions. In many cases, they are simply trying to get a better sense of the complete you! They are also trying to find out whether you have the qualifications to be successful and happy at the college.

Many colleges want students with different backgrounds. Students learn not only from teachers and books, but also from each other. Colleges may ask about your intended major. If they accept only students who plan to major in biology, for example, there may not be enough lab space to go around! By knowing more about you, colleges can plan for the kinds of services they will need to provide for you.

Colleges are required by federal and state law to ask certain questions, such as race and ethnic background, gender, and citizenship. You may not be required to answer all these questions. However, any information you provide must be truthful and accurate!

Your School Record

Colleges often ask that your high school transcript be sent directly from your high school. The **transcript** is an official record of your courses and grades.

Your school record—grades, grade point average, courses, and class rank—is an important part of getting into college. You may be asked specific questions about your performance in school. In addition, many applications include a form to be completed by your high school's college advisor or guidance counselor.

Colleges with selective admissions check to see whether you meet their standards for being accepted. Colleges with competitive admissions are not only looking at your record, but are also comparing it to records of other students who have applied.

Your Grades and GPA

Your grade point average is a number that summarizes your overall grades. An A is usually worth four points, a B is worth three points, a C is worth two points, and a D is worth one point. If your overall average is 3.3, you have the equivalent of a B+ average.

By themselves, neither your grades nor your GPA (grade point average) gives a complete picture of your school performance. For example, they do not show how difficult your courses have been.

Colleges look for patterns. Have your grades been consistent from year to year? Have you shown an ongoing improvement, or have your grades fallen over time? Are your grades consistent across your courses? Or are you strong in some subjects and weak in others?

Many schools use percentages instead of points or letter grades. For instance, 90 percent and higher may be equivalent to an A. If you want to learn more about your school's grading system, speak with your guidance counselor.

Suppose Terry earns all Cs freshman year, all Bs sophomore year, and all As junior year. During the same time, Pat earns all As freshman year, all Bs sophomore year, and all Cs junior year. Their overall grades and their grade point averages are the same. However, on this basis alone, Terry will be considered the stronger candidate. Why? Because Terry is showing ongoing improvement.

Your Courses

Colleges look to see what courses you have taken. They are interested in seeing the level of difficulty of your courses and the types of courses you have chosen. For example, if you apply to an engineering college, the college may want to see that you have taken precalculus.

The same subjects are taught at different levels. Many high schools offer courses at honors and other challenging levels. Some high schools also offer **Advanced Placement (AP)** courses. If you successfully complete an Advanced Placement class, you can take the AP exam. If you score well enough on the AP exam, you may be able to earn college credit. Some students take college courses while they are in high school. They earn college credit and, in some cases, high school credit, too. The level of your high school courses can affect your admission to selective and competitive colleges.

One student may have straight As in average courses, while another has As and Bs in honors courses. The first student has higher grades, but the second student will probably be rated higher by colleges. When schools calculate class rank, they often weight the courses so that students are recognized and rewarded for taking honors and AP courses.

What Is Class Rank?

One way that high schools have to compare performance is to rank each student. A student ranked number 1 is considered to have the highest academic achievement of all the students in that grade, at that school.

Many schools calculate class rank by using grade-point averages. In this case, the student with the highest GPA is ranked first. However, some high schools use a ranking system that gives students more credit for taking challenging courses.

If a senior class has 100 students, the 20 students with the highest rank graduate in the top fifth of their class.

Specific class rank is less important than rank relative to others. Suppose Lou's graduating class has 75 students and Reggie's has 500. Both Lou and Reggie have a class rank of 40. Lou's rank is not in the top half, but Reggie's is in the top 10 percent.

Your High School

Some colleges require a certain GPA or higher for you to get automatic admission. Competitive colleges accept only some of the students who apply. Check the college guide or Web sites to find out the typical class rank or GPA of students these colleges accept.

Colleges also compare your high school with other schools in your area. They learn about the courses offered, the grading system, and the performance of students who have gone on to college. Therefore, if you have attended a more challenging school with a proven track record, your grades and class rank may be looked at more favorably. These may include private schools with established records, or specialized schools or programs in your county that emphasize specific subject areas such as science, technology, or performing arts.

Essays

Many applications ask you to write essays. Some essays are very specific; others are fairly general. You may even be able to choose from several options. Essays serve several purposes. They provide a way for the college to get to know more about you. They also provide a sample of your writing and communication skills.

SAMPLE ESSAY QUESTIONS

A. If you could go back and change one day in your life, what would you change and why?

B. Choose one issue of international, national, or local concern that is of special interest to you. Describe your position on the issue, any personal involvement you may have had with the issue, and how you would resolve it.

C. You have just completed your 300-page autobiography. Please submit page 217.

D. If you could be anyone from the past, present, or future, who would you be and why?

E. Traditions are important to many people and their families. Describe a tradition in your family that is important to you and explain why.

Your Activities Outside Class

Colleges want to know more about you than just what you have done in the classroom. They also want to know about your achievements outside of class.

School Activities

Colleges depend on students to contribute to the college community. If students do not get involved in campus activities, the quality of that college suffers. Therefore, colleges are interested in students who have a track record of being involved.

You will have an opportunity to tell the college about ways you have participated in your school. Were you active in plays or choirs? Did you work on the school newspaper or yearbook? Did you participate in student government? Were you a member of any clubs?

Athletics

Students who participate in athletics develop important skills in both cooperation and competitiveness. They develop leadership skills. They also show their ability to balance the time demands of the classroom with the demands of their particular sport.

Work

Many colleges are interested in knowing about your work experiences. Students who have worked can show that they are mature and responsible.

Community Service and Activities

Colleges are increasingly interested in students who can show a proven commitment to their community through civic, religious, and other volunteer activities.

Many colleges look for students who combine a strong academic record with a good range of activities. Some will accept a B student who has been active before an A student who has not.

Extracurricular activities can help you get into selective and competitive colleges. They can even help you get scholarships. Most important, they're fun and fulfilling—and a great way to make friends.

Recommendations

Many colleges want to know what others think about you. Therefore, you may need to provide recommendations from others. Colleges usually want recommendations to come from one or two of your high school teachers or counselors. You may be able to provide additional recommendations, perhaps from your minister, employer, coach, or someone else who has known you for a while.

People writing recommendations are asked about more than just your proven ability. They are asked about your maturity, character, creativity, leadership, and potential for personal growth. They are asked to compare your abilities and potential to that of others the reviewer has known. Many recommendations, though not all, are confidential. In these cases, you will not know what has been written unless the person shares it with you.

Interviews

Although many colleges do not require interviews, many strongly recommend them. If you cannot get to campus, they may arrange for you to meet with alumni who live near you. Interviews help you learn more about the college or specific programs. They also help you make a good impression with someone at the college.

INTERVIEW TIPS

1. Know the time and place.
2. Be on time.
3. Dress appropriately.
4. Give a good handshake.
5. Use good posture.
6. Make eye contact.
7. Speak clearly.
8. Be yourself.
9. Have questions ready.
10. Express your interest.
11. Thank your interviewer.
12. Send a thank-you note.

Special Considerations

What do you do if the application does not give you the chance to let a college know information that you think is important? It's perfectly fine to add this information. Be sure, however, that you pick what is truly important and stay within the overall guidelines that the college provides.

Can I Submit Other Materials?

Students who are performers or studio artists may need to provide additional materials. In fact, if you apply to a college that specializes in the arts, you may be required to include a sample of your work: a portfolio with sample drawings or photos of sculptures or other artwork you have created, a CD of you playing an instrument or singing, or a recording of others performing a piece you have composed. If you are an actor or dancer, you may be required to audition in person. In other cases, you need to record yourself in performance. Check with the college about the best way to send them your supplemental materials.

If you have been active in sports, you may want to provide a video of your athletic performance.

Other Considerations

You may have had other experiences relevant to your overall record. Some may explain changes in your performance. Maybe your grades suffered when you were ill or facing serious family problems. Perhaps you have had to overcome obstacles, such as long-term physical challenges. You may have had special opportunities too, such as extensive travel, starting your own business, or learning another language. Essays often give you the opportunity to discuss these experiences. Be willing to share them with the college. They help the college get a more complete picture of who you are.

College Entrance Exams

Our single most important words of advice about college entrance exams: Do not wait until your senior year of high school to start thinking about them! Be prepared.

You can prepare for the exams in many ways: books, sample tests, software, special classes, and tutoring.

Selective and competitive colleges often require you to send them your scores from college entrance exams. These standardized tests are similar to ones that you may have taken in elementary and middle school. The two major exams, the **SAT** and the **ACT,** are offered several times a year throughout the country. You can take practice versions as early as seventh or eighth grade. Most students take these exams in their junior or senior year.

Some colleges require one test or the other. Other colleges will accept either. Test scores are only one factor in whether you are accepted, but they can be an important factor. Your guidance counselor can advise you about preparing for the tests, when to take them, test procedures, and special accommodations.

MAJOR COLLEGE ENTRANCE EXAMS

SAT. Three major parts: critical reading, mathematics, and writing; most reading and math questions are multiple choice; some math questions require you to supply the response; writing section includes a student-written essay.

SAT Subject Tests. Formerly called Achievement Tests; cover specific subjects such as biology, world history, and French; often requested by competitive colleges in addition to the SAT.

ACT. Multiple-choice tests in four areas: English, mathematics, reading, and science reasoning; an optional writing test is now available.

PSAT/NMSQT. Preliminary SAT/National Merit Scholarship Qualifying Test. Provides practice for the SAT and the chance to enter National Merit scholarship programs.

RECENT SAT SUBJECT TEST OFFERINGS

English

Literature

History

U.S. History

World History

Mathematics

Mathematics Level 1

Mathematics Level 2

Sciences

Biology (E/M)*

Chemistry

Physics

Languages

Chinese with Listening

French

French with Listening

German

German with Listening

Modern Hebrew

Italian

Japanese with Listening

Korean with Listening

Latin

Spanish

Spanish with Listening

After answering core questions, students select a section that emphasizes either ecological or molecular topics.

The SAT Subject Tests cover specific topics in depth. Many students take these tests toward the end of the school year in which they studied the particular subject. For example, if you take a chemistry course as a high school sophomore, you may take the SAT Subject Test in chemistry toward the end of your sophomore year.

Other important tests are the Advanced Placement or AP tests. Participating in the AP program gives you the opportunity to earn college credit and move more quickly into upper level courses of study at college. Students can take the AP test even if they have not taken an AP course.

Completing the Application

If you plan to apply for financial aid—money to help you with college costs—you will need to submit additional forms. We discuss financial aid in chapter 11.

Give yourself plenty of time to prepare your application. Whether you complete your application online or on paper, try to get the forms long before they are due. Be sure, however, to use the correct application. Forms and procedures often change from year to year.

A chart can help you keep track of application materials and deadlines. List the colleges where you are applying, the information you need to provide, due dates, fees, and the date you sent each application. Also, make sure that your materials have been received.

The application often provides the college's first look at you. Be neat, complete, and on time. Keep copies of your work. (Of course, don't forget homework, activities, and other responsibilities!)

Are There Other Ways of Applying?

Do not decide where to apply based only on whether a college accepts a common form. Choose colleges that are right for you. Then, if they happen to accept a common form, you can consider using it when you apply.

Another way to apply is to submit a form called the Common Application. Nearly 400 colleges accept the Common Application in place of their own, and this number continues to grow. You complete this standard form once, either on paper or online, and then send it directly to each college. To get more information about the Common Application, visit this Web site: *www.commonapp.org*

Over a million applications are sent in each year using the Common Application. However, not all colleges use the form. Also, many colleges that do use the Common Application have additional forms for you to complete. As always, check with the college's Admissions Office.

Many colleges have their forms available on their own Web site. Your guidance counselor will be able to help you learn more about online applications.

A Sampling of Colleges That Accept the Common Application

State	College or University
Arkansas	Hendrix College
California	Occidental College
Colorado	Colorado College
Connecticut	Fairfield University
Florida	Stetson University
Georgia	Emory University
Illinois	Knox College
Indiana	Earlham College
Iowa	Coe College
Kentucky	Centre College
Maine	Bates College
Maryland	The Johns Hopkins University
Massachusetts	Simmons College
Michigan	Kalamazoo College
Minnesota	St. Olaf College
Mississippi	Milsaps College
New Hampshire	Dartmouth College
New Jersey	Drew University
New York	Rochester Institute of Technology
North Carolina	Wake Forest University
Ohio	Case Western Reserve University
Oklahoma	University of Tulsa
Oregon	Willamette University
Pennsylvania	Franklin and Marshall College
Rhode Island	University of Rhode Island
Tennessee	Vanderbilt University
Texas	Texas Christian University
Vermont	Middlebury College
Virginia	Randolph-Macon College
Washington	Whitman College
Wisconsin	Ripon College
District of Columbia	The George Washington University

When Should I Apply?

Colleges have different timetables for when they accept students. Your deadline for applying to a particular college is determined by its timetable and the admissions option you choose.

Check with the college's Web site, catalog, or the admissions office to confirm application deadlines.

Competitive colleges with limited space usually have very strict deadlines for applications. Some colleges have priority deadlines—students who apply by the deadline may have a better chance of being accepted. Open-admissions colleges usually accept applications until the start of each term. They may, however, have deadlines for applying to certain programs.

Complete and send your applications as early as possible. At many colleges, applying early may enable you to be accepted earlier. You might also move to the head of the line for campus housing, financial aid, and enrolling in classes.

Rolling Admissions

Some colleges make their admissions decisions as they receive applications instead of waiting until the final deadline. If you are a qualified candidate, you have a better chance of being admitted if you apply early, before the available spaces are filled.

CONNECTICUT

Quinnipiac University in Connecticut considers applications on a rolling admissions basis. Students generally have until February 1 to submit their applications for fall. But once a program is filled, no more students are accepted into that program. For example, if you want to enter the physical therapy program, you should submit your application by November 1.

Types of Admissions

Regular decision. Selective and competitive colleges have cut-off dates for applications. Deadlines generally range from December through March. You are then notified of their decision in mid-March through mid-April. Specific dates vary by college.

Rolling admissions. Applications are considered in order of receipt. Space can run out. Students applying earlier have a better chance of acceptance. Final cut-off dates vary. Look for priority deadlines.

Open admissions. Applications are accepted until classes begin. Students are guaranteed admission with few requirements. Earlier application usually provides better access to special programs and class selection.

Early decision. A special opportunity for students with a clear first choice. Your application is due earlier than for regular admissions, often by November 15. You are notified earlier, often by December 15. If you are accepted and offered adequate financial assistance, you are obligated to attend. You must submit a nonrefundable deposit and decline any other admissions offers.

Early action. Similar to early decision, for students with a clear first choice. The biggest difference is that you usually have until the regular admission reply date to send in your deposit and your decision is not binding.

Early admissions. Allows students to attend college full time instead of their senior year of high school. For excellent and mature students. Apply during your junior year of high school.

Waiting list. Colleges accept more students than they have spaces for. They keep waiting lists in case space opens up. You may be accepted later. While waiting, accept another offer to be sure of space somewhere.

Transfer admissions. Special guidelines for students who have already taken classes at another college. Guidelines may differ based on where you have attended and when you plan to transfer. Many two-year colleges have special arrangements with four-year colleges. Transfer admission is also affected by how many courses you have already taken and at what level. (See "Transferring" later in this chapter to find out more.)

January and Midyear Admission

Colleges may offer students January or midyear admission even though the students applied for fall admission. In such cases, students may go to a second college for the fall term and then switch to the first one midyear. Sometimes students choose to apply for admission to a later term. If you make this choice, remember that fewer students are admitted midyear and that application deadlines are different.

Deferred Admission

Many colleges can provide a **deferred admission.** You apply at the same time as other students, and learn whether you have been accepted at the same time as well. However, the college allows you to take a term or even a full year off before you begin so that you can achieve other goals, such as completing an internship. Check with the admissions office about this option.

Conditional Admission

Colleges may offer you conditional admission. The college may want more proof that you can be successful at their school. Conditional admission often involves graduating high school with a certain grade-point average or completing a term at a community college.

MINNESOTA

On the one hand, Minnesota State University in Mankato (MSU) is a selective college. If you meet certain requirements, you will be admitted. Application deadlines for admission to most programs are fairly close to the start of each term. On the other hand, the nursing program is competitive, with limited spaces. The deadlines and requirements for applying are stricter than for other programs.

The Costs of Applying

Most colleges charge a **fee** when you apply. The fee covers the costs that the college has when it considers your application. Fees at competitive colleges can be higher than fees at other colleges because the staff and time needed to evaluate applications is greater. Fees also tend to be higher at private colleges than at public colleges.

Fees also discourage students from applying to colleges carelessly. These charges add up when you apply to several colleges. Fees encourage you to apply only to colleges where you really want to go and have a reasonable chance of being accepted.

Sometimes students cannot afford the application fee. Most colleges will waive the fee (not require the student to pay) in the case of financial hardship. Your guidance counselor or principal can help you learn more about fee waiver programs. They can also write a letter for you requesting a waiver.

Some colleges charge an application fee for "hard copy" applications sent through the mail, but do not charge if you apply online.

Some students qualify to get their fees waived for college entrance exams. These same students may also qualify for application fee waivers at many colleges.

SAMPLE APPLICATION FEES*

College or University	Fee	College or University	Fee
Athens State University (AL)	$30	Oklahoma City Community College	$25
Boston College (MA)	$70	Pomona College (CA)	$65
Bowdoin College (ME)	$60	Purdue University (IN)	$30
Concordia College (MN)	$20	Saint Louis University (MO)	$25
Duke University (NC)	$75	Shippensburg University (PA)	$30
Howard University (DC)	$45	University of Hartford (CT)	$35
Lansing Community College (MI)	$0	University of Vermont	$45
Marquette University (WI)	$30	University of Washington	$50
Montana State University	$30	University of Wisconsin	$44
Montgomery College (MD)	$25	Valencia Community College (FL)	$35
The Ohio State University	$40	Valparaiso University (IN)	$30

*Fees subject to change, based on regular application fee.

You're In—Now What?!?

After the admissions office has decided whether to admit you, it will notify you by either regular mail or e-mail. In most cases your application will be either accepted or rejected. In some cases, you may be placed on a waiting list—if space opens later, you could be admitted.

Make a Decision

After you are notified, the ball is back in your court. First, you must make a decision. Where will you go? If you have been accepted at several places, you must choose one.

Before deciding, visit the colleges if you can. Talk to family, friends, teachers, and counselors. Carefully weigh what each college offers. Finally, use your best judgment.

Now is the time to consider costs and what you can afford. Colleges usually try to notify you about financial aid at or near the time they offer you admission. You will not be expected to respond to an offer of admission until you know about the financial support you will be receiving from the college.

See chapters 10 and 11 for more information about college costs and paying for college.

If a college does not offer you enough money, you can contact the admissions office and explain any special circumstances you may face. Some colleges may be able to adjust the financial aid they offer you. There is no harm in asking, if you are serious about attending that college!

*May 1 is the **National Candidates Reply Date,** used by most colleges. Having one date gives students time to consider all their options.*

Once you have decided, notify the colleges of your decision. *You must respond to a college's admissions offer by its deadline (usually May 1), or you will lose your place.* Also, inform the colleges you are not choosing so that they can possibly offer your place to a student on their waiting lists.

Send the Deposit

Most colleges require you to make a **deposit** when you accept their offer of admission. The deposit goes toward your first year's expenses. It is often nonrefundable. The deposit is your commitment to the college. If you do not send the deposit by the deadline, you may lose your place.

If you are on a waiting list, you may find out later that space has opened up. Now you have a new decision to make. Evaluate again where you want to go—the college that has just accepted you or the college where you have already mailed your deposit. If you choose to go to the second college, you may not get back your deposit from the first one. However, do not base your decision on this. Instead, make your decision in terms of which college offers you the best overall opportunity.

Now Am I Done?

Not yet. True, you may have been accepted, responded, and paid your deposit. However, you must still successfully complete high school. If you do not, the college can withdraw its acceptance.

If you are placed on the waiting list of a college you truly want to attend, contact the college official who wrote to you. Let that person know—by letter, phone call, or e-mail—of your continued interest.

What If I Don't Get In?

Colleges with limited spaces often have many more applicants than spaces. Unfortunately, they cannot accept every qualified student who applies. Although you might be very disappointed if you don't get into your favorite college, focus on the positive.

Concentrate on the colleges that have accepted you. Many students look back on what at first seemed like a disappointment as the beginning of a wonderful opportunity somewhere else!

Transferring

Transfer students begin studying at one college and then switch to another college. Applying for transfer from one college to another is similar, though not identical, to applying to college the first time.

If you want to transfer, check with the college for any special forms, procedures, and deadlines you must follow to be admitted.

Why Would Someone Transfer?

Students transfer for many reasons. Money is a major one. Maybe you can't afford the college you are attending and want to switch to one that's less expensive. The reverse is also true. You might begin at a less expensive college, saving money so that you can afford to transfer to a more expensive one.

Students transfer all the time for many reasons. In fact, so many transfer that most colleges have counselors whose main job is to help students transfer to or from other colleges. College guides and online information are available specifically for students who are planning to transfer.

Grades and performance are another factor. You might find yourself in over your head and want to switch to a less challenging college. On the other hand, you may have been hesitant about college, but find you are doing better than you expected. You may decide to look for a greater challenge.

Sometimes students transfer colleges because they want to change majors. For instance, you might take sociology and psychology courses and discover that you are very interested in social work. You may decide to switch to a college with a program that specializes in social work.

You may transfer for many other reasons as well. Maybe your family has moved and you want to be closer to them. Maybe you started by going away to college and find that you're homesick. The most common reason that students transfer, however, is to continue their studies. Community college students frequently transfer to four-year colleges to continue their education.

Articulation Agreements

Many colleges have special partnerships with other colleges, enabling students to transfer from one to the other. These partnerships, called **articulation agreements,** clearly explain the conditions students must meet in order to transfer colleges.

Statewide public university systems have guidelines for students who transfer between colleges that are part of the system. Community college students are provided certain guarantees that ensure they can transfer to the state's four-year schools if they meet clearly defined conditions.

Some articulation agreements between colleges are referred to as 2 + 2 programs. Students attend one college, usually a community college, for two years. If they fulfill the requirements of the agreement, they are guaranteed admission to the second college to complete their junior and senior years. Other colleges have 3 + 2 programs. For example, you study physics and chemistry for three years at one school, and then study engineering for two years at another. Such programs allow students to study at both a liberal arts college and an engineering college.

Some articulation agreements between colleges are focused on students in a specific program, such as engineering or nursing.

Engineering science students at Hudson Valley Community College in Troy, New York, can transfer into their junior year at four-year colleges such as Clarkson University, Union College, and Rensselaer Polytechnic Institute. Their admission is guaranteed as long as they meet standards agreed on between Hudson Valley and the four-year college. Students who participate in such programs often receive more personal attention during their first two years of study, while also reducing their overall expenses.

NEW YORK

Changing Your Mind

Can you change your mind about where you will go to college? Absolutely! You can even change your mind after you have accepted an offer of admission. Of course, in that case, you may face some costs. If you have already sent a deposit to the college, do not expect to have it returned. And if you are receiving special grants or loans (see chapter 11), you may not be able to use them at another college.

However, if you find that the choice you have made is not the best one, you can look into other options. These include accepting another college's offer, applying to other colleges, or taking some time to work first and evaluate your goals. You may want to take a leave of absence—in this case, you leave the college for a short time, with an option to return. These choices are available to you whether you are already in college or have not yet started.

Again, be aware of costs. You may lose money you've already paid to the college. If you transfer, you may not be able to transfer all your credits. Even if you have already gone to one college for two years, you may have to attend the second college for more than another two years in order to earn your degree.

Any decision about changing your mind should be made as carefully as your first decision to go to college. As before, talk to others. Do not make your decision on impulse. Above all, establish clear goals for yourself, even if they are different from your original ones. Take charge of yourself!

10

How Much Does College Cost?

College can cost a lot. But exactly how much depends on many factors.

You might wonder whether college is worth the money. The answer is yes! The most important reason is that college is an investment in yourself. Many careers will not be available to you or will be harder to enter without a college education. If your future salary matters to you, people with college degrees generally earn much more than those without them. And remember, learning is important and enjoyable for its own sake!

In this chapter we look at the different types of college costs. We'll also look at some examples so that you can better understand these costs.

College Costs

Public colleges get support from state and local tax dollars. By comparison, private colleges get relatively little tax support. Public support helps keep tuition lower at most public colleges than it is at private colleges.

The total cost of college can vary a lot. Private (or independent) colleges, for example, tend to cost more than public colleges. Four-year colleges tend to cost more per year than two-year colleges. One of the biggest factors is whether you are a full-time or part-time student. And whether you live at the college, at home, or on your own can affect your overall costs.

College costs include tuition, fees, books and supplies, and room and board. In addition, you need to consider expenses such as transportation and other living costs.

Tuition

The part of your costs that pays directly for your education is the **tuition.** Your tuition helps pay for the college's faculty and staff. It also helps pay the general costs of running the college and providing certain services—costs such as books and other resources for the library, computers for student use, academic advising, and career counseling.

NEW YORK

The Cooper Union for the Advancement of Science and Art does not charge tuition to its students. Cooper Union, a top college for art, architecture, and engineering students, was set up in 1859 by Peter Cooper, an inventor and industrialist who had little schooling. Cooper believed that education, especially for children of immigrants and the working class, should be "as free as water or air." Money that Cooper and others set aside through the years has been invested and covers student tuition costs, although students have other expenses.

At many colleges (especially private, competitive colleges), tuition is your single biggest cost. At other colleges (especially public two-year and four-year colleges), other costs may be greater.

No matter how much tuition costs, it does not cover all of the college's costs. Taxes provide a lot of funding for public colleges and some funding for private ones. Contributions from alumni and other donors, grants from businesses and organizations, and earnings from a college's investments also help pay costs. Outside funding often pays for faculty research and special projects. This funding may come from federal and state governments, businesses, and charitable foundations. It may even come from individuals who are interested in specific research or services.

Students do not always pay full tuition. As you will see in chapter 11, many receive some form of assistance in paying for college.

New buildings on campus are paid for by special funds, not by tuition. Special contributions often pay for equipment such as an electron microscope for the science department or new pianos for the music department.

Many of California's public colleges and universities do not formally charge "tuition" to students who are residents of California. Instead, students pay college "fees" and living expenses. These fees may be more than $7,000 per year at some universities. The fees may increase depending on the level of funding that comes from the state.

Students who are not residents of California pay tuition in addition to the other fees. The amount they pay depends on the school they are attending.

California's many public colleges include the 10 schools in the University of California system (for example, the University of California–Berkeley. Almost two dozen more colleges form the California State University system (for example, Humboldt State University). California also has more than 100 two-year colleges (for example, American River College).

CALIFORNIA

Examples of Tuition at Four-Year Colleges

State	College or University	Full-Year Tuition
Alabama	Auburn University	$6,500*
Alaska	University of Alaska–Anchorage	$4,690*
Arizona	University of Arizona	$5,542*
Arkansas	Henderson State University	$4,885*
California	University of the Pacific	$30,880
Colorado	Colorado School of Mines	$11,239*
Connecticut	University of Hartford	$28,172
Delaware	University of Delaware	$8,646*
Florida	Rollins College	$34,520
Georgia	Agnes Scott College	$29,060
Hawaii	University of Hawaii–Manoa	$6,258*
Idaho	Idaho State University	$4,664*
Illinois	DePaul University	$25,490
Indiana	Indiana University–Bloomington	$8,231*
Iowa	University of Northern Iowa	$6,376*
Kansas	Kansas State University	$6,627*
Kentucky	University of Louisville	$7,564*
Louisiana	Grambling State University	$3,804*
Maine	Maine Maritime Academy	$9,605*
Maryland	St. John's College	$39,154
Massachusetts	Boston University	$37,050
Michigan	University of Michigan–Ann Arbor	$11,037*
Minnesota	Concordia College	$24,120
Mississippi	Alcorn State University	$4,488*
Missouri	Saint Louis University	$30,728
Montana	Rocky Mountain College	$19,080

In most cases, the amount includes student fees. Tuition figures are for full-time students in 2008–2009, and may have changed since this book was published. The tuition listed is for most programs at the college. Some programs, however, have a different tuition.

*College is a public college. Tuition listed is for in-state residents. Students from out of state have higher costs.

Examples of Tuition at Four-Year Colleges

State	College or University	Full-Year Tuition
Nebraska	Creighton University	$28,542
Nevada	Sierra Nevada College	$23,068
New Hampshire	Keene State College	$8,778*
New Jersey	Rutgers University	$11,540*
New Mexico	University of New Mexico	$4,874*
New York	Polytechnic Institute	$32,644
North Carolina	East Carolina University	$4,406*
North Dakota	Minot State University	$5,043*
Ohio	Oberlin College	$38,280
Oklahoma	University of Tulsa	$24,365
Oregon	Reed College	$38,190
Pennsylvania	Villanova University	$36,950
Rhode Island	Providence College	$31,394
South Carolina	Furman University	$34,588
South Dakota	Northern State University	$5,712*
Tennessee	Middle Tennessee State University	$4,700*
Texas	Texas Tech University	$5,654*
Utah	Weber State University	$3,856*
Vermont	University of Vermont	$12,844*
Virginia	Virginia Military Institute	$10,556*
Washington	University of Puget Sound	$33,975
West Virginia	West Virginia Wesleyan College	$22,880
Wisconsin	Marquette University	$28,128
Wyoming	University of Wyoming	$3,621*
District of Columbia	Trinity Washington College	$19,317

In most cases, the amount includes student fees. Tuition figures are for full-time students in 2008–2009 and may have changed since this book was published. The tuition listed is for most programs at the college. Some programs, however, have a different tuition.

*College is a public college. Tuition listed is for in-state residents. Students from out of state have higher costs.

Examples of Tuition at Two-Year Colleges

State	College or University	Full-Year Tuition
Alabama	Jefferson State Community College	$3,060
Alaska	Prince William Sound Community College	$3,790
Arizona	Yavapai College	$1,248
Arkansas	Rich Mountain Community College	$1,296
California	Napa Valley College	$506
Colorado	Community College of Denver	$2,227
Connecticut	Housatonic Community College	$2,984
Delaware	Delaware Technical and Community College	$2,684
Florida	Brevard Community College	$1,824
Georgia	College of Coastal Georgia	$1,994
Hawaii	Honolulu Community College	$1,734
Idaho	North Idaho College	$2,246
Illinois	Moraine Valley Community College	$2,466
Indiana	Vincennes University	$4,404
Iowa	Kirkwood Community College	$3,210
Kansas	Cloud County Community College	$2,400
Kentucky	Hopkinsville Community College	$2,904
Louisiana	Bossier Parish Community College	$1,848
Maine	Southern Maine Community College	$3,290
Maryland	Howard Community College	$3,993
Massachusetts	Bunker Hill Community College	$2,784
Michigan	Grand Rapids Community College	$2,080
Minnesota	North Hennepin Community College	$4,624
Mississippi	Hinds Community College	$1,700
Missouri	Jefferson College	$2,040
Montana	Fort Peck Community College	$1,940

In most cases, the amount includes student fees. Tuition figures are for full-time students in 2008–2009 and may have changed since this book was published.

*The tuition listed is the cost for area residents. In-state and out-of-state residents may have higher costs. All colleges on this chart are public colleges.

Examples of Tuition at Two-Year Colleges

State	College or University	Full-Year Tuition
Nebraska	Mid-Plains Community College	$2,370
Nevada	Truckee Meadows Community College	$1,920
New Hampshire	Manchester Community College	$5,792
New Jersey	Brookdale Community College	$3,274
New Mexico	Clovis Community College	$808
New York	Finger Lakes Community College	$3,642
North Carolina	Blue Ridge Community College	$1,431
North Dakota	Fort Berthold Community College	$3,240
Ohio	Columbus State Community College	$3,074
Oklahoma	Oklahoma City Community College	$2,521
Oregon	Clatsop Community College	$2,520
Pennsylvania	Community College of Philadelphia	$3,930
Rhode Island	Community College of Rhode Island	$3,090
South Carolina	Spartanburg Community College	$3,314
South Dakota	Sisseton Wahpeton College	$3,960
Tennessee	Jackson State Community College	$2,759
Texas	Alvin Community College	$1,006
Utah	Snow College	$2,346
Vermont	Community College of Vermont	$4,684
Virginia	Rappahannock Community College	$2,615
Washington	Big Bend Community College	$2,820
West Virginia	Southern West Virginia Community and Technical College	$2,470
Wisconsin	Western Technical College	$3,159
Wyoming	Laramie County Community College	$2,208

In most cases, the amount includes student fees. Tuition figures are for full-time students in 2008–2009 and may have changed since this book was published.

*The tuition listed is the cost for area residents. In-state and out-of-state residents may have higher costs. All colleges on this chart are public colleges.

Is Tuition More If I Attend a College Outside My Home State?

Most private colleges charge all students the same tuition no matter where they live. Most public colleges charge a higher tuition to students from other states. In these cases, the tax dollars that help support a state's public colleges enable students who are residents of that state to receive the benefit of a lower tuition.

You don't have to live in a particular state to attend its public colleges. But you should expect to pay a higher tuition than students from that state. Be aware that fewer spots may be available for out-of-state students, making those spots more competitive.

What About Community Colleges?

At Elgin Community College in Illinois, the 2008–2009 tuition for full-time area residents was about $2,200. For state residents outside the local area, full-time tuition was more than $9,400. Students from other states paid more than $11,000.

Many community colleges have three levels of tuition. Students from the county or nearby area pay the lowest tuition. Students from the state, but outside the local area, pay a higher tuition; and students from outside the state pay the most.

In some states, such as North Carolina, all of the community colleges charge the same tuition. State residents pay that tuition regardless of which community college they attend. A higher tuition is charged to out-of-state students. Although tuition is the same from community college to community college, other expenses may vary.

SOUTH DAKOTA

In some cases, neighboring states have agreements about tuition rates for their students at public colleges. Minnesota students at South Dakota State University pay less than students from other states. In addition, students from states in the Western Undergraduate Exchange (WUE) pay more than South Dakota residents but less than students from other states. For more information, see *http://wue.wiche.edu/*.

Residency Makes a Difference!

College or University	Resident Tuition*	Nonresident Tuition*
Albany State University (GA)	$3,710	$13,002
Appalachian State University (NC)	$4,333	$14,392
Austin Peay State University (TN)	$5,526	$16,418
Bluefield State College (WV)	$4,272	$8,568
Boise State University (ID)	$4,632	$13,208
Fort Hays State University (KS)	$2,832	$8,900
Frostburg State University (MD)	$6,614	$16,810
Humboldt State University (CA)	$4,148	$14,318
Morehead State University (KY)	$5,400	$14,040
Northern Michigan University	$7,079	$11,230
Oregon State University	$6,187	$18,823
Rhode Island College	$5,771	$14,482
Shippensburg University (PA)	$7,099	$15,229
Southeastern Louisiana University	$3,721	$9,721
Southern Connecticut State University	$7,179	$16,316
SUNY–Plattsburgh (NY)	$5,429	$11,689
Texas Tech University	$5,654	$12,398
University of Akron (OH)	$8,612	$17,861
University of Central Arkansas	$6,505	$11,605
University of North Dakota	$6,513	$15,325
University of North Florida	$3,020	$12,334
University of Northern Colorado	$4,680	$14,082
University of South Alabama	$5,512	$9,922
University of Wisconsin–Stevens Point	$6,196	$13,769
University of Wyoming	$3,621	$11,031
Virginia Commonwealth University	$6,779	$19,724
Western New Mexico University	$3,431	$12,718
Western Washington University	$5,535	$17,166
William Paterson University of NJ	$10,492	$17,050
Winthrop University (SC)	$11,060	$20,610

In most cases, the amount includes student fees. Tuition figures are for full-time students for 2008–2009 and may have changed since this book was published.

Fees

In addition to tuition, colleges charge students fees. Most fees are for very specific purposes. The amount may vary depending on your major or courses, the number of classes you take, and other reasons.

Why Do Colleges Charge General Fees?

The general fee may also be called a university fee or a consolidated fee.

Most colleges charge all students a general fee. This fee covers administrative costs—for example, the cost for the college to maintain your records. This fee may also cover activities and services, such as wellness programs or basic health services that can provide you some of your routine medical care while you are at the college.

What Other Types of Fees Do Colleges Charge?

Each college sets its own combination of fees. At many colleges, the general fee and the student activity fee are combined into one.

Some fees are very specific. Student activity fees help pay for student government, organizations, and publications on campus. Many colleges give the student government a block of money to divide among the different clubs and groups. The student leaders then set priorities and decide how much money each group receives. This fee may also cover your use of athletic, recreational, and other facilities on campus.

Colleges may also charge students fees if they are late registering for classes (see chapter 12) or for many other specific reasons.

Students who commute or keep a car on campus usually pay parking fees. Lab fees help pay the costs of equipment, supplies, activities, and special insurance. Transaction fees are charges students pay to register each term, to drop or add a class after the registration period ends, or to get a copy of their grades (a transcript). These fees are paid only by students who use the service. Many colleges also charge a graduation fee to pay for your diploma.

RECENT FEES AT THE UNIVERSITY OF MIAMI (FL)

*University fee	Included in tuition
*Student activity fee	$127.00 (per semester)
*Athletic fee	$57.00 (per semester)
*Wellness center fee	$140.00 (per semester)
Diploma fee (for bachelor's degree)	No charge for original
Transcript fee	$6.00 (per copy)
Nursing student insurance (liability)	$270.00 (per year)
Re-admission fee	$100.00
Late registration fee	$100.00 and up
Parking (for commuters and resident students)	$43–78 (per month)
Music lessons (for non-music majors)	$200.00 (per semester)

*These fees are required for full-time undergraduates. The amount may vary for other students. Other fees are charged based on a student's use of the service.

Books, Supplies, and Equipment

Most students are not used to buying books for their classes until they get to college. For most classes, you will need to purchase one or more textbooks. You may also need to buy study guides, lab manuals, solutions manuals, CDs, and DVDs. Book prices vary considerably, about $7 to $25 for small paperbacks and $100 or more for large textbooks.

> You'll also need notebooks, pens and pencils, highlighters, and more on a regular basis. These small costs can add up!

You will need to purchase other supplies. You may need a graphing calculator or software for some classes, lab kits, art supplies, and so forth. Many colleges estimate costs for books and supplies to be between $400 and $800 per term.

Some colleges also require you to buy a computer. Others simply recommend that you have one. Colleges may offer computers at discounted prices.

Room and Board

College living arrange-
ments are discussed in
chapter 13.

Living expenses are a major cost of college for many students, especially for those who live on campus. The cost of having somewhere to live is called **room** and the cost of meals is called **board.**

Even if you don't plan to live on campus, you still have to estimate room and board costs. You may live in an apartment of your own or with friends—your rent would be equivalent to room. And whether you eat on campus or off, you still need to budget a certain amount for meals, or board.

Many colleges require freshmen to live on campus. Colleges with on-campus housing list the amount of room and board in their catalog, along with tuition and fees.

You must be sure to eat properly. Select a meal plan that matches your eating habits and encourages you to follow a healthy diet.

College meal programs vary. Some may require on-campus students to buy **meal plans.** In many cases, you can choose different programs. You may pay a flat fee that covers all your meals for the term, or choose programs that pay for a certain number of meals or charge you meal by meal.

SAMPLE MEAL PLANS

Fixed plans. Students pay a set price. All meals are included.

Flexible plans. Students choose a plan based on how many meals per week they want. They may also purchase points to be used at restaurants, snack bars, and convenience stores.

Kosher/Halal plans. These are food plans for Jewish and Islamic students who observe the dietary laws of their religions.

Per-meal plan. Students pay on a meal-by-meal basis.

Sample Room and Board Costs

College or University	Annual Room and Board Costs*
Bay Mills Community College (MI)	$5,220
Berklee College of Music (MA)	$14,360
Connors State College (OK)	$6,692
Dartmouth College (NH)	$10,779
Emporia State University (KS)	$5,858
Fisk University (TN)	$7,725
Goucher College (MD)	$9,758
Hampton University (VA)	$7,422
Iowa Lakes Community College (IA)	$4,600
Jacksonville University (FL)	$8,360
Johnson & Wales University (RI)	$8,892
Kenyon College (OH)	$6,590
Nicholls State University (LA)	$6,798
Pacific University (OR)	$7,482
Paul Smith's College (NY)	$8,350
Ripon College (WI)	$6,770
Seattle University (WA)	$8,340
Stephens College (MO)	$8,730
Trinity College (CT)	$9,900
Tyler Junior College (TX)	$4,150
University of Idaho	$6,762
University of New Mexico	$7,080
Ursinus College (PA)	$8,800
Valparaiso University (IN)	$7,620
Yuba College (CA)	$10,152

*Numbers are for the 2008–2009 school year. Costs vary year to year and are based on the type of housing and meal plan chosen.

Northwestern University's meal plans provide lots of eating options. Dining halls offer everything from roast beef and chicken to lobster and vegetarian dishes. Students can also get lighter fare such as sandwiches, pizza, and salads. They can even visit *www.northwestern.edu/nucuisine/menus/index.html* to check out daily menus at individual dining halls!

Other Costs

You will also need to plan for several other costs. One major cost is transportation. If you commute to campus each day, you may have to pay for gas, tolls, insurance, and maintenance for your car or for public transportation. If you live on campus without a car, you still need to think about the cost of getting to and from college at the start and end of the year. You should also estimate the cost of any travel you have during the year.

You also will need to consider living expenses. You need to budget for basic supplies such as toothpaste. The same is true for laundry. Although many events on campus are free to students, others charge admission.

Many colleges offer laundry plans for students living on campus. The plans may cover only sheets and towels, or may cover other laundry as well.

Estimating and Comparing Costs

Your best bet is to make a chart for all of your expenses. In fact, you will need to make several charts, like the one on page 205, for each college you are considering. The different costs will vary from college to college. For example, your transportation costs for going to a college away from home will be different than for a nearby college.

Information for some categories, such as tuition and fees, can be found in guides and on Web sites. Other information, such as transportation or personal supplies, must be estimated based on your own situation.

Do not be too conservative when thinking about costs. It's much better to plan for higher expenses. Finding you have money left over is far better than discovering that you do not have enough resources to cover your costs.

Once you have estimated your costs for each college that interests you, use a chart like the one on page 206 to compare them. At this point, do not rule out any of the colleges based on costs until you have considered how to pay for them. Chapter 11 will help you learn more about paying for college.

Estimating College Costs

College name: _____

Tuition:	$ _____
Fees:	
University/General	$ _____
Activity	$ _____
Athletic	$ _____
Lab	$ _____
Courses (such as music)	$ _____
Parking	$ _____
Other fees	$ _____
Total of fees	$ _____
Books, Supplies, Equipment, and Technology:	
Books	$ _____
Supplies	$ _____
Computer	$ _____
Other equipment/technology	$ _____
Total for books, supplies, etc.	$ _____
Room and Board:	
Housing and meal plan	$ _____
Snacks/other meals	$ _____
Total for room and board	$ _____
Transportation (local and long-distance):	$ _____
Living Expenses:	
Clothing and laundry	$ _____
Personal supplies	$ _____
Entertainment	$ _____
Phone	$ _____
Other expenses	$ _____
Total for living expenses	$ _____
TOTAL ESTIMATED COST:	$ _____

Comparing Annual College Costs

Costs	College A	College B
College Tuition	Local college Could live at home $13,500	Suburban college in another state $7,000
Fees		
University fees	$175	$275
Parking	$120	$250
Other fees	$325	$500
Books	$1,200	$1,000
Supplies	$300	$300
Computer	$0 (use one at home)	$1,500 (purchase new)
Room and board	$2,100	$5,900
Snacks/other meals	$1,000	$500
Transportation	$700	$1,200
Living expenses		
Clothing and laundry	$450	$700
Personal supplies	$500	$600
Entertainment	$700	$500
Phone/Internet	$400	$500
Other expenses	$300	$425
Total cost	**$21,770**	**$21,150**
Minus grants and scholarships: (see chapter 11)	−$6,000	−$5,000
NET PRICE	$15,770	$16,150

Making a chart like this helps you see the big picture of how college costs compare. Notice that the net price is the cost actually charged after any aid has been subtracted from the total cost. (Chapter 11 discusses aid.) Within a few years, most college Web sites will have a built-in calculator to help you find the net price of attending that college. The U.S. Department of Education is also developing a net price calculator to be available at its Web site *http://studentaid.ed.gov.*

11

How Will I
Pay for College?

You can pay for college in more ways than you might expect! Estimating the cost of college is only one step. Another step is figuring out how much you can afford to pay. If college costs are more than you can afford, your remaining step is finding the money to pay the difference.

You're not alone in trying to find the money you need. Colleges work hard to provide you and your family as much support as possible. The government helps too, as do other sources. With good planning, some hard work, and, yes, a bit of luck, you may be able to afford a wide choice of colleges!

Ways to Pay

The different ways you can pay for college fall into five categories: family savings and income, payment plans, grants and scholarships, loans, and work. Most students pay for college using some combination of these financial resources.

The money to pay for college may come from both you and your family. Your parents' salaries may be enough to pay for your college costs, depending on the college and available payment plans. Some parents are able to set up a college savings fund for their kids.

Grants and **scholarships** provide money that you usually do not need to repay. You may need to make a certain commitment in order to receive this funding. For instance, programs such as ROTC cover some of your expenses in exchange for taking on a military service commitment.

Loans are funds that you borrow from others. You are expected to pay back this money over a period of time. Some loans must be repaid quickly, but others can be repaid over many years.

Another way to help pay for your education is by working your way through college. Whether you go to college full time or part time while working will depend on how much money you need, the kind of student you are, and the kind of job you have.

Many colleges have **work-study** programs that provide students with jobs on campus. Such programs either pay you a wage for your work or allow you to work in exchange for tuition and other expenses.

What Is Financial Aid?

The majority of students need some sort of help paying for college. Every college has a financial aid office that works with students to try to give them that help. The different kinds of support that you can receive—grants, scholarships, loans, and work-study—are all part of financial aid.

Where Does Financial Aid Come From?

Support comes from many different sources. The federal government is one of the most important. For many years, the federal government has provided a wide range of support to students. State governments also provide support. Each state has its own programs for helping students.

Corporations are an important source of aid. They are very interested in having well-educated students enter the workforce. Corporations help in several ways. Some give money directly to the colleges for scholarships. Others provide support directly to students. Many corporations have programs for their employees' children. And many companies support programs of study that are related to their business.

Special organizations called **foundations** are also important sources of aid. Foundations give money to special causes such as medical research and care, the arts, environmental protection, and help for the homeless. Educational support is among their top priorities.

Financial support also comes from religious groups, service and community organizations such as the Rotary Club and the Kiwanis, and interested individuals.

Depending on the state, scholarships may be awarded because of financial need or academic achievement. They may also be awarded to students in certain majors or those planning to enter certain professions.

Colleges themselves are a major source of aid to students. Many set aside part of their annual budget to provide support. Most colleges run special fund-raising programs aimed at providing financial aid.

How Do I Qualify for Financial Aid?

You can qualify for financial aid in several ways, including need, merit, and affiliation.

Most aid is **need-based** and is given to students who do not have the financial resources to pay for college. This kind of aid is available not only to students, but also to parents to help pay tuition.

Each year, thousands of students across the country receive National Merit Scholarships. Your qualification for these scholarships is based on your scores from the PSAT test that you take in high school (see chapter 9).

Merit-based aid goes to students who are successful in academics or other areas. For example, top academic students may receive merit-based aid. Some merit-based aid is also need-based.

You probably have heard about top athletes who receive aid when they play for a college. You can also get merit-based aid if you have special musical, artistic, or dramatic talent. You can receive aid by serving your community, organizing food drives, raising money for charity, and so forth.

Affiliation-based aid goes to students who meet criteria such as race, religion, and gender. For example, the United Negro College Fund provides support for African-American college students. Many religious groups provide support both at the national and local levels.

Some programs provide support for either male or female students. Every year, the Miss America Pageant provides millions of dollars of financial support to thousands of female students.

Where you live can also be a factor. Some aid is given to students from a certain geographical area. Still other aid is based on your future career. For example, some aid goes to students planning to become teachers in states that have shortages.

What Is Financial Need?

Need is the difference between a college's costs and what you and your family can afford to pay. The federal government estimates what your family can pay toward college costs. This amount is called your **Expected Family Contribution**, or **EFC.** Most states use the same formula.

Factors considered in calculating your EFC include family income, family size, the number of children attending college, benefits such as Social Security payments, and assets, including savings and checking accounts, savings bonds, and investments (for example, mutual funds and stocks). Factors such as high health-care expenses, alimony, a parent's job loss, and death of a family member can also be considered.

Your EFC may be more than your family believes it can afford. Do not worry. Colleges are simply required to use this number to estimate your "financial need" for federal financial aid.

How Is Need Calculated?

Each college financial aid office starts with an estimate of your *Cost of Attendance*, or *COA*. It then subtracts your EFC from this amount. The difference is your financial need. The COA estimate is based on many of the individual costs discussed in chapter 10. Colleges also include an estimate of living expenses for commuter students. (Remember, this estimate of expenses may differ from your actual costs.) The COA budget differs from one college to another, but your EFC remains the same unless your circumstances change.

After using the EFC formula, colleges also consider other areas of support, such as scholarships you may be receiving from other organizations, before deciding on the financial aid they will give you.

Suppose your EFC is $5,000. If a college's COA is $4,000, you would not be eligible for need-based financial aid: Your EFC is higher than the COA. If another college's COA is $20,000, your need is $15,000 to attend that college. However, the fact that you have $15,000 of need does not automatically mean that your full need will be covered.

What Are Grants and Scholarships?

Supplemental Educational Opportunity Grants (SEOGs) are federal government grants available to students with exceptional need. The individual colleges administer SEOGs, and students need to file a FAFSA to be considered for them.

Grants and scholarships provide college funds that do not have to be repaid. Grants are generally need-based. Scholarships may or may not be need-based and are often based on academics, special talents, community service, or athletics. They may be awarded to students in certain majors. Many scholarships are affiliation-based.

Pell Grants, available from the federal government, are awarded to a limited number of undergraduates who have the greatest need. For the 2009–2010 school year, the maximum grant was set at $5,350. Only the neediest students qualify, and not all get the full amount.

Congress sometimes provides other merit-based federal grants to high-need students, such as the Teach Grant. High-need students who excel academically should explore these additional opportunities for grants and scholarships.

You can also win monetary prizes and awards based on your high school performance. Although some of these are small amounts of money, every bit of additional aid helps.

Colleges themselves are a major source of aid, both need-based and merit-based. Companies and individuals also set up various scholarship programs, sometimes nationally and sometimes at specific colleges. For example, the Coca-Cola Company awards 250 merit-based scholarships every year. The Intel Science Talent Search, previously sponsored by Westinghouse, has provided merit-based scholarships since 1942.

TENNESSEE The University of Tennessee, Knoxville, has more than 1,400 different scholarships available to its students. These funds are in addition to grants and loans available from the federal or state government. Many are privately funded. The university's colleges and schools also provide awards to gifted students.

Most colleges have scholarships that have been set up to honor someone. Following the terrorist attacks of September 11, 2001, many groups set up scholarship funds for children of the victims or children of people serving in the military. Hood College (Maryland) and Hodson Trust offer a full-tuition Star Scholarship to selected veterans who have served in Afghanistan or Iraq.

When a donor's fund reaches a certain level, it becomes an **endowment.** The money is then invested and any earnings from the endowment are used to provide scholarships. In this way, the donor's relatives and friends have created a lasting memory, one that helps students for years to come.

Many scholarships are for one year only, though some can be renewed. Sometimes you must fulfill a requirement to get a scholarship; if you don't, you must repay the money. For example, you may need to major in a particular subject or maintain a certain grade point average. *Be sure you know the terms of your scholarships.*

Most states offer grants and scholarships to local high school graduates. In some states, these awards are portable, which means you can use the funds even if you go to an out-of-state college. Check with your state's higher education commission for more information.

OFFBEAT OPPORTUNITIES FOR SCHOLARSHIPS

Scholar Athlete Milk Moustache of the Year (SAMMY) Award. Awarded by the Milk Processor Education Program (MilkPEP) to 25 high school seniors, this scholarship is based on excellence in academics, athletics, community service, and leadership. Each award is $7,500.

Chick and Sophie Major Memorial Duck Calling Contest. This Arkansas-based contest is open to any high school senior who can call ducks. The first prize is a $1,500 scholarship for study in any major. Runner-up scholarships are available.

Duck Tape Brand Duct Tape Stuck at Prom Contest. Scholarships of $3,000 each are awarded to a prom couple that has the cleverest prom attire or accessories made completely from duct tape. The school where the prom is held also receives a prize. Prizes are awarded to runners-up.

For more information about unusual scholarships, go to *www.finaid.org.*

How Do Loan Programs Work?

In some cases, you may need to pay origination fees—fees that are charged when you first apply for the loan.

You may be able to borrow money for college from many sources, including the government, colleges, and banks. Loans are also available to parents. In a typical loan, you borrow a sum of money for a certain period of time. In addition to repaying the money, you pay **interest**—money that allows lenders to cover their costs for the loan.

Interest rates for educational loans vary, yet many educational loans charge less interest than loans for other purposes, such as taking a vacation. Educational loans are available to people at all income levels. However, loans with the lowest interest are often given to students with the greatest financial need.

When you repay a loan, you often send a payment every month for several years.

Many loans are **deferred loans**—you don't make any payments until you graduate. Sometimes no interest is charged while you are in college. Some loans may be deferred for a short while after graduation to give you time to find work.

FEDERAL STUDENT LOANS

Direct loans. The federal government is the lender; colleges administer the program. Repayment for need-based and non-need–based loans can be deferred for six months after school. For need-based loans, the government pays the interest while you are in school. For a non-need–based loan, you pay the interest, but not until you leave school. For parent loans, repayment plans vary. You may earn a tax deduction for interest paid.

Federal Family Education Loan (FFEL). Similar to Direct loans, except that funds for these federal loans come from private lenders, such as banks and credit unions. Repayment benefits may differ from those offered by the Direct Loan Program.

Perkins loans. Administered by colleges; funds come mostly from the government, with some college funds.

Private Student Loans

Some students supplement their federal loans with private loans from private lenders. These loans are based on a student's credit. They usually have higher interest rates, may require a cosigner, and often do not have benefits such as deferment.

Paying Back Loans

Many loan programs offer several repayment plans. Choices may change from year to year, depending on the loan and the lender. In most cases, you do not have to start repaying federal student loans until you leave college. Other loan programs may require you to make payments even while you are still in school.

As described on the previous page, loans can be deferred in some cases. For instance, if you go on to graduate school or are unable to find work, payments may be deferred.

Federal loans can even be "forgiven" in certain cases, which means you may not have to pay back all, or even any, of the loan. For example, some states forgive loans to students who fill certain jobs for a certain period of time in that state after they graduate. Peace Corps and Americorps volunteers may have some of their student loans forgiven. Sometimes loans can even be forgiven if you undertake community service or high-need work.

Follow two basic rules if you borrow money for college. First, be informed. Talk with the college financial aid officer before taking any loans in order to be sure that you understand all your options and responsibilities. Second, limit your debt. Do not borrow more than you think you can afford to repay.

The federal government limits how much a student can borrow annually from its loan programs. For example, your total borrowing limits for federal student loans may be $2,625 as a freshman, $3,500 as a sophomore, $5,500 as a junior, and $5,500 as a senior.

Many states have teacher shortages. Sometimes student loans are forgiven to attract new teachers or those who teach certain subjects such as math, science, foreign language, or special education.

What Are Tax Benefits?

The amount of taxes you or members of your family pay may be reduced if income or savings is used to pay for your education. These benefits will not help you with your upfront costs, but they may help out later. Talk with a tax advisor to learn about current tax benefits.

Tax Credits and Deductions

Each year people who earn income must figure out how much they owe the federal government for taxes. A tax credit directly lowers the amount of money a person must pay in taxes.

The actual tax benefits of the federal American Opportunity Credit will change over time. Search the Internal Revenue Service (IRS) Web site for up-to-date information at www. irs.gov.

Many students or their parents are eligible for the federal American Opportunity Credit and the Lifetime Learning Credit. If you qualify, a portion of your tuition payments may be credited against your taxes. Only those paying the tuition are eligible for these credits. Most families with high incomes do not qualify.

A tax deduction lowers the amount of your taxable income, which then lowers your taxes. Federal tax deductions vary from year to year. Some are based on payments for tuition and fees. Others are based on the interest paid on student loans.

Tax-Deferred Plans

If you withdraw money from an Education IRA to use for another purpose, you may have to pay a tax penalty on your earnings.

When you save or invest, your money earns money. Usually you have to pay taxes on these earnings, which, like salary, are considered to be income. In some cases, you can delay (defer) paying taxes on income set aside for postsecondary education. An Education Retirement Account, or Education IRA, allows you, your parents, and your grandparents to save for college without paying taxes until later. A financial advisor can help your family make the best decisions.

Tuition Savings and Prepaid Tuition

Many states, colleges, and other organizations offer additional opportunities for you to save money for college or to limit tuition costs. The state plans are often called **529 plans**. These plans allow families, often both in-state and out-of-state, to earn tax benefits while saving for tuition. The Web site *www.collegesavings.org* has more information about these plans and other programs.

The number 529 refers to the number of the Internal Revenue Service code that discusses these plans.

What Are Tuition Savings Plans?

The majority of states have tuition savings plans that are similar to Education IRAs—the money you set aside is not taxed in the year that you earn it. In many programs, the state does not tax the money even when you use it later for tuition or other state-approved costs.

In New York, for example, you can open a tuition savings account with a $25 contribution. You can arrange for automatic withdrawals from either a bank account or your paycheck to go into the account. Up to $5,000 per year can be deducted from your state taxable income.

You, your parents, grandparents, other relatives, and even friends can open up a savings plan and name you as the one who will receive the funds.

What Is a Prepaid Tuition Plan?

Some states and colleges have programs that allow you to pay now for college in the future. Essentially, you lock in the current tuition. For example, if you pay a lump sum of money now (or monthly installments, if the plan allows), you will have paid for tuition at the participating college. The state or college invests the money to cover your future tuition costs. Many plans allow you to choose whether to pay for all or part (for example, two years) of your tuition. In many cases, you don't even have to live in a state to participate in its plan.

Before participating in a prepaid tuition plan, learn whether the money can be used at a different college or in a different state. Also find out whether the money can be refunded if you choose not to attend college.

Work-Study Programs

Work-study programs provide aid to students by giving them jobs during the school year. Many of the jobs are on campus. Others may be with public agencies or non-profit organizations off campus. Some work-study programs are federally funded; others are funded by individual colleges.

In some cases, earnings from a work-study program are applied directly to tuition. In other cases, earnings provide students with spending money that they can use for basic living expenses while at college.

Work-study positions include community-service jobs, such as tutoring at a local elementary school.

A work-study job may match a student's major. For example, an art major might be able to get a job with an on-campus or local museum. If you are a biology major, you may be able to get a work-study job in an on-campus lab or at a biotechnology company in the area. You may even be able to get a work-study job as a lab or research assistant for a professor at the college. If you are majoring in allied health, your work-study program may have you working in the campus infirmary or at a health clinic in a neighboring community.

Many general on-campus jobs are offered through a work-study program. These jobs include sorting mail, serving meals, shelving books at the library, answering phones, or leading campus tours.

The pay rate for work-study jobs is often lower than for other jobs. The college may also limit the number of hours that students can work. However, the hours can usually be fit in easily around a student's classes and homework. Although federal work-study programs are available only to students with financial need, many other positions may be available to students who simply want to earn money for additional expenses while at college.

Financial Aid Packages

The financial aid office tries to develop the best combination of grants, scholarships, loans, and work-study jobs it can to match your needs. This combination is your financial aid package.

Two students might receive the same total amount, but different packages. One student's support may be mostly grants, while a second student's is mostly loans and work-study. The second student will then have more to repay after graduating than the first student will have.

When Will I Be Notified About My Financial Aid Package?

You should hear about your financial aid package about the same time that you hear whether you have been accepted to the college. If receiving financial aid is necessary for you to be able to attend a particular college, do not feel that you must commit to that college until you understand how much financial aid is available. The package you receive will help you compare your real costs at different colleges.

Some financial aid is restricted to freshmen. However, many scholarships and grants are set aside for juniors and seniors who have declared their majors and who have a track record of success at the college. When you learn about the financial aid that is being offered, try to find out how much of it is for one year only.

Students who receive loans have a responsibility to repay them to the lender. The bottom line: *Do not accept financial aid unless you fully understand and accept the responsibilities that go with it.*

Many expensive colleges are taking important steps to make college more affordable, especially for lower- and middle-income families. For example, Princeton University in New Jersey has replaced many of its loans with grants that do not need to be repaid.

A FINANCIAL AID SAMPLER: THE UNIVERSITY OF LOUISVILLE (KY)

Federal and State Programs

Pell Grant and Federal Supplemental Education Opportunity Grant (SEOG). For students with exceptional need.

Federal Work-Study Program. Campus and community-service jobs.

Federal Direct Loan Program. Students borrow money for college directly from the federal government. This program includes the following types of loans:

- *Federal Perkins Loan. Low-interest loans through the college.*
- *Federal Stafford Loan. Low-interest loans.*
- *Parent's Loan for Undergraduate Students (PLUS).* Low-cost loans for parents.

College Access Program (CAP) grant. A need-based grant for Kentucky residents.

Scholarship Programs

National Merit Finalists and Semifinalists.

Governor's Scholar Award.

Eagle Scout (Boy Scouts) Award and Gold (Girl Scouts) Award.

McConnell Scholars. Awarded to Kentucky residents who plan to major or minor in political science.

Woodford R. Porter Sr. Scholarship. Awarded to African-American students with strong academic records.

Grawemeyer Scholarship. Awarded to 10 Kentucky graduating high school seniors who have achieved a 3.75 grade point average.

Hallmark Scholarship. Awarded to Kentucky graduating high school senior who meets required levels of test scores and grade point average.

KCTCS Academic Transfer Scholarship.

Other Programs

Tuition Payment Plan.

Cardinal Covenant. Special program covering direct costs for students from families living at or below 150% of the poverty level established by the U.S. Census Bureau.

Emergency Loan Funds. Small short-term loans.

Nonresidents Scholarship Program.

Senior Citizens Program. Free tuition for older Kentucky residents, 65 and over.

Veteran's Educational Benefits.

Vocational Rehabilitation Assistance. For disabled students.

Tuition-Waiver Programs. For dependents of deceased or disabled Kentucky veterans, law officers, and firefighters.

Financial Aid Information on the Internet

You can find lots of information about financial aid on the Internet. Almost every college's Web site includes information about its financial aid office. You can learn about federal programs at the U.S. Department of Education Web site:

http://studentaid.ed.gov

FINANCIAL AID WEB SITES

http://finaid.org (FinAid! The SmartStudent Guide to Financial Aid). FinAid was established in 1994; it is a comprehensive and free guide to financial aid, with complete areas for loans, scholarships, and military aid. The site includes a scholarship search, calculators, parent seminars, and scam alerts.

www.nasfaa.org/ParentsStudents.html (National Association of Student Financial Aid Administrators Parent and Student Financial Aid Resource Center). This site lists resources and excellent links.

www.fastweb.com (FastWeb: Scholarships, Financial Aid, Student Loans and Colleges). Established in 1995, FastWeb helps match students with scholarships, based on eligibility requirements. The site has millions of users and a database of over 4,000 schools and more than a million scholarships.

www.hsf.net (Hispanic Scholarship Fund). HSF is the largest Hispanic scholarship-granting organization in the United States. Founded in 1975, it has awarded more than 90,000 scholarships totaling about $250 million.

www.studentscholarshipsearch.com (A Service of the Student Loan Network). This online site provides daily updates about grants, scholarships, and loans, with links to further information. It also covers loan repayment and loan forgiveness programs.

www.schoolsoup.com/ (School Soup). This site offers one of the largest free scholarship databases on the Internet, and encourages students to "feed their minds" with the wide range of available information. It has information about billions of scholarship dollars.

Financial Aid at Four-Year Colleges

State	College or University	Percentage of Freshmen Who Receive Aid
Alabama	Samford University	73%
Alaska	Alaska Pacific University	91%
Arizona	Northern Arizona University	79%
Arkansas	University of the Ozarks	98%
California	Occidental College	82%
Colorado	University of Northern Colorado	78%
Connecticut	Fairfield University	68%
Delaware	Delaware State University	93%
Florida	Florida International University	86%
Georgia	Oglethorpe University	99%
Hawaii	Hawaii Pacific University	41%
Idaho	University of Idaho	89%
Illinois	Knox College	96%
Indiana	University of Evansville	97%
Iowa	University of Iowa	78%
Kansas	Wichita State University	76%
Kentucky	University of the Cumberlands	100%
Louisiana	Dillard University	99%
Maine	Bates College	50%
Maryland	McDaniel College	93%
Massachusetts	Merrimack College	100%
Michigan	Kalamazoo College	99%
Minnesota	Bemidji State University	87%
Mississippi	Delta State University	89%
Missouri	Webster University	90%
Montana	Rocky Mountain College	100%

Minnesota's Carleton College grants over $27.6 million to its nearly 2,000 students. Carleton is a Dollars for Scholars college—students can earn up to $1,000 in outside awards without affecting their scholarships from Carleton.

Financial Aid at Four-Year Colleges

State	College or University	Percentage of Freshmen Who Receive Aid
Nebraska	Creighton University	92%
Nevada	University of Nevada–Las Vegas	84%
New Hampshire	Franklin Pierce University	99%
New Jersey	Stevens Institute of Technology	96%
New Mexico	Eastern New Mexico University	98%
New York	Fordham University	93%
North Carolina	Appalachian State University	56%
North Dakota	Dickinson State University	90%
Ohio	University of Dayton	99%
Oklahoma	University of Tulsa	91%
Oregon	Lewis & Clark College	80%
Pennsylvania	Slippery Rock University	89%
Rhode Island	Salve Regina University	81%
South Carolina	Clemson University	90%
South Dakota	Augustana College	100%
Tennessee	Vanderbilt University	65%
Texas	Rice University	84%
Utah	Southern Utah University	72%
Vermont	Saint Michael's College	89%
Virginia	George Mason University	60%
Washington	Western Washington University	60%
West Virginia	Marshall University	69%
Wisconsin	Ripon College	99%
Wyoming	University of Wyoming	97%
District of Columbia	Catholic University	96%

A recent study indicated that of all students attending public four-year colleges, about 61 percent had loans totaling almost $20,000 by graduation. For private four-year colleges, more than 70 percent had loans, with the average total being more than $27,000 per year.

What Aid Is Available for the Military and Dependents?

Many colleges offer grants and scholarships to veterans, active members of the military, and their dependents.

Do you have a parent who is or was in the military? If so, or if you plan to enter the military, you may be eligible for educational benefits during or after your service.

Students who attend military academies such as the U.S. Naval Academy do not pay tuition. In fact, they receive monthly pay to cover their costs. Many colleges offer Reserve Officer Training Corps (ROTC) programs affiliated with a specific branch of the military. Students enrolled in these programs may get full scholarships or monthly allowances in return for military service after graduation.

Students who apply to military academies must be nominated. Most nominations come from members of Congress, although there are other ways to be nominated.

You can find information about benefits currently offered by the Veterans Administration at *www.gibill.va.gov*.

Payment Plans

The University of Pennsylvania's Penn Monthly Budget Plan lets students pay costs over a 10-month period without any interest.

Most colleges send bills for tuition, fees, and any room and board in advance of each term. Many colleges also offer plans that allow you to spread out the payments during the school year.

For some people, a college with a payment plan is more affordable than a college where you must pay tuition all at once. Suppose tuition is $8,000 at College A and $12,000 at College B. At College A you must pay the tuition all at once. At College B, you may make 12 monthly payments of $1,000 each. Even though College B costs more than College A, it may be more affordable for someone who has a steady income but not a lot of savings.

Other Ways to Pay

As you look for ways to pay for college, you may be surprised at what's available, especially in your own community. You have to put in extra work to find this support, but the results can be well worth the effort. And even though these other grants and scholarships may be smaller, they can really add up!

Religious organizations often provide small college grants to members of their congregations. Many service and business organizations based in the community award scholarships to students with a track record of community service. Large companies often support students from the area as well. Company support is often geared to the children of employees.

Local businesses often work with area high schools. You may receive only $100 or $200, but every bit helps!

Become Money Smart

Many high schools, colleges, and banks offer courses and seminars in **financial literacy**—knowing how to manage your money and plan for the future. These courses are not just an opportunity to save for college but also an opportunity to gain an important life skill that will serve you for your entire life. You can learn about your credit history and credit score, identity theft, using credit cards wisely, and many more topics.

Thousands of scholarships are available, and they are given for all sorts of reasons. However, if you don't apply, the one thing you can be sure of is that you won't be selected.

LEARN MORE ABOUT MONEY

www.fdic.gov/moneysmart. The Federal Deposit Insurance Corporation has a program called Money Smart for Young Adults, aimed at youth ages 12-20.

www.jumpstart.org. Jump$tart is a coalition of more than 200 organizations working to help you develop important skills about managing your money.

www.mymoney.gov. An all-purpose site with many links to government information about your finances.

How Do I Apply for Financial Aid?

The information you need is usually available free of charge. If you decide to use a financial aid and scholarship service that charges a fee, check its qualifications and reputation very carefully.

Applying for financial aid starts with gathering information. Many resources can help you. School and college counselors can give you an overview and details about important changes and deadlines, especially with federal and state financial aid and local scholarships. They can provide the latest information and direct you to where you can find more. Schools and organizations may offer financial aid workshops, assistance completing forms, and access to computerized services, often free of charge.

Reference librarians can show you books written specifically about paying for college. They can also show you computer resources.

Financial aid offices can advise you about aid that is available specifically at their college. Much federal aid is the same from college to college. But state, local, college, and other types of aid vary.

The Internet connects you to lots of free information about financial aid. If you don't have access at home, use the computers at your school and local libraries.

And there's even more! Attend college fairs. Have your parents check the human resources office where they work about education benefits. Many funds are available for people who meet special criteria. Don't wait for financial aid to come to you. Take an active role!

College Goal Sunday is a national effort that helps families complete their financial aid forms. Each participating state schedules its own College Goal Sunday and arranges sponsors and volunteers. You can learn more at *www.collegegoalsundayusa.org.*

What Forms Will I Need?

The most commonly used form is the **Free Application for Federal Student Aid**, also known as **FAFSA.** You use this form to apply for federal financial aid. In addition, the form also provides many state and college aid programs the information they need about you.

The form asks for detailed information about your own background, your assets (as well as your family's), and your sources of income. Your parents must provide much of this information. The information is used to estimate your Expected Family Contribution (EFC). Colleges then use this figure to determine your financial aid package.

Many colleges have their own financial aid and scholarship forms, which you must file in addition to the FAFSA. In most cases, you should file the college's form at the same time you file your application for admission.

Many schools use, and may require, PROFILE, a form for students who are applying for nonfederal need-based aid. The form is handled by the College Scholarship Service. It is customized for each college, enabling each to collect the information it wants. You must pay a fee for *each* college you list when you file this form.

FAFSA is a free form. You will not be charged any fee to submit this form. FAFSA is also available in Spanish. You can find FAFSA on the Internet at http://fafsa.ed.gov.

Although PROFILE is not a free form, you can apply for a fee waiver. For more information, contact the College Board, college financial aid offices, or your high school counselor, or visit http://profileonline.collegeboard.com.

Ask your counselor about getting a free copy of *Funding Education Beyond High School: The Guide to Federal Student Aid* from the U.S. Department of Education. Other free guides include *Completing the FAFSA.* For more information, call 1-800-4FED-AID (TTY: 1-800-730-8913). You can also order copies through the Web site at *http://studentaid.ed.gov*.

227

Saving for College

Your parents may have already started saving for college. Get advice from them about opening your own account for college and keeping your savings in a safe place.

If you haven't already started saving for college, start now. The sooner you start, the more you will have available, and the more flexibility you will have in choosing where you go. Even if you decide not to go to college, your savings can help pay for vocational training or any of a number of important things—a car, a down payment on a house, or even the money you need to start your own business!

How Can I Save for College?

Upromise is an organization that helps families save for college through everyday purchases at the grocery store and certain restaurants. You can find out more at www.upromise.com.

Do you babysit? Do you have a paper route, mow lawns, shovel snow, or run errands for neighbors? All of these are fairly easy ways to earn money. When you're in high school, more opportunities may open up in fast-food and other restaurants, grocery stores, department stores, gas stations, and so forth.

Decide in advance that you will put a certain portion of what you earn into a college fund. You may also want to put another portion into savings for other reasons. Saving money is a great habit to develop—it will serve you well your whole life!

See page 216 for more information about tax-deferred savings, as well as tax credits that can help pay for college.

What you earn from working is not your only source for savings. Anytime you receive money from your allowance or from relatives or friends for a birthday or holiday present, you should put aside as much as possible for savings.

Where Should I Put My Savings?

Although the first place to put any money you save may be a savings account, you should look into tax-deferred savings (education IRAs), savings bonds, and certificates of deposit (CDs). But keep saving your money. You will be amazed at how quickly your savings can grow!

Where There's a Will, There's a Way

We have looked at ways to find money and ways to save. You should also look at ways of lowering your costs so your money can go further.

How Can I Lower My Costs?

Compare actual costs. Look at colleges that can help you achieve your goals. Compare their reputations. Lesser-known colleges may help you achieve your goals for less money, without sacrificing quality.

When you make your final decision about where to attend, look at the real cost of your choices. Consider your financial aid package and extra costs (for example, travel). For example, College A may cost $6,000 a year, but you get no financial aid. College B may cost $10,000 a year, but you get $5,000 a year in grants. At first, College B seems more expensive than College A. But because of the package, College B will cost you less.

Remember Community Colleges

Many students who attend two-year colleges go on to study at four-year colleges. Transfer programs can help students make the move to a four-year program without missing a beat. If you attend the two-year college and then transfer directly into your junior year at the four-year college, you can save a lot of money your first two years—more than half in many cases. Yet you still earn the same bachelor's degree as students who went only to the four-year college!

Be persistent. As the saying goes, where there is a will, there is a way. With enough hard work and determination, you will be able to afford to go to a college of your choice.

Many college and government Web sites have calculators to help you estimate the net price. Most are developing multiyear calculators to help you find the net price of all your college years, not just one year.

The Big Picture: Paying for College*

College name: _____

Personal savings: $ _____

Personal investments: $ _____

Earnings from work: $ _____

Contribution from parents: $ _____

Gifts from family and friends: $ _____

Local scholarships: $ _____

Other resources (such as tax
credits, tuition savings plans,
prepaid tuition plans, and bonds): $ _____

YOUR TOTAL RESOURCES: $ _____

TOTAL COLLEGE COSTS (from chapter 10 chart): $ _____

(subtract) YOUR TOTAL RESOURCES: $ _____

HOW MUCH YOU NEED: $ _____

(minus) Grants and scholarships: — $ _____

AMOUNT STILL NEEDED: $ _____

(minus) Loans: — $ _____

OUT-OF-POCKET COST TO YOU: $ _____

Estimates are on a per-year basis.

12

How Does College Begin?

College will be a new adventure for you. Like many new adventures, this one will be exciting, and maybe a bit scary. You might wonder how you will know what to do—what happens first?

Colleges have a lot of experience helping students through those first several weeks. In fact, many colleges help students prepare long before they actually arrive on campus. And once you do arrive, you will find lots of people to help guide you.

Remember, too, that you won't be alone. After all, many other first-time college students will be sharing the experience with you!

How Do I Get Started?

College begins in full swing once you're accepted and you've made your final decision about where to go. Now you can focus your attention on *going to* college rather than *getting into* college. And once the college knows you're coming, it focuses its attention on you and your fellow classmates!

You will probably start to get a lot of correspondence from the college. Carefully read what you receive. Keep this information with other important information that you have received about the college.

Even though you're now ready and excited to go, you still have several steps to take before your first class. You need to sign up for orientation; make arrangements to get to the college; find your way around campus; choose and sign up for your classes; and buy books, supplies, and equipment.

When preparing for your first year of college, think ahead to the end of the college year and to any other trips you might be taking—for instance, holiday and vacation travel. By planning your travel arrangements in advance, you may be able to save a lot of money.

In addition, if you plan to live on campus or anywhere else away from home, you also have some packing and moving ahead of you. You may need to arrange for housing and find a roommate, whether you live on or off campus (see chapter 13). If you are living away from home, you need to decide how you will move your belongings and how you will travel. And regardless of where you plan to live, you need to look into the various meal plans that the college offers and choose one that makes the most sense for you.

These steps take time—more, in fact, than you probably realize. Whatever steps you take, always try to take them on schedule—or even ahead of schedule!

What Is Orientation?

Most colleges offer at least one orientation program for incoming students. Orientation programs are designed to "orient" you to the college—they show you your way around campus. They help you understand what steps you need to take to get started and when to take them. They also explain campus rules and regulations and inform you about important campus services.

Larger colleges usually have more than one orientation program. Some programs are specifically planned for freshmen. Others may be designed for transfer students. In some cases, you can sign up for your classes during orientation. Reserve your spot for orientation as soon as you can and choose the earliest date possible. This will help you get a head start on the classes and schedule you want.

Colleges may have more than one kind of orientation program. Some may have programs that focus on certain majors or services. Other programs may be geared for specific groups, such as international students, athletes, honor students, or students with disabilities. Most likely, you will want to attend more than one program.

Some colleges have orientation programs for parents that answer their important questions.

Napa Valley College (CA) and the University of Hartford (CT) are just two of the many colleges that provide online orientation through their Web sites. Online orientation is especially helpful for students who live a long distance from the college.

Several colleges have special programs for new students. For example, freshmen at Colby College in Maine can participate in a Colby Outdoor Orientation Trip (COOT) the week before regular orientation. Small groups of new students—led by upperclass students, faculty members, or staff—get a taste of Maine. Trips may include canoeing in the Belgrade Lakes, shooting the rapids on the Penobscot River, hiking Mt. Katahdin, or working as a volunteer in Portland. Students who participate in programs like these make new friends who help make their first days easier.

MAINE

Finding Your Way

You may have already toured the campus when you first considered applying to the college. Still, take time to learn your way around. You might even take another tour. Get a copy of the campus map. (You may already have one from materials you received.) Find the important places: your room (if you plan to live on campus), parking, classroom buildings, the student union, the bookstore, the library, and the dining hall. Also find where student services are located.

Once you know where classes will be held, make a trial run. Be sure you know how to get from one place to another and how much time you need. On some campuses, classroom buildings are pretty far apart. Be sure you have time to get from one class to the next. Know the fastest route!

If you will be commuting to campus, drive or ride the route ahead of time. See how long you need to get to and from campus during the time of day that you expect to be making the trip.

Some colleges offer online and iPod tours. Checking things out in person is important for finding specific offices or rooms.

Maps are available online at most campuses. This map shows Goucher College in Baltimore, Maryland.

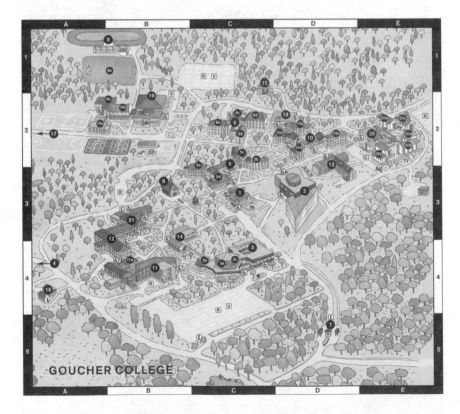

GOUCHER COLLEGE

What Is Placement Testing?

The college may give you one or more **placement tests.** These are not tests that you pass or fail. The college tests you in order to learn more about your level of skill and to make sure that you do not take courses that are too difficult or too easy for you. The college then uses the test results to place you into courses that match your skills.

Placement tests are most frequently given in math and English. However, colleges also test in other areas, such as foreign language, study skills, and technology. Placement tests are especially important in subjects where the material learned in one course is directly needed for other courses.

Open admissions colleges almost always give placement tests. These colleges do not restrict admission to the college. Therefore, they need a way of evaluating each student's skills. At most colleges (open, selective, and competitive), you may be excused from placement testing if your college entrance exam scores are high enough or if you have already taken certain high school or college classes.

Many colleges give placement tests as part of their orientation program. Sometimes, you can walk right into the placement office to take the test. Other times, you can schedule your tests in advance.

In either case, take your placement tests as soon as you can. The sooner you learn the results, the more time you will have to figure out which courses you should select. In addition, many colleges will not let you sign up for courses until you have taken your placement tests.

The college may provide materials that will help you prepare for placement tests. These materials may include sample questions. It's important to prepare so that the tests accurately reflect your skills.

Arrive on time for tests. Bring the required materials, including photo identification, if needed. For math tests, find out what type of calculator, if any, you may use.

Registering for Classes

A lot of students do not really feel that they are college students until they have registered (signed up) for their first set of classes. Although you have many decisions to make when you register, this period of time can be exciting—you're taking charge of your future!

What Is Registration?

In a nutshell, **registration** is the process of choosing the courses you would like to take, seeing that they all fit together into a good schedule, getting approval to take those courses, signing up for them, and paying your bill. You may be able to fine-tune your schedule if needed.

You must register for classes before each term. Keep in mind that you cannot register unless your bill is paid or payment plans are in place.

Who Can Help Me with Registration?

Advisors are the college's experts on choosing, scheduling, and registering for classes. As a freshman, you may be assigned an advisor to help you through your first registration. At many colleges, you will be assigned either a faculty member or someone from the advising or counseling center who will act as your advisor. Some colleges may also assign you a peer advisor—another student who can help answer your questions.

Faculty advisors usually teach in the program in which you are majoring.

Advisors can help you choose the right courses in the right order so that you will graduate on time. They can also help you prepare a planning form that tracks the courses you have taken and those courses you still need to complete a major and to graduate. They can help you even if you haven't selected a major. Advisors help you balance your courses so that you aren't overwhelmed.

Meet with your advisor early when you are planning your schedule. Check whether you need to make an appointment. You may also be able to talk with your advisor by e-mail.

Where Do I Learn About Courses?

The college **catalog** lists all the available courses, along with a brief description of each course. It tells you about general requirements that you must complete, as well as specific requirements for your major.

The catalog is your contract with the college. The course requirements listed at the time you begin classes generally don't change if you continue to attend the college and keep the same major.

The next handy tool is the **schedule of classes.** This schedule, which is revised each term, tells you when courses are offered and who teaches each course. In many cases, a course is offered at several different times. For example, precalculus may be offered at 10 different times. Each of these classes is a *section*. The number of sections that are offered depends on the demand for the course. Professors may teach one or more sections.

Class schedules list the name and number of each course (see the next page). If the course has more than one section, each section is listed individually. The schedule lists the days and times each section is taught, the way each section is taught (for example, lecture or online), and where each section is taught. The person teaching the course is often listed. Usually the schedule lists the number of credits or units you earn when you take the course.

In most cases, online schedules are updated regularly so that you can tell if courses and sections have been added, dropped, or filled as students register.

You often see staff, instructor, TBD, or TBA listed as the teacher. These mean that the actual teacher was not known when the schedule was first published. TBD means "to be determined" and TBA means "to be announced."

Many classes are taught three times a week on Mondays, Wednesdays, and Fridays for 50 minutes. These will be listed as MWF on a schedule. Classes that are taught twice a week, often for an hour and 15 minutes, are usually held on Mondays and Wednesdays (MW) or Tuesdays and Thursdays (TTh).

How Do I Know Which Courses to Take?

If you took advanced high school courses or earned high scores on achievement and Advanced Placement tests, you may not have to take all the general requirements courses.

You take some courses to meet general requirements. For example, most freshmen take composition or literature courses. Meet with your advisor to discuss which requirements you have already met and which remain. Your advisor can also help you figure out which courses to take for certain subjects.

*A **prerequisite** is a course that you are required (-requisite) to take before (pre-) taking another course.*

The catalog tells you which courses are needed for different majors. It also tells you about course prerequisites. For example, you may need to take general biology before taking genetics. However, you may need to take both general biology and general inorganic chemistry before you take a cell biology course.

Not all courses are offered every term. Some are offered once each year. Some are offered only every other year. Be aware of how often courses are offered when you make your selections.

The class schedule or catalog explains how courses are numbered.

Colleges have different ways of numbering courses. Courses below certain numbers may be remedial courses. Those with higher numbers may be restricted to juniors and seniors.

COURSE NUMBERING AT IOWA STATE UNIVERSITY

Course Numbers	Types of Courses
1–99	Courses have no credit toward degree
100–299	Mostly for freshmen and sophomores
300–499	Mostly for juniors and seniors
500–599	Mostly for graduate students
600–699	Only for graduate students

For example, Accounting 284 (Financial Accounting) is mostly for freshmen and sophomores, and Accounting 497 (Introduction to Auditing) is mostly for juniors and seniors.

How Do I Register for Classes?

Registration has become more convenient for students. Most colleges offer several different ways to register, both on and off campus. The person in charge of registration is called the **registrar.**

Try to register as soon as you can. Courses and sections fill up. You may get blocked from taking some courses because of space limitations. The earlier you register, the better your chances will be for getting the courses you want. You will also have more time to find other choices, if needed.

Most colleges have a time period when you can adjust your schedule. During this period, you can add and drop courses. You may be able to switch sections as well, enabling you to have a better schedule or a different instructor. Sometimes space opens up in a course that had been closed. If you are on a waiting list, you may be able to get into that class.

Some colleges run registration on a first-come, first-served basis. Other colleges decide the order in which students can register. Seniors and juniors often register first. Other students may be picked in alphabetical or some other order that is fair to all students over time. Colleges can usually accommodate students with special situations.

WAYS TO REGISTER FOR CLASSES

Freshman orientation. Students register as part of the orientation program.

Online registration. Students use computers linked to the college's registration system; the Internet enables more students to register by computer; students get an instant response about the availability of classes.

Walk-in or in-person registration. Students come directly to the college to register; this method is often used in the last days before classes start.

Telephone registration. Students either speak to college staff handling registration or use the phone to link to the college computer.

Mail-in or fax-in registration. Students complete forms indicating the courses and schedule they want; materials are mailed to the registrar and processed.

How Do I Plan My Schedule?

When you first plan your schedule, you need to know what courses you want to take and when you want to take them. Sometimes certain sections or even entire courses are filled by students who register before you. You may not be able to get everything you want when you want it. Therefore, you'll need back-up plans.

When you plan your schedule, expect to be in class one hour each week for every credit you take. For example, if you take a three-credit course, expect the class to meet for three hours each week. In addition, for every hour you are in class, you can expect to spend two to three hours studying and doing homework. College students are usually considered to be full-time students if each semester they take the equivalent of 12 to 15 credits or more, depending on the college.

Many classes have required labs, which meet for two or more hours per week. Some classes and labs are scheduled together. In other cases, the two are independent of each other. Check which is the case for any labs you have.

In this schedule, Spanish has 4 credits; English Literature, Biology, and Precalculus each have 3 credits; and Biology Lab and Internet Research each have 1 credit.

SCHEDULING FOR CLASS CREDITS

TIME	Monday	Tuesday	Wednesday	Thursday	Friday
8:30					
9:30	Spanish	Spanish	Spanish	Spanish	
10:30		Biology		Biology	
11:30	English Literature		English Literature		English Literature
12:30					
1:30	Precalculus	Internet Research	Precalculus	Biology Lab	
2:30					
3:30					
4:30					
5:30					

TEN STEPS TO PLANNING YOUR SCHEDULE

1. *Organize information.* Review the catalog, schedule of classes, and your placement scores. Locate any planning and registration forms.

2. *Meet with your advisor.* Talk with your advisor about how to register and which courses to take.

3. *Consider your needs and preferences.* Would you prefer early or late classes, or online classes? Be honest about your study skills and how they affect the number and kind of classes you take. Think about the time you need for work, commuting, or extracurricular activities.

4. *Balance your courses.* Think about the kind of homework the courses require (reading, writing, problem-solving, or projects), your study strengths and weaknesses, and the difficulty of each course.

5. *Schedule required courses first.* Begin with the required courses that have the fewest sections or meet only one term per year. Do all you can to get into them, including registering online. Schedule all other classes and activities around them. Next, schedule required courses that have many sections.

6. *Schedule nonrequired courses.* List these courses in order of preference. Go down the list until you find one that fits with your required courses and your preferred schedule.

7. *Prepare required information.* Complete the information you need to register: course names and numbers, section numbers, and other related information.

8. *Be on time.* Your planning is wasted if you do not register on time or make your payments on time. If you stay ahead of schedule, you will get more classes you want and have time to solve problems that develop.

9. *Have a backup plan.* Be ready with your next move if a required course or a section is closed. Do not be shy about asking your advisor or others for help if you have trouble getting it.

10. *Make a final schedule.* Once you have registered, create a final schedule that also includes your study time, work, meals, rest, and activities. Make extra copies for yourself.

Odds and Ends

Registering for classes is not the only step that you take before classes begin. Some other steps still remain.

Physicals, Health Forms, and Insurance

You may need to get a physical examination before you begin college, especially if you plan to live on campus or are studying in certain fields. Colleges need to ensure, for instance, that all students have been vaccinated for measles and meningitis. You need to make sure you have proper health insurance, whether provided by you or by the college. If you have specific health concerns—such as diabetes or epilepsy—be sure that you notify medical officials on campus.

IDs, Permits, and Forms

Your student ID can even save you money away from campus. For instance, you might get special rates when you travel if you can show a student ID.

At some point early on, you will get a student identification (ID) card. You will need your ID to check out library materials, use the fitness center, attend football games or other campus events, and more. Your ID might also save you money at local shops and restaurants.

If you need a parking permit, you should handle the paperwork before classes begin. If you receive financial aid, you will have tasks to complete each term. If you will be living in college housing, you have forms you should complete as soon as possible.

Get Your Books and Supplies Early!

Once your schedule is confirmed, buy your books. Bookstores do not always have enough copies. If you wait too long, the store may run out and have to reorder. You can often order books online, but not always. Having your books and supplies early helps you get off to a strong start.

Starting Classes

Little compares to the first day of classes! You already know this feeling: It combines excitement, nervousness, motivation, and a bit of uncertainty. But the day has arrived. You're ready to begin!

Double-check the location of your classes. (Sometimes, classes are moved to different rooms or buildings.) In most cases, you can choose whatever seat you want. College classes usually do not have seating charts. Pick a seat close enough to the front of the room for you to hear clearly. You also want to be able to see anything the teacher writes on the chalkboard or shows on a screen.

What Is a Syllabus?

Most teachers provide a course **syllabus** to students on the first day of class. The syllabus is an outline for the course. It often provides an idea of what will be taught each day of the class. It includes reading assignments and sometimes detailed homework assignments. The syllabus will also tell you when major projects such as papers are due and when you can expect to have major tests.

The syllabus often includes your teacher's office location and hours, phone number, and e-mail address. It may also explain attendance and grading policies.

Is Homework Graded?

It may or may not be. Homework in college is not quite the same as what you are used to now. Daily homework is often assigned to help you learn the lessons and prepare for each class. You usually do not have to turn in this kind of work, although teachers may check to see if you have completed it. However, larger assignments, including essays and research papers, may take several days or weeks to complete and may be an important part of your grade.

In some classes such as math, professors may go over only the most difficult problems in class. Otherwise, students check their own homework. Always complete your homework regardless of whether it is checked in class or graded.

YOUR STUDIES OUTSIDE OF CLASS

Exercises and problems. More traditional homework that involves solving problems or answering questions about reading material; questions often come from textbooks; used often in math, statistics, accounting, chemistry, physics, and foreign language.

Journals. Reports you maintain on a regular basis; may be creative writing, daily observations, or a collection of data.

Papers and essays. Brief explorations of certain topics; may require a certain amount of research, but usually from a limited number of sources; you may be asked to analyze a particular topic; can include informational writing, but can also include more creative writing and English compositions.

Research papers. More formal and lengthy papers; usually require you to use many sources of information; often involve formal use of footnotes, sources, and a bibliography; usually very important to your grade.

Discussion groups. Extra sessions outside the regular class; smaller groups discuss topics related to the class; may be run by the professor or teaching assistant; all students are expected to participate.

Computer/technology applications. Special computer projects, including engineering and business simulations, programming, and large statistical studies.

Lab reports. While some labs are for practical experience, other labs require follow-up reports; these reports show that you are learning proper research methods and provide practice in summarizing your findings.

Field exercises and labs. Required sessions outside the lecture class; provide students with a chance to conduct experiments.

Keeping Up with Tests and Assignments

Keep up with your ongoing assignments. They are important on their own. They also help you prepare for tests and exams. Pay close attention to information about tests. Find out what kind of questions you can expect and how much the tests will count toward your grade.

TYPES OF TESTS

Final. An important test given at the end of the term; test usually lasts two to three hours and may cover the entire course; the grade often counts for one-third to one-half of the grade for the course.

Hourly. Important test usually given once or twice during the term; the test takes up the entire class session; covers either the material from the start of the term or the material covered since the previous exam; the grade may count for as much as one-third to one-half of your grade for the course.

Midterm. Same as hourly, but offered halfway through the term; may count for up to one-half of your grade for the course.

Pop quiz (see quiz). A brief test, usually not announced until the day it is given; used to check your progress with the material and look for weak spots; also used to encourage you to keep up with daily work.

Quiz. A brief test; usually takes up less than half of the class period; often focused on a specific amount of material; unlike pop quizzes, this type of quiz is usually announced in advance.

Completing Your Schedule

Once you have your class schedule and the syllabus for each course, you should create a master schedule for the term. This schedule should include your classes and all your tests, major assignments (including research papers), special events, and vacations.

You can choose from many formats for scheduling your time: formal daily or weekly planners, index cards, calendars, or e-mail or cell phone applications.

You should also create weekly and daily schedules with more detail. In these, you can add more information; for example, times that you meet with study groups, play sports, rehearse for a performance, meet with a club, or simply relax. If you have any special events or meetings (for example, a guest lecture or a meeting with your advisor), you can add them to your weekly schedule, too.

How Will I Be Graded?

For the most part, courses are graded the same way as in high school. But your grade may depend on fewer projects, tests, and assignments. In many courses, your class participation may be an important part of your grade.

Some colleges even offer credit/no credit courses. These are often experimental courses, some even taught by other students. No one is graded. You earn credits toward graduation, but not toward your major or general requirements.

Many colleges allow you to take some courses on a pass/fail basis. You don't receive a letter or numerical grade (for example *A* or *93*) as you do in other classes. Most pass/fail courses do not count toward your major. This system encourages students to take challenging courses outside their main area of study, but without the pressure of being graded.

Getting Extra Help

Some professors require freshmen to meet with them at least once in their office. A professor's office hours are for you—for questions, advice, and simply getting to know your professor.

All sorts of resources are available to you. Many students find that studying with others helps. You may want to team up with other students early in the term to form a study group that meets regularly to go over class notes, homework, and reading assignments. Study group members can help each other with difficult portions of the course and help prepare for tests.

Professors have office hours or e-mail so that you can ask them any questions. Some have teaching assistants who can help. Many departments have learning labs—for example, math labs—where you can get extra help or practice. Colleges also provide tutoring. If you need help and are uncertain how to get it, contact the advising office or the counseling center. They'll point you in the right direction to get the help you need.

Enjoy the Ride!

All the new experiences that you will face, particularly in the first few weeks, can feel overwhelming at times. But they can also be fun—new learning opportunities, new people, new adventures. Embrace them all!

13

What Happens at College?

Lots of activities and opportunities happen on a daily basis! Your studies, of course, are very important. But the many opportunities that take place outside your classes are also important.

You'll meet new people; some will become lifelong friends. You'll also participate in many activities, some of them new to you. And you'll be challenged by others to expand your horizons.

In this chapter, we look at student life—all the things available to do on campus when you are not in class. We also look at what you can do to feel at home and take full advantage of college.

Where Will I Live?

Some colleges require incoming freshmen to live on campus. Other colleges do not provide any housing—in this case, the decision of where to live is entirely yours. Still others give you a choice about where to live. Your decision is an important one.

Colleges often have drawings to determine who gets to live in college housing or the order in which students pick their rooms. Some colleges fill rooms on a first-come, first-served basis.

In some cases, the college doesn't have enough housing for everyone. Usually, the college sets aside enough space so that freshmen who want to live on campus can do so. However, many students enjoy living off campus. Students who live off campus often rent apartments or rooms near the college. Students attending a college near where they went to high school often live at home, at least during their freshman year.

What Is a Dormitory?

Some larger rooms, called suites, have two or more small bedrooms and a larger shared living area.

Many college students live in college-run **dormitories** (often called dorms or residence halls). Dorms may provide housing for small groups or for hundreds of students. Although some students (usually juniors or seniors) have their own rooms, most have roommates. Most rooms are doubles (two students), triples (three students), or quads (four students). Most dorm rooms include a bed, a desk, a chair, a dresser, and a closet. You bring everything else!

Most colleges today provide wireless Internet service (Wi-Fi) in some areas of the dorms.

Some dorms have dining halls and study rooms in them. Most have lounges where students can spend free time just relaxing, watching television, playing games, or listening to music. Many dorms have small kitchens available for student use. Students usually share bathroom facilities with other students. Students can easily use their computers in most dorm rooms to access e-mail, the campus intranet, and the Internet.

COMMON LIVING ARRANGEMENTS IN DORMITORIES

Male or female. Students in the dorm are either all male or all female.

Coed by floor. Both male and female students live in the dorm; some floors are all male, and some floors are all female.

Coed within floor. Each floor has both male and female students.

Freshmen only. These dorms focus on the needs of new students.

International. Students in these dorms are from countries all around the world, including Americans who would like this experience.

Honors. Dorm space is reserved for students in special honors programs; these dorms may have advantages (such as larger rooms or a better location).

Alcohol-free and smoke-free. Students sign pledges in which they agree to ban alcohol and cigarettes in the dorm.

Who Runs the Dorms?

The people who live in the dorms and are in charge of them are the dorm staff. Each dorm has a **head resident** (or resident director) who manages the dorm. In some cases, head residents are seniors who have previously been members of the dorm staff. They usually report to the dean of housing or the director of resident life. They keep an eye out for the entire dorm and are informal counselors to students who live there.

Resident assistants, or **RAs,** live on each floor. They watch over all or part of a floor, depending on the size. They work to prevent problems and help solve them when they do occur. They provide safety and other information to students on their floor—for example, information about safety drills. They usually report to the head resident.

Deans of housing and directors of resident life are responsible for making sure that campus housing is safe and comfortable. They and their staff oversee housing assignments, determining who lives where. They also assign roommates.

Colleges may also have area directors who oversee groups of dorms.

What Other Types of Housing Are Available?

Students may also have opportunities to live in fraternities, sororities, and other group housing, discussed later in this chapter.

Many colleges have student apartments, both on and off campus. Unlike dorm rooms, apartments have their own bathrooms and kitchens. Some colleges maintain apartments to ensure a steady supply of student housing. College-run apartments usually go first to married students, graduate students, students with children, and upperclassmen. Students may also arrange their own off-campus housing.

How Do I Get a Roommate?

When you live off campus, you usually need to find your own roommate. Many colleges have student referral programs that help students find other students to be roommates. Many cities also have programs that help students find both off-campus housing and roommates.

If you plan to live on campus, the college will send you a questionnaire to complete. It will ask you about your personal likes and dislikes and the kind of person with whom you might want to share a room. For example, the questionnaire might ask whether you prefer to study with music playing or with no background noise. The college tries to match you with a roommate who has similar preferences.

The college usually takes responsibility for matching freshmen with their roommates. After that, you can continue with the same roommate, find one on your own, or have one chosen at random. As a freshman, you may be allowed to room with someone you already know. Many colleges want you to room with someone you do not know so that you will get to meet new people. Some colleges have single rooms available for freshmen.

You have adjustments to make even if you live at home. Your relationship with your family changes. You also need to make sure you stay connected to the campus.

Many students must learn to make adjustments in getting along with their roommates, even when they're a lifelong friend. Learning to make these adjustments is an important part of the college experience. The dorm staff, counselors, advisors, and the dean of students are available to help you.

What Should I Take with Me to College?

A lot of what you need depends on how far from home you will be going. If you are able to get home easily on weekends or even during the week, you can always pick up things that you forget. But if you are going to college far from home, you need to think more carefully about how you will pack.

For many students, going away to college is the first time they have gone away from home for more than a week or two. Items that you are used to having around—as simple as toothpaste and shampoo—now become your responsibility. Besides basics such as clothing, toiletries, and medicine, you will probably want to bring things that make you feel at home or which you can use for rest and recreation. These may include some favorite music, an iPod or DVD player, favorite books, athletic gear (tennis racket, baseball glove), and photos. Bringing your own computer to campus is important.

Your college may send a list of suggested supplies as well as optional items you can rent. Talk with your roommate to coordinate who will bring larger items such as a TV or a rug.

If you forget something, you can buy many supplies after you arrive on campus.

Students often overlook the need to have good, sound sleep. Pack a comfortable pillow or two—and a favorite blanket if you want.

You may want to split the cost of certain items (like a small refrigerator) with your roommate.

PACKING THE BASICS

Computer and printer	Backpack or knapsack
College dictionary*	Supplies (pens, highlighters, etc.)
Calculator	Good desk lamp
Calendar*	Daily planner*
Sports equipment	Comfortable pillows and linens
Alarm clock	Raincoat or poncho
Seasonal clothing	Toiletries (shampoo, comb, etc.)
Laundry supplies	Music or DVD player

*could be on computer

What Are Fraternities and Sororities?

Together, fraternities and sororities are known as the Greek community, *or the* Greeks. *The name of each organization consists of two or three letters of the Greek alphabet. For example, ZBT, or Zeta Beta Tau, is one of many fraternities. AKA, or Alpha Kappa Alpha, is one of many sororities.*

You may have a chance to join a **fraternity** or **sorority.** These are national membership organizations that offer opportunities for strong friendships, development of leadership skills, and participation in athletic, social, and community events. They set up chapters at various colleges. Fraternities are for males, and sororities are for females. (A few individual chapters are coed—they admit both males and females.) Many colleges have both fraternities and sororities, though some do not permit either.

Many chapters operate houses on or near campus and provide housing for members who pay room charges. Each house may provide rooms for a few dozen members. Some chapters require their members to live in the house for at least a year; others do not.

The process of recruiting new members is often called rushing.

Fraternities and sororities are not groups anyone can join. In most cases, you must be invited to become a brother (fraternity) or sister (sorority). You then go through many steps, during which time you are a pledge. The process of joining (called *pledging*) places significant demands on your time—all at a time when you are still trying to adjust to college life. Some colleges will not allow you to pledge until you have completed one or more terms.

What Are Cultural Centers?

Many colleges have multicultural centers where students from different backgrounds share their experiences. Multicultural centers may be located within dorms or at independent locations on campus.

Many colleges have centers where students can share their interest in particular cultures, regardless of whether they are from that cultural background. At Wright State University in Ohio, you will find several cultural centers, including the Asian/Hispanic/Native American Cultural Center, the Bolinga Black Cultural Center, the Women's Center, and the University Center for International Education.

The Student Union

The **student union** is one of the first places you should find when you get to campus. It is an important place for students to gather.

Not all colleges have a separate student union. But most have some sort of student center that serves the same purpose.

Meals and Books

Many student unions have places to eat, both regular dining halls and places open late at night. The student union is also where you might find the campus bookstore. You can buy textbooks and other class materials at the bookstore, as well as other books and magazines, college clothing (for example, sweatshirts with the college name on them), snacks, and many other items.

Getting Mail

As a student, you may have your own mailing address at the college. The mail is sent to a central location, often the student union, where you have a mailbox and key. Larger colleges may have several locations where mail is received and sent out.

Student Services

The student union is also the place where many student services are located. You might find counseling, advising, placement, and employment offices there. The offices that coordinate student activities (concerts, clubs, intramural sports) may be in the union, along with the student government. You will also find meeting rooms, lounges, coffeehouses, and small performance sites for plays, music, stand-up comedy, and readings.

The student union sometimes houses the campus health office.

Larger student unions may have even more: hair stylists, travel agencies, banking services, fast-food restaurants and shops, game rooms and bowling alleys, and even movie auditoriums and hotel rooms.

253

Clubs and Organizations

When you go to college, you will be able to choose from dozens of different clubs and organizations. You may decide to play a sport, either with an official team or an intramural team. You may want to become active with a college publication such as the campus newspaper or literary magazine. You may also be interested in student government.

Academic and Career Organizations

Members of student groups often share an academic or career interest. For example, a biology club might bring leading biologists to campus for guest lectures or plan a field trip to study plant life in a nearby forest. In addition, these organizations often help members find jobs, internships, and career advice.

Religious Organizations

Groups of students who share a common faith often organize special worship services, discussion groups, and other religious and social events. For example, Newman Centers serve the needs of Roman Catholic students. Many campuses have interfaith centers serving the needs of students from Christian, Jewish, Islamic, Buddhist, and other religious backgrounds. Campus groups often have ties to houses of worship or religious organizations in the local community.

Performance Organizations

Most colleges have a campuswide choir, often called a glee club. You may also be able to play with a marching band, an orchestra, or a small chamber group. Colleges also have theater and comedy groups, smaller singing groups, dance companies, and bands.

Service Organizations

Many organizations are formed to serve the campus or the surrounding community. For example, Big Brothers and Big Sisters programs match college students with kids from the community. College students often help build homes in the community or volunteer at nearby shelters. They also hold lots of special events, such as dance-a-thons, to raise money for groups like the Muscular Dystrophy Association. Service groups also run programs on campus. For instance, some groups provide an escort service so that students do not have to walk alone across campus at night.

Social Organizations

Many groups provide ways for students with similar interests or backgrounds to get together for fun. For example, the University of Michigan in Ann Arbor has different groups for students who are Filipino, Pakistani, Serbian, Latino, and more. Other groups center on activities, such as chess, debate, martial arts, juggling, water skiing, swing dancing, and ultimate Frisbee.

Political Organizations

Students who share the same views on politics and issues often have their own organizations. For example, you might find clubs for both Young Republicans and Young Democrats at many colleges.

Support Organizations

Some groups help students share their problems or concerns. These groups can provide opportunities for students to voice their views, and find and give comfort and advice. For example, you may find groups that provide support for students with eating disorders or depression or for students with other physical or personal challenges.

Some of the Student Organizations at Auburn University

Performance Groups
Concert Choir
Gospel Choir
University Singers
Marching Band
Symphonic Band
Concert Band
Jazz Ensembles
Basketball Pep Band
The Telfair Peet Theatre
AU Summerstage
Theatre Upstairs

Service Organizations
Action Campus Civitan Club
Alpha Phi Omega
Best Buddies
Circle K
Tiger Habitat

Religious Organizations
Baptist Campus Ministries
Catholic Student Organization
Eastern Orthodox Christian Association
Jewish Student Organization
Muslim Students' Association
St. Dunstan's The Episcopal Church
Wesley Foundation

Military Organizations
Kadettes
Mariners
Semper Fidelis Society
Steerage Society
Trident Society

Special-Interest Groups
African and Caribbean Students
   Alliance

Amateur Radio Club
College Democrats
College Republicans
Computer Gaming Club
Egyptian Student Association
Environmental Awareness Organization
Film Society
Indian Student Association
Karate Club
Korean Student Association
Libertarians
Outdoor Adventure Club
Tennis Club
Volleyball Club

Leadership and Honor Groups
Cardinal Key
Golden Key International Honour
   Society
Lambda Sigma
Phi Kappa Phi
Sigma Xi

Academic and Career Groups
Agronomy Club
American Institute of Architecture
   Students
Chemistry Society
Horticulture Forum
International Interior Design
   Association
Mathematics Club
Marine Biology Club
Public Relations Council of Alabama
Society of Women Engineers
Student Dietetic Association

Extra! Learn All About It!

Another way you can become active at college is to work on a student publication. Most colleges have at least one campus newspaper. The paper comes out once a week on some campuses. At larger colleges, the paper is often published daily.

Campus newspapers provide information about important issues on campus; a summary of the news both on and off campus; reviews of films, concerts, and plays; sports results; and calendars of upcoming events. They also have editorial pages that print the ideas and opinions of both the newspaper staff and the college community.

Many colleges have literary magazines that give students a chance to publish stories, essays, drawings, poems, and photographs. Colleges also have student yearbooks. Other publications may be available depending on student interest.

In addition to publications, many colleges have student-run radio stations. These stations may combine music with news, issue-oriented shows, and call-in talk shows. Faculty, staff, and members of the community often get involved as well, frequently hosting their own shows.

Students have lots of other ways to communicate. There are all the ways you communicate now—e-mail, phone including voice mail and text messaging, and social networking sites. On many campuses, students can easily set up their own home pages. Some colleges run public-access television programs, providing students with both on-air time and behind-the-scenes experience. And nothing beats getting together with others at a favorite spot on campus!

College newspapers need reporters, editors, columnists, photographers, graphic artists, advertising coordinators, and publishers. At many colleges, some students are paid for their work.

WNUR FM is the student-run radio station at Northwestern University in Illinois. On the air 24 hours a day, this student-run station can reach millions of listeners every day. Mt. Hood Community College broadcasts KMHD—Portland, Oregon's all-jazz radio station.

Sports at College

Sports are an important part of campus life. Most colleges have college-run teams in a variety of sports; these teams play teams from other colleges. Most colleges are organized into groups called **conferences.** Teams within the conference play each other often and develop long-term rivalries.

Official teams with the top players are often called *varsity* teams. Many colleges have *junior varsity* teams as well. These often feature athletes who are freshmen or sophomores, or students who are waiting for openings on the varsity teams. Teams play according to rules established by groups that set policies for college participation in sports.

The NCAA has very strict rules about how athletes are recruited, the financial aid they can receive, their academic performance, and their conduct on and off the field. See your counselor or advisor for more information.

The National Collegiate Athletic Association (NCAA) is the most prominent group overseeing college sports participation. The NCAA divides colleges and conferences into several different divisions: I, II, and III. Division I, which generally represents colleges with larger athletic programs, has two subdivisions for football, formerly known as I-A and I-AA. In some cases, colleges may play in two different divisions in sports other than football and basketball.

The West Coast Conference is an NCAA conference made up of eight colleges that play each other in basketball and other sports. Six members of the conference are in California (Loyola Marymount University, Pepperdine University, Saint Mary's College, Santa Clara University, University of San Diego, and University of San Francisco). The other two members are the University of Portland (Oregon) and Gonzaga University (Washington).

What Are the Academic Requirements for Athletes?

In recent years, the standards for playing college sports have become stricter. Athletes are expected to maintain certain grade point averages in order to play for a team. Organizations like the NCAA establish guidelines and review them regularly. Individual conferences or colleges may set even higher standards.

In many cases, athletes must have a certain score on their college entrance examinations in order to play during their freshman year.

What Athletic Opportunities Are Available for Women?

Over the past 30 years, opportunities for women to play varsity sports have skyrocketed. Women are also finding jobs as sports writers, broadcasters, and commentators. Sports like swimming, diving, tennis, and track and field have provided opportunities for many years. More recently, basketball, softball, volleyball, lacrosse, and soccer have caught up. Opportunities will continue to grow, especially as more scholarships become available to top female athletes.

Time Commitment

In order to play on a varsity team, you must make a huge time commitment, even to keep in shape during the off-season. You must be very self-disciplined and organized to play a varsity sport while maintaining your grades. Play on the team if you have the desire, the ability, and the time. Do not be pressured by others, and do not sacrifice your academic performance.

College athletics are also important at two-year colleges, which offer most of the same sports as the four-year colleges. Among the major groups overseeing athletics is the National Junior College Athletic Association (NJCAA).

Can I Play on Other Types of Teams?

You can be involved with college athletics without playing for a team, for example, by being a sports announcer or sportswriter or a member of the cheerleading squad or marching band. You may also have the opportunity to be an assistant trainer or a student manager.

At most colleges, anyone can join an **intramural** team for fun. Intramural teams are made up of groups of students within the college, often organized into leagues. They play most games against each other. For example, different fraternities and sororities may have their own intramural teams. A team may also be made up of students from a specific dorm, a specific club, or any other group of students who want to play together. Colleges have their own rules about how intramural sports are organized.

In some cases, students who have an interest in a particular sport form a club. They may play clubs from other colleges or clubs from the community. Sports clubs are often formed for sports that are not covered by college-run varsity teams and that do not have enough interest on campus to set up a league of intramural teams.

SPORTS AT TEMPLE UNIVERSITY (PENNSYLVANIA)

Varsity sports. Baseball (M), basketball (M/F), crew (M/F), cross country (M/F), fencing (F), field hockey (F), football (M), golf (M), gymnastics (M/F), lacrosse (F), soccer (M/F), softball (F), tennis (M/F), track and field (M/F), and volleyball (F).

Intramural sports and events. Basketball, dodgeball, flag football, floor hockey, indoor and outdoor soccer, softball, and volleyball.

Sports clubs. Bowling, cricket, diving, equestrian, fencing, field hockey, Frisbee, ice hockey, indoor rock climbing, jujitsu, lacrosse, rugby, roller hockey, swimming, taekwondo, and volleyball.

Key: M—male, F—female, M/F—male and female.

School Spirit

Sports have a way of bringing people together at many colleges. In one way, they physically bring people together—athletes, cheerleaders, the band, and spectators. Students, faculty, staff, alumni, parents, and members of the community all gather in the same place to support the team and the college.

They also bring people together emotionally. The school spirit that is generated by sports is very important to a lot of colleges. Of course, sports are not the only source of school spirit. All the other activities and organizations are also very important to how the people at a college feel about themselves and their college community.

Mascots and Nicknames

Most colleges have figures, or **mascots,** that symbolize the college. The name of the mascot often becomes the nickname of the college and its sports teams. One of the best-known mascots is the Nittany Lion of Penn State University.

Certain mascots and nicknames are popular for teams because they represent strength or bravery. Many colleges pick mascots and nicknames that have special meaning based on the college's name (the Bonnies of St. Bonaventure University in New York), history (the Pilgrims of New England College), or educational specialty (the Miners of New Mexico Institute of Mining and Technology).

The mascots appear in all sorts of places—mugs, bumper stickers, sweatshirts and other clothing, notebooks, and so forth. They may also appear live at sporting events and other campus activities, usually played by students in costume.

As at high schools, most colleges also have school colors (usually two) that are used in uniforms for athletes, cheerleaders, and others. Most mascots display these colors. Colors are even included in some college nicknames, for example, the University of Delaware's Blue Hens and Alabama's Crimson Tide.

It's All in the Name!

State	College or University	Nickname/Mascot
Alabama	University of Alabama	Crimson Tide
Alaska	University of Alaska–SE	Humpback Whales
Arizona	Arizona State University	Sun Devils
Arkansas	Southern Arkansas University	Muleriders
California	University of San Diego	Toreros
Colorado	Colorado School of Mines	Orediggers
Delaware	University of Delaware	Blue Hens
Florida	Stetson University	Hatters
Georgia	Oglethorpe University	Stormy Petrels
Hawaii	University of Hawaii	Rainbow Warriors
Idaho	University of Idaho	Vandals
Illinois	Knox College	Prairie Fire
Indiana	Purdue University	Boilermakers
Iowa	St. Ambrose University	Fighting Bees
Kansas	Wichita State University	Shockers
Kentucky	Western Kentucky University	Hilltoppers
Louisiana	University of Louisiana–Lafayette	Ragin' Cajuns
Maine	University of Maine	Black Bears
Maryland	University of Maryland	Terrapins
Massachusetts	Brandeis University	Judges
Michigan	University of Michigan	Wolverines
Minnesota	Concordia College	Cobbers
Mississippi	Mississippi Valley State University	Delta Devils
Missouri	University of Missouri–Kansas City	Kangaroos
Montana	Montana State University–Northern	Northern Lights

The University of California at Santa Cruz has an unusual mascot—the banana slug! Student demand and a strong publicity campaign led to the replacement of the previous mascot, the sea lion, in 1986.

It's All in the Name!

State	College or University	Nickname/Mascot
Nebraska	Nebraska Wesleyan University	Prairie Wolves
Nevada	University of Nevada–Las Vegas	Runnin' Rebels
New Hampshire	New England College	Pilgrims
New Jersey	New Jersey City University	Gothic Knights
New Mexico	University of New Mexico	Lobos
New York	Yeshiva University	Maccabees
North Carolina	University of North Carolina	Tar Heels
North Dakota	Jamestown College	Jimmies
Ohio	Xavier University	Musketeers
Oklahoma	University of Oklahoma	Sooners
Oregon	University of Oregon	Ducks
Pennsylvania	Lafayette College	Leopards
Rhode Island	Providence College	Friars
South Carolina	Coastal Carolina University	Chanticleers
South Dakota	South Dakota School of Mines	Hardrockers
Tennessee	Vanderbilt University	Commodores
Texas	Texas Christian University	Horned Frogs
Utah	Westminster College	Griffins
Vermont	University of Vermont	Catamounts
Virginia	University of Richmond	Spiders
Washington	Evergreen State College	Geoducks
West Virginia	Marshall University	Thundering Herd
Wisconsin	St. Norbert College	Green Knights
Wyoming	University of Wyoming	Cowboys
District of Columbia	Georgetown University	Hoyas

Among the most popular college nicknames are the Tigers, the Bulldogs, the Pioneers, the Cougars, the Wildcats, the Panthers, and the Lions. But easily the most popular nickname of all is the Eagles, used by more than 50 colleges, including Boston College.

Student Government

Each class (freshman, sophomore, and so forth) may have its own officers and committees. The senior class officers play an important role in planning any special events that will be held during graduation week.

One of the most important student organizations at any college is the student government. Student governments have officers and people in charge of important committees. Some have a senate or an assembly as well.

At most colleges, all the students vote for the president, vice president, treasurer, and secretary. They may also vote for other officers and committee heads. In some cases, students elect representatives from different student groups: dormitories, fraternities, sororities, commuters, and other groups. In these cases, the students within each group vote for their representative.

WHAT DOES STUDENT GOVERNMENT DO?

Distributes money to student organizations. The student government budget comes from student activity fees and fund-raising events. Student government decides how money will be spent, sometimes including how much goes to different clubs and organizations.

Sponsors special events. Student government plays an important role in a college's social and cultural life. It sponsors concerts, guest speakers, dances, festivals, barbeques, debates, and other events.

Works with faculty and administration. The student government can influence areas of the college such as academic or student policies, new programs and services, and changes to existing services. Students often serve on important college committees.

Oversees certain parts of the student code of conduct. Disputes between students are often heard by student judiciary boards. These boards may deal with other violations, including honor code violations. (Many honor codes deal with honesty, cheating, and other student behavior.)

Special Events

In addition to your ongoing activities, you can participate in special events on a regular basis. Each week brings lectures, seminars, concerts, and other events. Some are sponsored directly by the college. Many others are sponsored by student clubs and academic departments.

For example, during a typical week, you may be able to attend lectures by a politician discussing the economy and a biologist explaining climate change. You may attend a debate on health care or a symposium in which experts from many different fields discuss the media's bias in covering elections.

During the same week, a rock band may play a concert on campus, an English professor may read a collection of newly written poems, and the college's art gallery may open a special exhibit of paintings and sculptures created by students.

Meanwhile, the business club may have the head of a software company meet with its members to discuss *entrepreneurship*—starting your own company. Several of the religious organizations on campus may sponsor an interfaith dinner. The outing club may sponsor a weekend kayaking trip to a nearby state park. And some of the fraternities, sororities, and service clubs may hold a dance marathon to raise money for a homeless shelter.

Colleges publish weekly and daily calendars of all these events. These calendars are usually posted around the campus as well as on the college Web site. Be on the lookout for information about the various events, and try to fit some of them into your regular schedule.

Many colleges hold a homecoming weekend in the fall when they invite alumni back to share in special events. The weekend often includes an important football game, a big dance, picnics and dinners, and, in many cases, a parade.

Feeling Like You Belong

At some point, you might find yourself feeling somewhat lost or lonely. You may feel overwhelmed by the amount of work, the difficulty of the work, or all the choices you have. These reactions can make you feel like you chose the wrong college or don't belong in college at all.

You wouldn't be the first student to feel that way—nor would you be the last. Try to relax. Take positive steps! Remember, you're not alone.

Taking Care of Yourself

Going to class all day, studying all night, and fitting in activities and special events—not to mention taking time to make new friends or to handle a job or other responsibilities—may make you feel like you are burning the candle at both ends. Be sure you get enough sleep. Being rested will help you make more efficient use of your time. You will also lower your chances of getting sick.

Be sure to eat properly and get exercise. The healthier you are, the more easily you will be able to handle your commitments.

What If I Have Trouble with My Classes?

You are better off asking for help early and then finding you don't need it than waiting until your problems get worse. Don't be shy! Colleges offer many services because lots of students need them—not just you!

Don't waste a moment. Get some help. You have all sorts of choices open to you. They include getting a tutor, working with a study group, going to a learning lab, and improving your study skills. You can talk to your advisor, a counselor, your professors, members of the dorm staff, or even other students. But don't delay. If you tackle your obstacles the moment you run into them, you can take full control of them quickly.

Spreading Yourself Too Thin

One problem a lot of students face is taking on too many commitments. The extra activities and special events make your college experience more complete. Remember, however, that your commitment to your studies must take first priority.

But don't go in the other direction, either. Your classes will (and should) take up much of your time. But with careful planning and self-discipline, you should be able to enjoy college activities and special events as well.

Manage your time by developing weekly and daily schedules that work for you. Schedule time for your studies and your job, if you have one. Also schedule time for friends and recreation. Make necessary adjustments, but stick to your overall schedule. The same people who can help you with your classes can help you learn to manage your time.

Many colleges offer classes that help you learn to manage your time. Check with the counseling, advising, or tutoring office.

What If I Feel Lonely or Homesick?

A lot of freshmen and even sophomores have to adjust to being away from home and starting in a new place where they don't know anyone. Sometimes you are simply caught off guard. You have been so excited about starting college that it never occurred to you that you could miss home and old friends. You may be worried about what others will think and try to hide how you're feeling.

Being lonely or homesick is natural. But if it gets to you in a way that interferes with your studies or your enjoyment of college, then talk to someone. Speak to a counselor, a favorite professor, your advisor, or a minister. They can provide you with lots of tips for feeling more at home and receiving more support if you need it.

Going to college can be like going to summer camp for the first time. A lot of people feel lonely, but only until they get the hang of it!

What Can I Do to Fit In?

Remember why you picked your college in the first place. Focus on the positive. Find things that make you glad you're there—a favorite class, a place on campus where you like to spend time, an activity you enjoy.

Suppose you don't get the part you want in a play. Find other ways to be involved—building sets, helping with publicity, and so forth.

Become active. Don't be discouraged if your first choices are not available. The more you participate, the more likely you are to make new friends and feel like you are fitting in.

Look for events that bring the college together. Football and soccer games provide opportunities early in the year. Try to get involved in school spirit. Colleges have events like winter carnivals and spring festivals that involve the entire campus and will give you a sense of belonging.

And, as we've noted before, remember that you can change your mind. If you have addressed the issues discussed here and still don't feel like you belong, you can always consider opportunities at other colleges. What is important, as always, is that you recognize college as an opportunity. You are in charge of making it the best you can. If you take charge, your college experience—wherever you go—will be a rewarding one that will shape your dreams and plans for the rest of your life!

NEW YORK

Each winter brings the Big Red Freakout to Rensselaer Polytechnic Institute in New York. The Freakout is more than a hockey game in February. Thousands dress in red, or red and white paint, and bring the loudest noisemakers they can find. Through television and live webcasting, this event is shared nationwide with alumni and fans.

14

Is College My Only Choice?

Education leads to opportunity. The more education you have, the more opportunities you will open for yourself. In today's world, a lot of jobs require special skills above and beyond those that you can learn in high school. Not all careers require a college education, but they do still require training that you can get elsewhere.

For many reasons, you may not be able to go to college right after high school. You may not be interested in a career that requires you to attend college. You may choose to work before deciding whether college is right for you. You have other options. Several of them are discussed in this chapter.

Career-Technical Education

Career-technical (career-tech) education focuses on teaching you the skills you need for specific occupations. Its purpose is to prepare you for immediate employment in your chosen occupation once your studies are complete. In many cases, career-technical education leads to the licensing or certification that is required for some occupations (cosmetology or plumbing) and valuable for others (computer technology or automotive repair).

What's Different About Career-Tech Education?

Most colleges provide a broad general education as part of their program. By contrast, a career-tech program emphasizes job knowledge and practical training experience.

Some career-tech programs are based entirely on job skills. Other programs may require that you take general education classes, but the classes will still relate to job skills. For example, at a college you may need to study general writing skills in an English composition course. A secretarial school, however, may require that you take Business English instead, in which you will learn to write office reports, letters to customers, and other business correspondence.

How Long Will I Be in Training?

The amount of time required to complete a career-tech program varies considerably. A course that provides a certificate of completion could require just a few weeks or even a few hours if the training is learning a specific pro-cedure, such as testing a part on an appliance. Programs can also take as long as two years or even more for cer-tain technical and allied health professions.

Alternatives to College

Technical institutes and career schools. Also called proprietary or trade schools. Generally private, focusing on hands-on instruction in specific occupations. Programs often lead to diplomas or certificates of completion. In some cases, classes may satisfy the instructional requirements for eligibility to take certification or licensing exams.

Community and technical colleges. Offer certificate and degree programs in occupational areas. Generally public. Usually require general education courses as part of completing program. Often have noncredit coursework in many occupational areas. Courses may satisfy the eligibility requirements for licensing or certification in occupations such as food-service manager, real estate agent, day-care provider, and nursing assistant.

Apprenticeships. An organized and supervised program of direct, hands-on training, instruction, and practice. The student often works with a mentor. Prepares students for employment in specific trades and technical fields, such as plumbing, construction, carpentry, and culinary arts.

Military. Each branch of the military has many specialized areas of training, with different levels of expertise within each area. Army and Marine Corps refer to these areas as Military Occupational Specialties, or MOS. The Navy uses Navy Enlisted Ratings (NER), Navy Limited Duty Officers (LDO), and Navy Warrant Officers (WO). The Coast Guard uses Aviator, Enlisted, and Warrant. The Air Force uses Air Force Specialties (AFS). Occupational training within the military often satisfies requirements for occupations after leaving the military.

Government training programs. A variety of job training programs designed especially for disadvantaged students. Programs include Job Corps, school-to-work, training for people who are unemployed or on welfare, and regional training centers that teach a variety of occupational skills.

Business and industry programs. Offer training programs for specific skills. Range from one-hour seminars introducing specific software to long-term programs teaching telephone system installation and repair.

Sample Career Schools Across the States

State	Career School (year established)
Alabama (Birmingham)	Southeastern School of Cosmetology (1994)
Alaska (Anchorage)	Career Academy (1985)
Arizona (Chandler)	Golf Academy of America–Phoenix (1996)
Arkansas (Hot Springs)	Arkansas Career Training Institute (1961)
California (Morgan Hill)	American School of Piano Tuning (1958)
Colorado (Denver)	United States Truck Driving School (1959)
Connecticut (Stratford)	Porter and Chester Institute (1946)
Delaware (Newark)	Schilling-Douglas School of Hair Design (1977)
Florida (St. Petersburg)	SeaSchool (1977)
Georgia (Atlanta)	Montessori Institute of Atlanta (1968)
Hawaii (Honolulu)	Travel Institute of the Pacific (1974)
Idaho (Boise)	ITT Technical Institute (1906)
Illinois (Melrose Park)	Lincoln College of Technology (1946)
Indiana (Hobart)	College of Court Reporting (1984)
Iowa (Mason City)	World Wide College of Auctioneering (1933)
Kansas (Manhattan)	Manhattan Area Technical College (1965)
Kentucky (Louisville)	ATA College (1994)
Louisiana (Baton Rouge)	Baton Rouge School of Computers (1979)
Maine (Bangor)	New England School of Communications (1981)
Maryland (Baltimore)	Baltimore School of Massage (1981)
Massachusetts (Boston)	Rittners School of Floral Design (1945)
Michigan (Troy)	Carnegie Institute (1947)
Minnesota (Minneapolis)	Miami Ad School–Minneapolis (1993)
Mississippi (Jackson)	Magnolia College of Cosmetology (2001)
Missouri (Earth City)	Midwest Institute (1965)
Montana (Laurel)	Northern Skies Aviation (1994)

Source: RWM Vocational School Database

Professional umpires for Major League or Minor League Baseball attend an approved training school such as Harry Wendelstedt Umpire School or Jim Evans Academy of Professional Umpiring, which both operate in Florida and other locations around the world.

Sample Career Schools Across the States

State	Career School (year established)
Nebraska (Omaha)	The Creative Center (1993)
Nevada (Carson City)	Carson City Beauty Academy (1988)
New Hampshire (Amherst)	Granite State Dog Training Center (1996)
New Jersey (Camden)	Divers Academy International (1977)
New Mexico (Albuquerque)	Albuquerque Career Institute (1974)
New York (New York)	Lee Strasberg Theatre and Film Institute (1969)
North Carolina (Charlotte)	Carolina School of Broadcasting (1957)
North Dakota (Bismarck)	St. Alexius School of Radiologic Technology (1950)
Ohio (Cincinnati)	College of Art Advertising (1977)
Oklahoma (Purcell)	Oklahoma Horseshoeing School (1973)
Oregon (Portland)	Western States Chiropractic College (1904)
Pennsylvania (Philadelphia)	Academy of Vocal Arts (1934)
Rhode Island (Newport)	International Yacht Restoration School (1993)
South Carolina (Columbia)	South Carolina Criminal Justice Academy (1968)
South Dakota (Sioux Falls)	Southeast Technical Institute (1968)
Tennessee (Madison)	Middle Tennessee School of Anesthesia (1950)
Texas (Dallas)	Dallas Institute of Funeral Service (1900)
Utah (Salt Lake City)	Violin Making School of America (1972)
Vermont (Montpelier)	New England Culinary Institute (1980)
Virginia (Roanoke)	ECPI Technical College (1966)
Washington (Vancouver)	School of Piano Technology for the Blind (1949)
West Virginia (Bradley)	Appalachian Bible College (1950)
Wisconsin (Sun Prairie)	Diesel Truck Driver Training School (1963)
Wyoming (Lander)	National Outdoor Leadership School (1965)
District of Columbia	The National Conservatory of Dramatic Arts (1975)

Source: RWM Vocational School Database

For some careers, like computer programming, you can choose from among hundreds of career schools and colleges. But even for more unusual careers, like violin making or clock repair, you can still find places to study.

Preparing for Work

Chapter 5 describes the degrees you earn by completing a four-year program (bachelor's degree) or a two-year program (associate's degree). Many community colleges also offer certificates. At many career schools, you earn either a **diploma** or a **certificate** to indicate that you have completed the program of study. A diploma is awarded for programs that are at least a full year, but less than two years in length. Certificates are often awarded for programs a year or less in length.

What Are Licenses?

For many jobs, you need a license before you can begin work. Licenses are issued by either states or the federal government. Before you can be licensed, you must often pass an exam. States often have their own exams.

Although many exams are written, you may also need to demonstrate your skills. For example, you must pass a specialized driving test to be licensed to drive a diesel truck or a bus. In a growing number of jobs, such as school bus driver, you must pass a background check that looks not only at your skills, but also at your personal character and history.

Many people can cut your hair. But before cosmetologists can apply chemicals (such as hair dye) and cosmetics to others for hair and skin care, they need to be licensed by their state.

Jobs that require licenses include electricians, plumbers, private investigators, real estate brokers and appraisers, insurance agents, nurses, barbers, and cosmetologists. If you work with pesticides, you may need a license. Therefore, if you simply groom dogs, you may not need a license; but if you use pesticides to remove fleas, you will need a license. Similarly, exterminators and landscapers who use pesticides need licenses.

What Is Certification?

Although some fields do not require a license issued by the government, they may require **certification**—evidence that you have completed an approved program of study or passed a test demonstrating your competence in the field.

Earning a certificate is not quite the same as earning your certification to practice in your field. For example, you may complete studies in cardiovascular technology, which teaches you about the heart, how to use equipment that monitors the heart, and how to evaluate information from that equipment. You may earn a certificate of proficiency, showing that you have successfully completed your studies. You still have to take a national certification examination to become a Certified Cardiographic Technician (CCT). In short, your studies prepare you to apply for certification.

In some fields, especially medical fields, you must have certification or a license to practice. In other cases, being certified may not be required, but it can help you find better jobs with higher wages and more opportunities for advancement.

Certification can cover an entire field or specific parts of it. For example, if you are an office equipment technician, you may be certified to work on a type of equipment, such as a photocopier. Your training may be even more specific, based on a brand such as Xerox or Canon copiers, or even a specific model of copier.

You can study automotive repair at a number of career schools and community colleges. The National Institute for Automotive Service Excellence (ASE) certifies professionals—assuring consumers that an individual is competent in a specific area of automotive repair. They conduct tests twice a year, administered by ACT (which also conducts college entrance exams), in dozens of categories. If you pass, you are certified in that area for up to five years. For more information, visit *www.asecert.org*.

What Are Apprenticeship Programs?

In many ways, being an apprentice is similar to serving as an intern (see chapter 6). The main focus is on-the-job training, often supported by classroom instruction and independent opportunities to learn more about the field in which you are working. **Apprenticeship** programs often allow you to work very closely over a period of time with an experienced worker or manager who supervises and instructs you.

Some states have agencies that oversee apprenticeship programs. Although many excellent programs are not registered with the state agencies, you can expect that registered programs will meet certain minimum standards. In addition, many large corporations have their own apprenticeship programs.

Apprenticeship programs are especially important in fields where your studies are not enough—where you need to have lots of hands-on experience. You will often see apprenticeships in applied trades. For example, if you want to become an electrician, plumber, carpenter, or welder, an apprenticeship would be extremely valuable and, at times, required.

Many trade and technical schools can help you find an apprenticeship program. Apprenticeships are often run by individual employers, trade associations, or labor groups. The armed services and government agencies, especially the Department of Labor, either have apprenticeship programs or can help you find them. In some cases, completing an apprenticeship program can lead you to earning a license or certification to work in your chosen field.

The Employment and Training Administration (ETA), a branch of the U.S. Department of Labor, coordinates job programs and provides information about career opportunities. In addition, the Office of Apprenticeship supervises apprenticeship programs nationally. To learn more, visit the following Web sites:

www.doleta.gov

http://oa.doleta.gov

The Wide Range of Opportunities

Depending on your field of interest, you have lots of choices. For fields that require more theory and less hands-on training, you should consider pursuing a degree at a two-year or four-year college. But for many technical fields, you will be able to choose between career schools and community colleges.

Regardless of your path, completing a program of study and being licensed or certified in your field opens up many job opportunities, including the opportunity to be self-employed. For example, you can study to be an electrician through a community college, a career school, or an apprenticeship program. Eventually, after you have earned a license from the state, you have more choices. You can work for a larger electrical contractor. You can work as an in-house electrician for a company; a school district; a utility company; or a state, county, or local government. Or you could be self-employed, finding your own clients and even hiring other electricians to work for you.

You may not be required to have any formal training to start up your own company, but the training will help. For example, you don't need specific education to open your own restaurant. However, you need to know how to meet regulations for the health and safety of your workers and customers, as well as regulations involving electrical work, plumbing, and fire codes. You need to know how to interview and hire employees, maintain financial records, pay bills, order supplies, and promote your restaurant, as well as hundreds of other details. To gain this knowledge, you can take courses to study how to be a restaurant manager.

Choosing a Program

If you have decided that some sort of occupational program is the right choice for you, you have many important steps to take. Start by asking: "Do I know which occupation I want to enter?" If you have a clear idea, you will have an easier time finding a school or program that is right for you.

Suppose you know you want to work specifically in radio. You can look for programs that can train you to be a broadcast technician, a radio announcer, or some other position in radio. You may find an apprenticeship program—maybe even with a radio station—that teaches you the big picture of how a radio station operates and also trains you for a specific career in radio.

On the other hand, you may know you want to work in broadcasting, but do not know the specific field, such as radio or television. In this case, you want a program that offers more choices and flexibility, allowing you to try out various areas before making a commitment. A school of broadcasting might be the better choice for you.

What If I'm Not Sure What to Study?

The way you explore jobs and careers that interest you is the same whether you plan to go to a college or a career school. See the discussion in chapter 2 about exploring careers.

You may not even know what interests you, except that you want to pursue a career-tech program. In this case, a technical or community college that offers a broad range of programs as well as general education courses may be best for you. You will be able to keep your options open while you take courses that will help you decide. If you think that you may want to continue your education after you have started your career, you will want to select a program that allows you to apply your courses toward a college degree.

How Do I Find Out More?

Begin by talking with your school guidance counselor about your options. The counselor can give you a variety of standard tests and surveys that will help you determine your likes and dislikes, and how they match specific types of careers.

Looking for a career school is very similar to looking for a college. A lot of guidebooks are available that list thousands of different schools or focus on specific fields. The reference librarian can help you find many of these print materials.

The Internet, employment organizations, and some of the resources through the Department of Labor can also help. CareerOneStop (*www.careerOneStop.org*) is a national resource for jobseekers and businesses. CareerInfoNet (*www.acinet.org*) has information about job trends, wages, training requirements, state profiles, and more. America's Service Locator (*www.servicelocator.org*) can help you find the One-Stop Career Center closest to you.

Don't forget to talk to people who work in your field of interest. For example, if you would like to be a plumber, speak to some of the licensed plumbing contractors in your area. Ask them how they learned their trade. Also contact the agency that licenses plumbers in your state and ask about training.

Many high schools have counselors and teachers with special knowledge about career-technical opportunities. The career center and career counselors at your local community college may also be able to help you.

If you know of a company for which you would like to work, contact its human resources or personnel department and ask for advice about the training and education you would need.

Many libraries carry *National Trade and Professional Associations of the United States,* a guide to organizations that represent companies and individuals who work in specific fields. Check with the reference librarian at your school or public library.

Accreditation

Chapter 7 describes organizations that accredit colleges, providing a formal assurance that either the college or one of its departments has met a set of standards. Career schools also have accrediting organizations.

In addition to checking a school's accreditation, try to talk to graduates of the school to learn more about their experiences.

Some organizations, such as the American Dental Association or the Society of American Foresters, represent specific professions. Still others represent specific populations, such as visually handicapped students. In some cases, the groups focus on the type of programs or instruction. The Distance Education and Training Council Accrediting Commission is one example.

Find out whether a school's accreditation is recognized by the U.S. Department of Education. This recognition determines a school's qualification for awarding financial aid to students.

EXAMPLES OF ACCREDITING ORGANIZATIONS FOR CAREER SCHOOLS

Accrediting Bureau of Health Education Schools

Accrediting Council for Independent Colleges and Schools

Accrediting Commission of Career Schools and Colleges

Accrediting Council for Continuing Education and Training

American Board of Funeral Service Education

American Council for Construction Education

American Culinary Federation

American Occupational Therapy Association

Association for Biblical Higher Education

Commission on Accreditation of Allied Health Education Programs

Committee on Accreditation for Respiratory Care

Distance Education and Training Council

National Accrediting Agency for Clinical Laboratory Sciences

Career School Costs

College costs vary a lot. So do the costs of career schools. These costs vary because of the wide range of programs offered by different schools.

Some career schools charge a flat tuition for the programs they offer, similar to an annual charge or per-term charge at a university. At other schools, the tuition varies because the number of hours needed to complete a program varies. Whether a career school is public or private can also affect its charges.

Most career schools do not offer housing. Therefore, when you estimate your costs, you will have to factor in living costs. You also need to find out whether books, supplies, and any special equipment are included. For example, if you take a weeklong real estate course, books or other handouts may be included in the tuition. If you attend barbering school, you need to find out whether shears and other equipment are included.

Some programs require you to attend on a full-time basis; you may not be able to work while you go to school. Other programs easily fit into your work schedule. In some cases, your employer may even pay your costs of attending school.

Many career schools have financial aid plans. You may qualify for low-interest loans to help pay your tuition. Some schools are able to offer government-sponsored aid.

Some career schools are eligible to award grants and loans from the federal government. Also, the American Opportunity and the Lifetime Learning tax credits can be taken for many career schools. See chapter 11 for more information about ways to pay.

Some real estate programs or other individual courses may require as little as eight hours of classroom time to learn a basic introduction, with a tuition as low as $125 or even less. Other programs in technology and applied trades can take over two years with tuition of more than $10,000 per year.

Other Considerations

When you consider attending a career school, you should ask as many questions as you would when considering a college. The following is a list of some of the most important questions.

CAREER SCHOOL CONSIDERATIONS

- When was the school established?
- Are the founders still involved with the school?
- If the founders are still involved, what is their background?
- Is the school accredited?
- How many students attend the school?
- How many students are enrolled in the program in which you are interested?
- How are courses taught—how much is classroom time vs. hands-on experience?
- Are apprenticeship programs available?
- What are the admissions requirements?
- Are there additional requirements for enrolling in certain programs?
- If the school offers more than one program, can you make a change?
- What credentials do students receive upon completing the program, such as certificate, diploma, degree, or other?
- For fields where you need a license or certification to practice, does the instructional program satisfy the requirements?
- What training do the teachers have?
- How much are the tuition costs and fees?
- Are there additional costs? If so, what are they?
- Is financial aid available?
- What is the refund policy?
- What is the graduation rate for the program?
- What is the success rate of graduates who take exams to earn licensing and certification?
- Does the school have a job-placement service?
- What is the placement rate for the school?
- How successful is the school in helping students find a position in their chosen occupations?
- Where have students been employed and what has been their average salary?
- What other services does the school offer?

15

What Should
I Do Now?

You should plan for your future! Whatever age you are and whatever grade you're in, now is a great time to start looking ahead.

Everything we have discussed in this book up to now boils down to a few basic points: Know who you are, develop your skills, make your decisions with care, and follow your heart.

College may or may not be the best path for you. But you can always learn more. And you have the opportunity to learn who you are and to make decisions about your future—decisions that will help you achieve your goals!

Take a Picture of Yourself

In chapter 8, we looked at steps that you can take to know yourself better when you're ready to apply to college. These steps will help you when you are trying to find colleges that are the best fit for you.

By the time you are a junior or senior in high school, you will have created much of the record that affects where you will be accepted to college. But in the school years before—while you are in middle school as well as your freshman and sophomore years of high school—you still have time to make changes that will shape your record.

Start now to get to know yourself better. Gather good information and get a clear picture of yourself. One of the most important things you can do is become aware of what interests you. You don't need to set long-term goals yet, but you can start exploring them and thinking about ways to make your dreams come true.

If there are subjects that come naturally to you and that you like, challenge yourself to go further with them. If other subjects are harder, learn why you are having trouble with them. Talk to your parents, teachers, and guidance counselors.

Look at your abilities now. Ask where they should be if you are going to accomplish your goals. For example, if you want to be a journalist, you need strong writing skills. If you don't have them now, you will need to work to improve them.

You have the time now to make these changes. And because you have that time, more doors of opportunity are still open to you!

Explore Your Options

In chapters 2 and 14, we discussed career opportunities. We looked at some of the steps you can take to explore specific careers. And you can take many of these steps at any time, beginning today!

Learning about careers can help you in several ways. You can make choices that will improve your opportunities later. For example, if you are interested in being a veterinarian, you can choose courses in high school that will help you get into colleges with good preveterinary programs. You can also use school projects and work to prepare yourself further. For instance, you could get a job at a veterinarian's office, a farm, a pet store, or even a kennel—something that will enable you to work with animals.

Another advantage of exploring careers early is that you may be able to rule some out. In this same example, you might discover—through the courses that you take or jobs you have—that you really are not interested in being a veterinarian. If so, it's better for you to learn this early instead of finding out after you have started college.

In high school, Marcus Bryant knew he wanted to become a computer scientist. He took challenging courses and participated in a mentoring program. His guidance counselor told him about the local community college's honors program, which he chose over many other schools. When it was time to transfer, Marcus had many offers, all with scholarships. He chose to attend The Johns Hopkins University to earn a B.S. in Computer Science. Marcus has now earned a master's degree.

Find Role Models and Mentors

Some people cannot even imagine that they will ever go to college. Perhaps no one in your family has gone or you feel that you are not a strong enough student to go to college. Perhaps concerns about money stop you from thinking about college.

How Can Role Models Help?

We often pick athletes or celebrities as role models. But the best role models are often relatives, teachers, coaches, police officers, clergy, doctors, and others close to our daily lives.

Finding a role model is a great way for you to overcome your concerns about your future. Even if you know that you are headed to college, a role model can help you. A **role model** is someone whom you admire and who has been successful in ways that you too would like to be successful.

The best role models are people with backgrounds similar to yours who can inspire you to go after your dreams. They can share with you what they did to achieve their goals and to overcome any mistakes they made or any obstacles in their way. They can give you ideas about steps that you should now be taking.

ASPIRA is a national organization devoted to educating Latino youth and to developing their leadship skills. Its name comes from the Spanish verb *aspirar*, which means to aspire, or to hope. ASPIRA has community-based offices in eight states— Connecticut, Delaware, Florida, Illinois, Massachusetts, New Jersey, New York, and Pennsylvania—and Puerto Rico. Its staff members work with over 85,000 youths and their families every year. ASPIRA provides leadership training, career and college counseling and support, cultural activities, and opportunities to coordinate special projects in the community. To learn more, visit *www.aspira.org*.

What Are Mentors?

Mentors are similar to role models. A role model may be someone you know; but often he or she is someone you admire from far away. A mentor, however, is someone who works side-by-side with you.

In some cases, mentors can help you learn about a particular career. They may be able to answer your questions about the career, let you spend time with them on the job, or help you with courses that will prepare you for that career. They can help introduce you to others whose work is closer to your interests. In other cases, mentors help you in the same way that advisors or counselors do. Instead of guiding you toward a specific path or career, they help you get a clear picture of yourself.

Many schools, as well as after-school and summer programs, work with local colleges to put you in contact with current college students and alumni. Business, community, and religious organizations also have mentoring programs. Ask your guidance counselor, teachers, or youth group leader to learn more.

A good place to find out about support programs for kids is America's Promise Alliance, founded by General Colin Powell. The Web address is *www.americaspromise.org*.

Your town's chamber of commerce is made up of local businesses and professionals who care about their community. Similar groups include the Jaycees, Rotary Club, and Kiwanis. Many of their members are willing to be mentors.

The organization Big Brothers Big Sisters (BBBS) is one of the nation's oldest and largest youth mentoring organizations. It serves young people ages 5 to 18 years old in more than 5,000 communities. You can find a BBBS near you at *www.bbbsa. org*.

Check Your Study Habits and Skills

Now is the time to take a close look at your study habits and skills. Evaluate what you do well and where an improvement could make a difference.

Study Habits

Start with your study habits, asking: When? How? What? Where?

Believe it or not, sometimes you can study too hard. If you study long hours, be sure you take study breaks. Get up, stretch, walk around; take a few moments now and then to refresh yourself.

When do you study? Do you study when you first come home from school, late at night, early in the morning, or on weekends? When do you complete your homework: when it is first assigned, or at the last minute? When do you start working on big projects?

How do you organize your work? How do you keep track of homework assignments? Do you write them down in an easy-to-find place? How do you organize school papers and class notes? Are the subjects all jumbled together, or is each organized?

What do you need to study? Do you have the books and supplies you need? How about access to technology and equipment? Do you play music or the television while studying, or do you need a quiet place?

Where do you study? Do you study in your room, at the library, or somewhere else? Do you work at a desk, on your bed, on the floor, or elsewhere? Have you ever experimented with different surroundings?

No single study method works best for everyone. If you know your habits, you can figure out what works best for you and what doesn't work at all. You can experiment with different ways of studying. What works for others may not work for you. And what works for you in some subjects may not work for you in others.

Study Skills

Studying hard is not quite the same as studying wisely. For example, you might be in the habit of taking notes during class. But your note-taking skills may need work. Your notes might be unclear and hard to follow. They might be so sketchy that they don't help you when you review for a test. Or they might be so detailed that you use lots of time that could be spent elsewhere. Then when you review for a test you need to wade through everything rather than just the key points.

Perhaps you have excellent study habits but weak study skills. For a while, your habits may lead to good results in school. But as your subjects get more difficult, or as you tackle new subjects, you need to strengthen your skills. Even if you already have good skills, you should always look for ways to improve them.

Your school counselor and teachers can help you figure out which areas need the most work. If you look at yourself honestly, you too will be able to figure out the skills that need your attention. For example, you might do well remembering what your teachers have said in class, but struggle to remember anything you read in a textbook. In this case, you might need help learning how to get the information you need out of a book.

You may do well on essay tests and short-answer tests, but struggle with multiple-choice tests. In this case, you would want special help that focuses on multiple-choice tests.

In addition to getting help from people at your school, you may want to take special courses that focus on study skills. Tutors can often give you one-on-one attention that is very helpful.

Many community and religious groups provide tutoring services for students who might not otherwise have access to such help.

You may find companies that specialize in study skills. CDs, DVDs, Web sites, television, software programs, and all sorts of guides and books can also help you build your study and test-taking skills.

IMPORTANT STUDY SKILLS

Listening. How closely do you pay attention when your teacher or classmates are speaking? Do you jump to conclusions before they are done? How well do you remember what was said?

Vocabulary. Do you understand most of the words you read? Do you keep a dictionary and thesaurus nearby? (How often do you use them?!) Do you try to figure out what words mean before looking up their definition? How often do you practice using new words?

Reading speed and comprehension. How long do you need to read your assignments? Do you need the same amount of time for fiction as you do for facts? Do you understand most of what you read? When you read, do you skim the material first, then go back and read it more closely? Do you answer sample problems and review questions?

Memory. How well do you remember what you have heard or read? How long are you able to remember material? What methods do you use to help you remember?

Writing. Does writing come easily to you? Are there types of writing that you prefer (essays, stories, poems, reports, and so forth)? Are you organized when you work on a report? Do you know how to outline a report? Are you able to summarize your thoughts clearly?

Note-taking. Do you take very detailed notes? Do you have a way of highlighting important information? Do you rewrite your notes? How often do you review them? Are they helpful when you study for a test?

Test-taking. Do certain types of tests (essay, short answer, matching, and so forth) come more easily to you than other types? Do you wait until the last minute to start studying for tests? Do you run out of time when you take tests? How do you prepare for tests?

Using study tools. How well do you know how to use the library? How comfortable are you with a dictionary, thesaurus, or other reference resources? How are your skills with computers, calculators, CDs, DVDs, and software applications? How are your technology skills, such as word processing or working with databases, charts, tables, and graphs? Do you know how to use the Internet properly to research information?

Read, Read, Read!

Make reading a lifelong habit. Read to relax, read to learn, read to have fun. Try to read as much as possible between now and the time you go to college. Even if you are a senior who has already been accepted to college, you should continue to read as much as you can.

Be an active reader, not a passive one. Read to build your vocabulary. Read to learn information. Read to understand new ideas and complicated theories. Being a good reader is like being a good athlete or a good musician. All take practice and then more practice.

What If Reading Is Hard?

If you have a reading problem, deal with it right away! Maybe you missed out on certain skills and have simply fallen behind. Or you may have a learning disability, like dyslexia, which could possibly be overcome with special teaching. Don't be shy or embarrassed. You are not alone. Speak to your parents, teacher, or counselor. Get the support you need. You'll be amazed at how quickly you can tackle most problems. Once you do, the world opens up in ways you cannot imagine!

Schools and colleges often put together reading lists for students. Many books on these lists are classics—they've stood the test of time and deal with important themes that tell us about ourselves. Some are simply great stories that also provide the opportunity to practice reading and build vocabulary.

The books listed on the next pages frequently appear on reading lists. Many are fiction. You may want to read more poetry and drama, as well as history, biography, and other nonfiction. The important thing is to read some of these books, but also to read the news, magazines, other books, and other sources simply for pleasure.

Your teacher or librarian can add more recent books to this list, including ones that tell stories that address your personal interests. Also, the admissions office or college English departments may be able to suggest other ideas.

291

Read, Read, Read…

Author	Title
James Agee	*A Death in the Family*
Louisa May Alcott	*Little Women**
Maya Angelou	*I Know Why the Caged Bird Sings*
Anonymous	*Beowulf*
Jean Anouilh	*Becket*
Jane Austen	*Pride and Prejudice*
Jim Bishop	*The Day Lincoln Was Shot**
Ray Bradbury	*The Martian Chronicles**
Charlotte Brontë	*Jane Eyre*
Emily Brontë	*Wuthering Heights*
Dee Brown	*Bury My Heart at Wounded Knee*
Pearl Buck	*The Good Earth**
John Bunyan	*Pilgrim's Progress*
Albert Camus	*The Stranger*
Lewis Carroll	*Alice's Adventures in Wonderland**
Rachel Carson	*Silent Spring*
Willa Cather	*My Antonia**
Miguel de Cervantes	*Don Quixote*
Geoffrey Chaucer	*The Canterbury Tales*
Joseph Conrad	*Lord Jim*
James Fenimore Cooper	*The Last of the Mohicans*
Stephen Crane	*The Red Badge of Courage*
Daniel Defoe	*Robinson Crusoe*
Charles Dickens	*Great Expectations* *A Tale of Two Cities*
Fyodor Dostoyevsky	*The Brothers Karamazov*
Sir Arthur Conan Doyle	*The Hound of the Baskervilles*
Alexandre Dumas	*The Count of Monte Cristo*
Daphne DuMaurier	*Rebecca*
George Eliot	*Silas Marner**

*Appropriate for young adult readers

Read, Read, Read...

Author	Title
Ralph Ellison	*Invisible Man*
Euripides	*Medea*
William Faulkner	*As I Lay Dying*
Henry Fielding	*Tom Jones*
F. Scott Fitzgerald	*The Great Gatsby*
Gustave Flaubert	*Madame Bovary*
Esther Forbes	*Johnny Tremain**
Anne Frank	*Diary of a Young Girl**
Benjamin Franklin	*Autobiography of Benjamin Franklin*
Robert Frost	*Complete Poems*
Hamlin Garland	*Main-Traveled Roads*
Johann Wolfgang von Goethe	*Faust*
William Golding	*Lord of the Flies*
Alex Haley	*Roots*
Edith Hamilton	*Mythology*
Dashiell Hammett	*The Maltese Falcon*
Thomas Hardy	*The Mayor of Casterbridge*
Bret Harte	"The Outcasts of Poker Flat"
Stephen Hawking	*A Brief History of Time*
Nathaniel Hawthorne	*The Scarlet Letter*
Ernest Hemingway	*For Whom the Bell Tolls*
John Hersey	*Hiroshima*
Thor Heyerdahl	*Kon-Tiki*
S.E. Hinton	*The Outsiders**
Homer	*The Iliad* *The Odyssey*
Victor Hugo	*Les Misérables*
Aldous Huxley	*Brave New World*
Henrik Ibsen	*A Doll's House*
Washington Irving	*The Sketch Book**

*Appropriate for young adult readers

Read, Read, Read...

Author	Title
Franz Kafka	*The Metamorphosis*
MacKinlay Kantor	*Andersonville*
Helen Keller	*The Story of My Life**
Thomas Keneally	*Schindler's List*
Ken Kesey	*One Flew Over the Cuckoo's Nest*
Rudyard Kipling	*Kim**
Harper Lee	*To Kill a Mockingbird*
Madeleine L'Engle	*A Wrinkle in Time**
Gaston LeRoux	*The Phantom of the Opera*
Jack London	*The Call of the Wild*
Henry Wadsworth Longfellow	*The Song of Hiawatha*
Bernard Malamud	*The Natural*
Gabriel García Márquez	*One Hundred Years of Solitude*
Carson McCullers	*The Member of the Wedding**
Herman Melville	*Moby-Dick*
Arthur Miller	*Death of a Salesman*
Molière	*Le Tartuffe*
Toni Morrison	*Beloved*
John O'Hara	*Appointment in Samarra*
Eugene O'Neill	*Long Day's Journey Into Night*
George Orwell	*Animal Farm*
Baroness Orczy	*The Scarlet Pimpernel*
Edgar Allan Poe	*Tales* ("The Cask of Amontillado")
Chaim Potok	*The Chosen**
Erich Maria Remarque	*All Quiet on the Western Front*
J.K. Rowling	*Harry Potter and the Sorcerer's Stone**
J.D. Salinger	*The Catcher in the Rye*
Sir Walter Scott	*Ivanhoe*
Maurice Sendak	*Where the Wild Things Are**
Anna Sewell	*Black Beauty**

*Appropriate for young adult readers

Read, Read, Read...

Author	Title
William Shakespeare	*Macbeth* *A Midsummer Night's Dream*
George Bernard Shaw	*Pygmalion*
Mary Shelley	*Frankenstein*
Aleksandr Solzhenitsyn	*One Day in the Life of Ivan Denisovich*
Sophocles	*Oedipus the King*
John Steinbeck	*The Grapes of Wrath*
Robert Louis Stevenson	*Kidnapped!**
Bram Stoker	*Dracula*
Harriet Beecher Stowe	*Uncle Tom's Cabin*
William Strunk Jr. and E.B. White	*The Elements of Style*
Jonathan Swift	*Gulliver's Travels*
Henry David Thoreau	*Walden*
J.R.R. Tolkien	*The Hobbit*
Leo Tolstoy	*Anna Karenina*
Mark Twain	*The Adventures of Huckleberry Finn*
Various	*The Bible**
Jules Verne	*Journey to the Center of the Earth*
Booker T. Washington	*Up From Slavery*
James Watson	*The Double Helix*
H.G. Wells	*The Time Machine*
Edith Wharton	*The Age of Innocence*
E.B. White	*Charlotte's Web**
Walt Whitman	*Leaves of Grass*
Oscar Wilde	*The Importance of Being Earnest*
Thornton Wilder	*Our Town*
Tennessee Williams	*The Glass Menagerie*
August Wilson	*Fences*
C. Vann Woodward	*The Strange Career of Jim Crow*
Richard Wright	*Native Son*

Appropriate for young adult readers

Computer Skills

An important part of being fully prepared for college is having good technology skills. You should know how to operate a computer and develop the skills that will enable you to use different types of software. You should also know how to access and navigate the Internet and organize your favorite sites.

Even if you don't have your own computer, you may be able to use one at your school or public library. Also, as people upgrade their computers, they are often willing to sell, or even give away, their old computers.

Personal computers are an essential part of your toolkit. They are far more important than the portable typewriters that students relied on a generation ago. What hasn't changed is the need for typing, or keyboarding, skills. You need to know how to type on a keyboard without looking at your fingers. You must also develop the skills needed for basic tasks such as saving your work, managing your files, installing software, and protecting both your computer and your files from viruses. Having these skills will save you more time than you can imagine—and open up job opportunities as well!

You should learn at least one basic word-processing program. You can use this kind of program to type and edit papers. It has features that help you create tables, charts, and graphics. Also learn how to use spreadsheet, database, and graphics programs. Spreadsheets help with calculations. Databases help you organize lots of information. Your address book is essentially a database. Graphics programs are great for creating and editing illustrations, photos, and charts. If you need help developing your skills, talk to your teachers or school counselors, librarian, mentor, or youth group leader.

A lot of information is available on the Internet—some of it is reliable, and some is not. Learning to tell good sources from bad ones is an important Internet skill. Even though Internet sources can be quite helpful, it is important that you still complete your own assignments.

Know how to access the Internet and to use e-mail properly, safely, and ethically. Protect your privacy. Learn how to use search engines such as Yahoo! and Google. Practice researching information. You may even find Web sites that can help you when you are having difficulty with your homework!

Consider Your Courses Before College

Choices you make about middle and high school courses can influence where you are accepted to college. As you prepare for high school, you will learn about what you need to study to receive a high school diploma. What you need to graduate from high school may be less than what you need for the more competitive colleges. For example, you may need three years of general science to graduate. But a college may specifically require that you study biology and chemistry in high school.

Many high schools offer different programs, or tracks. For example, a college program is for those preparing to go to college. (As discussed in chapter 9, there are different levels of courses, such as honors and AP.) A vocational track is for students heading to careers in areas such as plumbing, auto repair, and medical assistance. Some schools have special tracks for high-technology fields such as computer or science technology. Your school may also have a business track for office skills. General education tracks do not provide specific college or career preparation.

Some high schools, often called *magnet schools* or *academies*, focus on special areas such as the arts, the sciences, technology, or communications. Some schools have articulation agreements with nearby colleges, enabling you to earn high school and college credit at the same time. These programs may be called dual or concurrent admissions programs.

If you are not in a college track, you can still go to college, but your initial choices may be limited. Know your options before signing up for ninth-grade classes. Talk to a school counselor about your best plan of action. Parents, teachers, and mentors can also help.

If you are taught at home, learn how your home-schooling may affect college admission. Contact colleges that interest you for more information. Essays, college entrance exams, and interviews are likely to be more important. Your school district may have a home-schooling coordinator who can help.

What Other Choices Will I Have in High School?

Not all of your high school courses are required. Just as in college, you can choose some electives. Colleges will be interested to see which electives you choose. Some are every bit as challenging as your required classes. Others challenge you less, but let you develop long-term skills (computer keyboarding) or express yourself creatively (choir and art). Try to get a sense of what mix of courses is of most interest to the colleges where you might be applying.

Consider computers and foreign languages. Colleges do not expect incoming students to be computer scientists. But colleges do expect students to be *computer literate* (at ease with computer basics).

The International Baccalaureate Program (IB) is a two-year diploma program offered at some high schools. It allows you to study college-level coursework during your junior and senior years. For more information, visit the International Baccalaureate Organization Web site: www.ibo.org.

As our world becomes increasingly small, the ability to communicate in another language grows in importance. Many colleges prefer students who study a foreign language in middle and high school. In fact, many require you to show a certain level of skill in a foreign language.

Should I Graduate Early from High School?

At some high schools, you can graduate in three years rather than four by completing more courses each year. This option gives you a jump start on college. However, you sacrifice many of the extracurricular activities that high school offers and that help you round out your background. (You also lose a year of saving for college.) You do need to consider whether you're ready socially and emotionally to take on the greater demands beyond high school. One option to explore is whether your high school offers a concurrent enrollment program that allows you to take some college courses for credit at the same time that you continue with your high school studies.

What Are Gifted and Talented Programs?

Many school districts have special programs for their strongest students. These programs start as early as elementary school. They often give students the chance to work at a higher level and, in many cases, to keep moving ahead at their own pace. If you find that certain subjects come very easily to you and that you are receiving the highest grades with little effort, you may want to talk to your parents, teachers, and school counselor about being evaluated for gifted and talented courses.

The Johns Hopkins University in Maryland sponsors the Center for Talented Youth (CTY), which provides opportunities every year for thousands of younger students throughout the world. Visit the Center's Web site at http://cty.jhu.edu.

Do Colleges Offer Special Programs for Kids?

Many do. Lots of colleges have special programs for juniors and seniors. And many colleges now offer programs for freshmen and sophomores, as well as for elementary and middle school students. To find out more, contact admissions offices; college Web sites; and other print, software, and Internet guides such as CollegeView (*www.collegeview.com*). In particular, look for programs at nearby community colleges. They are committed to serving their community, and often have many interesting and affordable summer opportunities.

Michigan's Lansing Community College (LCC) offers summer sports camps for kids as young as fourth grade. High school juniors and seniors can participate in the dual-enrollment program, taking college courses at LCC while finishing high school requirements. Freshmen and sophomores can apply for the special admissions program, which allows them to take college courses. The Saturday School program reaches gifted and talented students in both elementary and middle schools, providing multiweek courses in arts, science, math, and geography.

MICHIGAN

Participate in Activities

How do you spend time when you are not in class? If you are someone who comes home and spends hours just watching television, playing computer games, or social networking, now is the time to change your habits.

Hobbies and Organizations

You can choose all sorts of ways to spend your extra hours productively. Many activities are available through your school. You can participate in the band, try out for the cheerleading squad, write articles for the school newspaper, take photos for the school yearbook, or develop an exhibit with other science club members for a science fair.

Many of these same activities are also available in your community: playing soccer in a neighborhood league, acting in a play or helping out backstage with your local community theater, taking dance classes and being part of a dance recital, or joining a book club that meets regularly to discuss books.

You can also become active with groups such as Boy Scouts of America, Camp Fire USA, or a youth group at your place of worship. A lot of these groups combine social activities with volunteer work, leadership activities, and career development.

For example, the Girl Scouts of the USA have a wide range of activities—everything from athletics to zoology. During the course of a year, you may have the opportunity to learn to canoe, go to a zoo, tour a nearby factory, practice arts and crafts, visit a college, plan a fundraiser, and explore careers. You may have the chance to work with a mentor while being a mentor yourself to someone younger.

Community Service and Volunteering

Another way to be active is through volunteer work. When you are old enough, you can help out at the local hospital, publicize a rally for a political candidate, serve meals at a community shelter, or work with your town's chamber of commerce to promote special projects around town.

The public library may need volunteers to help stack books on shelves. The local firefighters may want volunteers to help around the station. You might participate in a walk or run to raise money for charities. You may work behind the scenes for the Special Olympics. Volunteering gives you a chance to learn skills, have fun, and feel great about yourself.

Many service organizations in your community sponsor special activities for students. For example, your local Kiwanis organization may sponsor a Kiwanis Builders Club at your school.

Work

In addition, you can get a job. Babysitting, delivering papers, shoveling snow, and, when you are older, working for a restaurant, department store, landscaping service, or office all provide valuable experience as well as money that you can put toward college.

Other Experiences

Traveling provides another great learning experience. Going to camp gives you a chance to develop skills and hobbies and to make new friends from other places. You may even have the chance to become a camp counselor.

Any and all of these activities will improve your chances for getting into the college you want. (But you must always be sure that they don't interfere with your studies.) They help you develop interests and skills that carry over into other parts of your life. But the best reason of all for participating in these activities is not to help you get into college. It's simply because they enrich your life and the lives of others.

Prepare for College Costs

One of the things that you can do at any time is start saving for college. Even if you get a lot of financial aid when you get to college, you will still need money to pay for day-to-day expenses or for major purchases such as a computer. As we noted earlier, if you decide not to go to college, you still will have saved money that can help you in other ways.

Suppose you are 10 years old and start saving $5 per week in a savings account. You could have over $2,000 by the time you turn 18. While that may not pay your tuition, it will help a lot with books and supplies.

One of the other things you can do now is to start looking into the types of scholarships and grants that are available. When you are in the process of applying to colleges, your life can be hectic. You may not have time then to look into scholarships. Spending time now will give you a better chance of finding some of the more unusual scholarships and grants that often go unused each year because no one applies for them.

You can also develop contacts with local organizations that award money to students from your area. Suppose a service club gives out a couple of grants each year. If you have worked with that club over several years as a volunteer, the members will know who you are. You may then have an advantage for receiving the grant.

In short, the sooner you start to learn, save, budget, and plan for college costs, the more prepared you will be.

Develop a Plan

Between now and the time you go to college, you will be working with a lot of information. You will be gathering information about colleges and career opportunities, sources of financial aid, and the different college entrance exams. You'll be building a record, not only of grades, but also of books you've read, your activities, places you've visited, volunteer work, and paid work. You will be thinking about and evaluating your goals and your preferences. And you will also want to set financial goals to help pay for college.

You can choose all sorts of ways to stay on top of this information. What is important is that you develop an overall plan. Having a plan doesn't mean having a strict program or schedule that you must follow at all times. *It does mean that you are an active participant in your own future.* Choices that you make have consequences, for better or for worse.

Few people achieve their goals by luck alone. Some people may seem lucky; but in almost all cases their success is built on self-discipline and a lot of effort.

Making a chart may be the best way to develop your plan. Create a checklist of what you want to accomplish each year—colleges to visit, how much to save, classes to take, habits to develop, skills to learn, activities in which to participate, information to gather, tests to take, and so forth. Good choices help you keep doors open. Having a plan tailored to your needs and goals is the best way to stay in charge of your future!

Mapping Your Future is a free Web site that helps students plan for college, careers, financial aid, and more, starting with middle school. You can visit its Web site at http://mappingyourfuture.org.

Many other organizations have free or low-cost resources to help you and your parents develop your plan.

The Road Ahead

We began this book by telling you that college is a bridge to the future—your future! We hope we've been successful in answering many of your basic questions about college and helping you identify where you can go to learn more about the opportunities ahead of you.

The road ahead of you is an exciting one! As you travel it, we want to end our portion of your trip with three overall thoughts:

1. If you truly want to go to college, you *can* go and you *will* go. Do not let anyone tell you that you cannot go to college, no matter what reason they give you.

2. Do not let your financial resources stop you from thinking about college or applying. *First get accepted*; then find a way to pay for it.

3. The journey is as important as the destination. *How you get there*—what you learn, the skills you develop, the experiences you encounter, and the friends you make—*matters*. We wish you well.

Glossary

4-1-4—college calendar made up of a four-month term followed by one month of separate study and another four-month term.

4-4-1—college calendar made up of two four-month terms followed by one month of separate study.

529 plans—state plans that provide an opportunity for families to earn tax benefits while saving for tuition.

academies—high school programs for qualified students interested in specialized studies, such as performing arts, engineering, or technology; may exist within a high school or in a separate school; see *magnet schools*.

accreditation—proof that a college or program meets educational standards established by the government or a professional organization.

ACT—American College Testing; college entrance exam that tests students' skills in English, mathematics, reading, and science reasoning; also, career-related tests.

administration—the group of people who run a college; group often includes the president, vice presidents, deans, and directors.

admissions office—the college office that provides information and assistance to students interested in applying to the college; also the office that determines who will be accepted; also known as enrollment services or entry services.

Advanced Placement courses—special high school courses taught at a college level; see *AP exams*.

Advanced Placement exams—see *AP exams*.

advisor—also adviser; specially trained staff member, teacher, or counselor who is assigned to help students with academic planning and success; students meet with their advisors at least once each term to prepare for the next term and for other reasons.

affiliation—the relationship a college has with a particular group or organization, for example, with a religious denomination.

affiliation-based aid—money for education that goes to students who belong to a certain group or meet criteria such as race, religion, and gender.

alumni—the graduates of a college or any other educational institution; an individual graduate is called an alumnus (male) or alumna (female).

American Opportunity Credit—a federal tax credit program that reduces the amount students or their parents pay in taxes when income or savings are used for tuition; see *tax credit*.

AP exams—standardized tests given nationally to students who have completed Advanced Placement or other high school courses taught at the college level.

application fee—the fee most colleges charge to process a student's application form.

apprenticeship—an organized and supervised program of hands-on training, instruction, and practice that prepares students to work in specific career and trade fields, such as plumbing and electricity.

articulation agreement—a special agreement between colleges and schools that defines how students transfer from one college or school to the other.

assessment—a test or evaluation.

associate's degree—degree given for completion of a two-year program; generally awarded by community colleges.

bachelor's degree—degree given in most cases for completion of a four-year program. Common abbreviations include B.A. (for bachelor of arts) and B.S. (for bachelor of science).

block calendar—college school year system in which students take one course at a time. Each course lasts about three and a half weeks, with a few days off between courses.

blog—short for Web log; a journal or diary that individuals write online.

board of trustees—the group with overall responsibility for a college; also called the board of directors.

branch campus—an additional location for a college other than the main location.

campus—a college's physical surroundings; its buildings and grounds.

career center—the place on campus where students can get a wide variety of information, advice, and assistance about employment; also known as a career counseling or career development center.

career counselor—someone who helps students identify their interests and skills, match those to career fields, and develop the skills necessary to obtain a job.

career day—a special day a school uses to focus on jobs and the education and skills required to do them; people in the community often come to share information about their jobs with students.

career school—a school that teaches specific, hands-on job skills to prepare students for work.

career-technical education—studies that emphasize practical skills and training for specific careers; also called vocational education, vo-tech, or occupational education.

catalog—a book that describes a college's requirements, rules, and courses in detail.

certificate—recognition that a student has completed specific training or study in a specialized career area.

certification—evidence that a person has completed a program of study or passed a competency test; gives the person permission to practice in a chosen field.

chancellor—the highest-ranking college administrator, usually at a university or multicampus college.

class rank—a measure of a student's academic performance compared to all other students in the same grade at the same school.

coed—short for coeducational.

coeducational—the education of both males and females at the same college or university.

college—school after high school that is either a two-year program of studies leading to an associate's degree or a four-year program of studies leading to a bachelor's degree; see also *community college* and *university*.

college calendar—the way in which a college divides its school year into terms; most often semesters, trimesters, or quarters.

college entrance exams—standardized tests used to measure skills related to college success; many colleges require applicants to take the SAT or the ACT; some require SAT subject exams; also called college admissions tests.

college fair—a special event where high school students pick up informational materials and speak with representatives from many different colleges.

College Navigator—a government Web site run by the National Center for Education Statistics; it enables students to search for colleges by a wide variety of areas such as location, size, setting, cost, and more; also provides links to college Web sites.

Common Application—a college application form that is accepted by almost 400 colleges in place of their own forms.

community college—school after high school that offers programs leading to associate's degrees and certificates; full-time programs can usually be completed in two years; sometimes called junior college.

commuter—a student who travels to and from college each day and lives away from campus.

competitive admissions—applicants must meet or exceed specific standards; qualified applicants are then compared to determine who will be admitted.

concurrent enrollment—refers to students who take college courses while still enrolled in high school; also see *dual enrollment*.

conference—an organized group of colleges whose athletic teams play each other often and develop long-term rivalries.

consortium—a group of colleges that allow students at one college to take advantage of courses, facilities, and additional benefits at the other colleges.

cooperative education—a program that combines studies with practical work experience, sometimes paid, in a student's chosen field; also called co-op program.

core courses—see *distribution requirements*.

cost calculator—a tool found on college and federal government Web sites that helps students and their parents estimate how much they will have to pay for college; see also *net price calculator*.

course section—one of many times a course is offered (for example, Mondays and Wednesdays, 10:00–11:30 a.m.); may also refer to different teaching methods (for example, online or telecourse) or locations.

credit—a measure of how much a particular course counts toward completing overall graduation requirements; usually based on the number of hours a course meets each week; often used to calculate tuition; also called credit hour.

cum laude—a mark of distinction awarded to top students at graduation; Latin for "with praise." See also *magna cum laude* and *summa cum laude*.

deadlines—definite dates by which time college application, financial aid, and other processes *must* be completed.

dean—a person responsible for a major portion of the college, such as dean of students or dean of housing.

deferred admission—selection process that enables students who have been accepted to a college to delay their enrollment; also refers to a college admitting an applicant, but for a later term than requested.

deferred loan—borrowed money that does not need to be repaid right away.

degree—the title a college grants to students who complete specific programs of study; most common are bachelor's degree (four-year college) and associate's degree (two-year college); advanced studies can lead to master's degrees and doctorate degrees.

department—a group of professors who teach in the same subject area; the head of the department is often called the department chair.

deposit—money a student sends to save a place at a college after accepting its offer of admission. This money applies toward the student's first year's expenses and is often nonrefundable.

developmental studies—programs that help students bring their basic skills up to a college level; also called remedial studies or college preparatory studies.

diploma—a formal document that recognizes a student's completion of a specific program of study, usually of one to two years.

direct loan—the federal government loans money to the student, but the college administers the loan program.

discipline—a subject area such as English, biology, or psychology.

discussion group—a group of students who meet regularly (usually weekly) to discuss course topics; usually headed by a faculty member or graduate assistant.

distance learning—instruction that takes place when the teacher and the student are in different locations all or much of the course; assignments and discussions can take place online through television, video, and audio; see also *hybrid class* and *online course*.

distribution requirements—courses that students are required to take from a variety of different subject areas before they can take most courses in their major or graduate; also called core requirements or general education requirements.

diversity—differences in personal characteristics, background, and experience, such as race, ethnicity, religion, gender, and geography.

division—a group of related departments that often make up a unit within the college; for example, the natural sciences division.

doctorate—an advanced degree; also called doctor's degree; the Ph.D. (doctor of philosophy) is a common one.

dormitory—a building that houses students who live on a college campus; also called residence hall.

double major—studies to complete degree requirements in two subject areas at the same time; see *major*.

dual enrollment—high school students take college classes at their high school or at a college; courses may count for both high school and college credit.

early action—college application and selection process; it enables students to be admitted early *without* an obligation to attend.

early decision—application and selection process enabling students to be admitted earlier than all other applicants and obligating them to attend that college or university.

electives—courses students choose (or elect) to take, but are not required to take; can be general (students choose any course they want) or specific (students must choose from a particular group of courses).

endowment—the total of a college's investments and savings; often includes both general and individual scholarship funds that have been donated to the college in memory or in honor of someone.

entrance exams—see *college entrance exams.*

entry services—see *admissions office.*

ESL—English as a Second Language; refers to special services and classes for students whose native language is not English; also called ESOL for English for Speakers of Other Languages.

ethnicity—ethnic background; the common national, religious, racial, tribal, linguistic, or cultural backgrounds that bond groups of people.

exchange program—a program that allows students at one college to attend a different college for one or more terms.

Expected Family Contribution (EFC)—the amount that, according to a government formula, a student's family should be able to pay toward the student's college costs wherever the student attends.

extension center—an additional campus that a college sets up in another location; similar to a branch campus.

extracurricular activities—activities a student participates in outside of class, such as sports, music, or clubs.

faculty—the teachers at a college: professors, associate and assistant professors, lecturers, and instructors.

FAFSA—Free Application for Federal Student Aid; the form students use to apply for financial assistance from the government; available in English and Spanish.

fees—charges for particular services, equipment, or facilities; can include a general fee, a student activity fee, a parking fee, class or lab fees, and so forth.

field studies—studies that take place outside traditional classrooms and labs, in a setting where subjects can be studied firsthand.

financial aid—money provided to a student to help pay for college.

financial aid package—the combination of grants, scholarships, loans, and work-study that a student receives to help pay for college.

financial literacy—basic financial knowledge everyone should have, such as budgeting, careful use of credit score, identity and privacy protection, and Internet use.

first-generation student—a college student whose parents did not attend college.

foundation—a special organization, often focused on a specific cause, that may provide money for scholarships and other educational support.

fraternity—a national membership organization for men, with individual chapters at various colleges.

freshman—a student who is in the first year of college.

GEAR UP—Gaining Early Awareness and Readiness for Undergraduate Programs; a government program that works with partners to prepare elementary, middle, and high school students for college.

general education courses—see *distribution requirements*.

gifted and talented programs—classes and activities that enable strong students the chance to work at a higher level and faster pace; may focus on broad or specific talents and abilities.

grade point average (GPA)—an average of all of a student's grades for a term, a year, or several years; see also *weighted grade point average*.

graduate assistant—a graduate student who helps a faculty member with teaching, grading, leading discussions, or conducting research; also referred to as a teaching assistant or TA.

graduate school—usually found within larger universities, a school that offers advanced studies to people who have already earned their bachelor's degrees; completion of the program often leads to master's degrees and doctorates.

graduate student—a student who has already earned a bachelor's degree and is continuing to study at an advanced level.

grant—a financial award to a student; generally does not need to be repaid.

head resident—person who manages a dormitory; also called resident director; see also *resident assistant*.

HEATH Resource Center—the national clearinghouse for information about post-secondary education for individuals with disabilities.

home page—the main starting point for a Web site; it provides links to the other pages on the site.

honors courses—courses that challenge students at a higher level.

hybrid class—a class that combines online and classroom instruction; students are in class part of the time and online part of the time; sometimes called campus web.

independent study—an opportunity to study a topic in depth outside of a traditional classroom; usually involves working individually with a teacher.

infirmary—the health facility on campus; also called the health center or wellness center.

information literacy—the knowledge necessary to perform effectively as a student and citizen; the lifelong ability to acquire and evaluate information in many ways, including information obtained electronically.

interdisciplinary—courses, or a major, that combine studies from more than one field.

interest—money paid to a lender in addition to the amount of a loan.

International Baccalaureate Program—a two-year college-level diploma program offered at some high schools.

internship—a program that lets students apply their studies in a work setting.

intramural sports—athletic programs that enable students within a college to compete against each other in various sports; open to all students.

intranet—a private computer network that only users in a certain organization can use; for example, a college's faculty, staff, and students.

Ivy League—a group of distinguished and older colleges in the northeastern United States.

job placement—the office that assists students in getting jobs; also called the career center.

junior—a student who is in the third year of studies at a four-year college.

junior college—see *community college*.

junior year abroad—semester or year-long overseas study experience offered during the third year of college.

laboratory or lab—a setting where students conduct experiments; also, settings where students can practice specific skills, such as a computer lab.

land-grant colleges—colleges established in the 1800s with federal land and funds, designed to provide a college education to a broader range of students.

learning resource center—see *library*.

lecture—a class setting where the teacher speaks in front of the students.

liberal arts—studies that cover broad knowledge in a wide variety of subjects.

liberal arts college—a college where students study a wide range of subjects.

library—the place on campus that houses books, reference materials, electronic databases, and other information sources and study services.

license—formal permission required by and obtained from a state or the federal government to work in a particular field.

loan—financial assistance that must be repaid by students or their parents, depending on the type of loan.

logo—a symbol that visually represents a college; often includes the college's name and motto.

magna cum laude—a mark of distinction awarded to top students at graduation; Latin for "with great praise." See also *cum laude* and *summa cum laude*.

magnet schools—public high schools that serve students with special interests and abilities in specific areas, such as performing arts, technology, or allied health.

main campus—usually the largest campus of a college, where the greatest number of resources and services are located.

major—the area of study in which a student chooses to specialize; sometimes called learning program.

mascot—a figure that symbolizes a college, often becoming the nickname for the college and its teams.

master's degree—an advanced degree following a bachelor's degree.

meal plan—a program that covers payment for meals and other campus food services.

mentor—a person who actively helps another achieve academic and career goals.

merit-based aid—financial assistance based on a student's talents.

midyear admission—offer of admission for the middle of an academic year; see also *deferred admission*.

minor—a second area of study that a student emphasizes, although without completing all of the requirements of a major.

multimedia—combining two or more types of media, such as film, audio and video, CDs, DVDs, Internet, and other electronic formats.

National Candidates' Reply Date (NCRD)—May 1, a shared deadline by which students must notify colleges where they will attend; most colleges use this date, but not all.

NCAA—National Collegiate Athletic Association; organization that oversees college athletic programs and related rules and regulations.

need-based aid—financial assistance based on a student's ability to pay for college.

net price calculator—a tool found on many college and federal government Web sites that helps students and their parents compare the cost of attending different colleges; it includes tuition and fees, but not other expenses such as room and board or books.

occupational education—study and preparation for a particular field of employment. See also *career-technical education.*

online course—a class that uses the Internet for instruction and for communication between the teacher and students; also see *hybrid class.*

open admissions—applicants are admitted with very few requirements.

open houses—a college event that enables prospective applicants to visit the campus; talk with the faculty, staff, and students; and learn more.

orientation—a program designed to introduce students to the college or specific programs in the college.

payment plan—a program that permits some or all college costs to be paid in smaller amounts rather than all at once.

Pell Grants—federal government grants that are awarded to the neediest undergraduate students; see also *SEOG.*

placement tests—exams given after students are admitted; help determine which courses students need to take.

portfolio—an organized collection that represents a student's work in a particular area, such as art.

prepaid tuition—a program that allows parents and others to pay many years in advance, locking in tuition rates; see *tuition.*

preparatory course—see *developmental studies.*

prerequisite—a course that is required before another course can be taken.

private college—an independent college set up by individuals or organizations; receives limited taxpayer support.

professor—a full-time teacher with a high level of education and experience; a teacher may be an instructor, assistant professor, and associate professor before becoming a full professor.

PROFILE—a form many private colleges require students to complete in order to qualify for need-based aid; completed in addition to any necessary federal or state financial aid forms.

proprietary school—a privately controlled school; specializes in areas such as business, technical, and vocational training.

provost—see *chancellor.*

PSAT/NMSQT—Preliminary Scholastic Achievement Test/National Merit Scholarship Qualifying Test; provides practice for the SAT and enables students to qualify for scholarship programs; generally taken in the fall of the eleventh grade.

public college—a college set up with government support; receives strong taxpayer support.

quarter—a college term lasting about 11 weeks; full-time students usually attend three quarter terms each year. See also *semester* and *trimester.*

recruiter—college representative who will answer students' questions and encourage eligible students to apply to the college; also called admissions counselor.

recruitment—the process of finding qualified students to apply to the college.

registrar—the person responsible for registration and for maintaining student records.

registration—the process of signing up for or enrolling in classes.

remedial studies—see *developmental studies.*

research college—a college at which the faculty and staff spend a lot of time on original research, often with student participation.

residence hall—see *dormitory.*

resident assistant—someone who supervises a portion of a dormitory; often called an RA.

role model—someone whom a person admires and who has been successful in ways that person would like to be successful.

rolling admissions—admissions decisions are made as applications are received.

room and board—the cost of housing (room) and meals (board).

ROTC—Reserve Officer Training Corps; a program that combines military training with studies at colleges and universities other than military academies.

SAT—Scholastic Aptitude Test; college entrance exam that tests students' skills in critical reading, writing, and mathematics.

SAT Subject Tests—college entrance exams that test students' knowledge in specific subject areas; for example, world history, literature, biology, and German; one or more may be requested by some colleges.

schedule of classes—a listing of courses offered each term along with dates, times, and locations; also called class schedule.

scholarship—a financial award that does not need to be repaid.

search engine—a Web site used to help find information on the Internet.

secondary school—middle school, junior high school, and high school.

selective admissions—applicants must either meet or exceed specific standards to qualify for admission.

selectivity—the level of difficulty involved in getting into a specific college; levels include open, selective, and competitive admissions.

self-paced classes—classes in which students work at their own speed.

semester—a college term lasting about 16 to 18 weeks; full-time students attend two semesters each year. See also *quarter* and *trimester.*

seminar—a small, discussion-oriented class, often for upperclassmen.

senior—a student in the final year of classes at a four-year college.

SEOG—Supplemental Educational Opportunity Grants; federal funds awarded to the neediest Pell Grant recipients; the amounts available differ by campus; timely application is extremely important.

social networks—Web-based communication used to exchange information, ideas, and opinions among students, alumni, and others. Examples include Facebook, MySpace, Twitter, YouTube, and blogs.

sophomore—a student in the second year of college.

sorority—a national membership organization for women, with individual chapters at various colleges.

STEM—an abbreviation for Science, Technology, Engineering, and Math programs; as in STEM scholarships, programs, and studies.

student body—all the students enrolled at a college.

student-faculty ratio—the number of students for every teacher.

student portal—a special entry point on a college Web site designed for easy access to information enrolled students frequently want and need; often requires a personal password to use.

student services—the services colleges provide to help students enroll, succeed, and enjoy campus life; for example, advising, counseling, tutoring, and athletics.

student union—the building that is central to student activities and services; often includes the dining hall, mailroom, and bookstore.

summa cum laude—a mark of distinction awarded to top students at graduation; Latin for "with highest praise." See also *cum laude* and *magna cum laude*.

syllabus—a course outline provided by the teacher that tells which topics will be covered in the class and when; may include exam and assignment dates as well as the teacher's contact information.

tax credit—an expense that reduces the amount of taxes owed.

tax deferment—an allowable delay in paying taxes.

teaching assistant—see *graduate assistant*.

teaching college—a college that places special emphasis on the relationship between teachers and students as part of the learning process.

technical institute—a postsecondary school that emphasizes practical career and job skills, especially in technology and applied trades.

technology college—a college that emphasizes programs such as engineering, computer science, and the natural sciences; may be called polytechnic institute or institute of technology.

telecourse/teleclass—a course taught through television, including cable and public television as well as DVDs and video.

tenure—a guarantee of job security given to professors who meet teaching, research, or publishing requirements set by the college.

term—a period of time during which courses are taught.

TOEFL—Test of English as a Foreign Language; a test often required for students from outside the United States.

trade school—see *career school.*

transcript—a summary of a student's academic record.

transfer—the process of switching from one college to another.

trimester—a college term lasting about 15 weeks; full-time students attend two out of three trimesters each year. See also *quarter* and *semester.*

TRIO programs—a group of federal programs, including Student Support Services, Talent Search, and Upward Bound, designed to help students with disadvantages prepare for and succeed in college.

tuition—the portion of college costs that pays directly for classes.

tuition savings plan—a state program that encourages saving for college costs.

tutoring—small group or one-to-one academic and study skill assistance.

two-year college—See *community college.*

underclassmen—freshmen and sophomores at a college.

undergraduate—a student who has not yet completed graduation requirements nor earned a bachelor's (or associate's) degree.

university—an institution of higher learning that usually combines one or more colleges with other schools, such as medical or law school.

upperclassmen—juniors and seniors at a college.

viewbook—a booklet that provides both photographs and general information about a college.

virtual tour—a way of touring a campus online; DVDs, CDs, or other multimedia methods are often available.

vocational-technical education—studies that emphasize practical skills and training for specific careers; also called vo-tech.

waiting list—a college's list of students who cannot be accepted at first but *may* be accepted later.

weighted grade point average—an average of all of a high school student's grades for a term, a year, or several years with additional points based on the difficulty of specific courses.

work-study—a financial assistance program that provides students with jobs, usually on campus.

Map of the United States

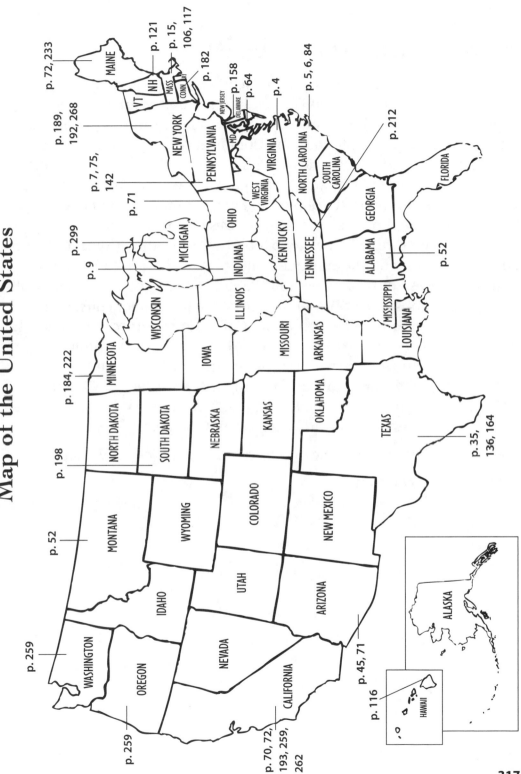

MAINE — p. 121

NH — p. 15, 106, 117

VT — p. 72, 233

MASS — p. 182

CONN — RI

NEW YORK — p. 189, 192, 268

PENNSYLVANIA

NEW JERSEY — p. 158

MD. — p. 64

DELAWARE

VIRGINIA — p. 4

NORTH CAROLINA — p. 5, 6, 84

SOUTH CAROLINA — p. 212

GEORGIA

FLORIDA

OHIO — p. 7, 75, 142

WEST VIRGINIA — p. 71

KENTUCKY

TENNESSEE

ALABAMA — p. 52

MISSISSIPPI

LOUISIANA

MICHIGAN — p. 299

INDIANA

ILLINOIS — p. 9

WISCONSIN

MINNESOTA — p. 184, 222

IOWA

MISSOURI

ARKANSAS

NORTH DAKOTA — p. 198

SOUTH DAKOTA

NEBRASKA

KANSAS

OKLAHOMA

TEXAS — p. 35, 136, 164

MONTANA — p. 52

WYOMING

COLORADO

NEW MEXICO

IDAHO

UTAH

ARIZONA — p. 45, 71

WASHINGTON — p. 259

OREGON — p. 259

NEVADA

CALIFORNIA — p. 70, 72, 193, 259, 262

ALASKA

HAWAII — p. 116

317

Photo and Art Credits

Page 5, courtesy of the University of Nebraska–Lincoln; page 9, photo gravityshots.com, courtesy of Flathead Valley Community College; page 12, photo Angel Art, courtesy of University at Buffalo Publications Department; page 20, photo Colby Communications; page 33, courtesy of Paul Bither; page 34, courtesy of Southwest Airlines; page 38, photo Bill Kiefer, courtesy of Gregory Jbara; page 39, courtesy of Eddie George, The EDGE Group; page 48, photo Kip Evans Photography; page 49, photo NASA; page 50, photo Peter Simon, courtesy of Judy Blume; page 51, courtesy of The Honorable Ed Pastor; page 61, photo Colby Communications; page 62, courtesy of Miami-Dade College; page 63, photo Franklin Muñoz, courtesy of UTEP News and Publications; page 113, photo Colby Communications; page 119, photo Lawrence Greenfeld, courtesy of Jonathan Hamburg; page 121, photo Colby Communications; page 126, photo Colby Communications; page 149, photo Colby Communications; page 151, photo University of Denver, courtesy of Michelle Kwan; page 231, photo Colby Communications; page 234, courtesy of Goucher College's Office of Communication; page 263, courtesy Boston College; page 285, courtesy of Howard Community College.

Other photos: PhotoDisc, Inc.; Comstock, Inc.; I Stock; and Digital Vision

Artwork: Art Explosion

Index

Crowley, Candy, 48
CTY (Center for Talented Youth), 299
culinary arts, 96, 102
Culinary Institute of America, 11
cultural anthropology, 89
cultural centers, 252
cultural studies, 104
cum laude, 79, 308
Cuyahoga Community College, 62

D

Dallas Institute of Funeral Service, 273
Dana College, 47
dance, 91
Dartmouth College, 4, 7, 49–50, 121, 165, 181, 203
Davidson College, 59, 155
day students, 45
deadlines, 182–184, 308
deans, 19, 308
declaring a major, 83
deferred admission, 184, 308
deferred loans, 214, 308
degrees, 78–80, 308
Delaware State University, 17, 158, 222
Delaware Technical and Community College, 196
Delgado Community College, 139
Delta State University, 222
demography, 88
Denison University, 49, 73
dental hygiene, 99
departments, 85, 308
DePaul University, 47, 62, 194
DePauw University, 73, 158
deposits, 187, 308
developmental biology, 86
developmental psychology, 88
developmental studies, 114, 308
deviance, 88
Dickinson College, 8, 58, 75
Dickinson State University, 159, 223
Diesel Truck Driver Training School, 273
dieticians, 99
difficulty level, researching colleges, 147
Diggs, Taye, 49
digital resources, 128
Dillard University, 51, 222
Dimon, Jamie, 49
diplomas, 274, 308
direct loans, 214, 308

disabled students, 60
  researching colleges, 146
  services for, 124–125
disciplines, 85, 308
  agriculture and forestry, 102
  arts and humanities, 90–91
  business, 100
  communications and mass media, 103
  computers and information systems, 95
  cultural studies, 104
  education and library sciences, 101
  engineering, 92–93
  hospitality and tourism, 102
  interdisciplinary studies, 104
  languages, 97
  mathematics and statistics, 94
  medicine and allied health, 98–99
  military programs, 103
  natural and physical sciences, 86–87
  social and behavioral sciences, 88–89
  technology and trades, 96
discussion groups, 111, 308
distance education, 45
distance learning, 65–67, 115, 308
distribution requirements, 82, 309
Divers Academy International, 273
diversity, 145, 309
divisions, 85, 309
doctorate, 79, 309
dormitories, 248–249, 309
double major, 83, 309
Dove, Rita, 49
Drew University, 16, 181
Drexel University, 35
dual enrollment, 309
Duck Tape Brand Duct Tape Stuck at Prom Contest, 213
Duke University, 47, 59, 165, 185
Duncan, Tim, 49
DVDs for college information, 132

E

Earlham College, 16, 73, 181
early action, 183, 309
early childhood education, 101
early decision, 183, 309
early graduation from high school, 298
earth and atmospheric sciences, 87
East-Asian studies, 104
East Carolina University, 195
East Tennessee State University, 48

M

About the Authors

Barbara C. Greenfeld is Associate Vice President of Enrollment Services at Howard Community College in Columbia, Maryland, where she administers admissions, academic, advising, testing, registration, and financial aid services. She is an honors graduate of the University of Maryland at College Park and received her M.S. with honors from The Johns Hopkins University. The programs that Ms. Greenfeld has developed have received local and national recognition, including the National Academic Advising Association's Outstanding Advising Program Award (for Howard Community College's Freshman Focus Program). She has also been instrumental in developing many other unique programs at the college, including the innovative James W. Rouse Scholars, Silas Craft Collegians, Early Entrance Programs, the Rouse Scholar–Dickinson College Study Abroad Partnership, HCC's Pay for College initiative, and a variety of early college awareness programs for elementary, middle, and high school students and their parents. She also has been a consultant to other colleges in developing similar programs. In addition, Ms. Greenfeld has served on the LPN Standards Committee of CGFNS International. Throughout her career, Ms. Greenfeld has worked extensively in the areas of outreach; open, selective, and competitive admissions; assessment; physical and learning disabilities; international student admissions; transfer programs; and the development of learning communities.

Robert A. Weinstein has worked in educational publishing for more than 25 years. He is an honors graduate of Colby College and received his M.B.A. from Harvard University. As an editor for McGraw-Hill and other publishers, he has visited hundreds of colleges across the country and has published dozens of successful texts as well as numerous supplements using a wide range of media. As head of Gerson Publishing Company, Mr. Weinstein edited much of the HarperCollins College Outline Series and is the author of numerous materials aimed at helping high school students make a successful transition to college. He is active in community theater and is president of Oasis Players in Monmouth County, New Jersey, where he directs, produces, and performs in family theater and musical concerts.